THE HIDDEN C's OF COMMON CORE

Orlean Koehle

Copyright 2014 ©

ISBN Number
978-1-4951-0863-1

Turn the Helm Publishing
Santa Rosa, CA
707-539-8393

James 3:4 "Behold the ships, which though they be so great and are driven by fierce winds, yet are they turned about with a very small helm…"

Acknowledgments

One of the mantras of those supporting Common Core is that now teachers can go "a mile deep and an inch wide" into subjects, where before they had to spread the information too thinly. This book is my attempt to do that with Common Core itself. We are going to go much deeper into it and take a much closer look at it. This is the 401 course, in place of the 101 course, which was my previous book, *Common Core, The Trojan Horse for Education Reform.*

I would like to thank some amazing people who have been in the forefront fighting Common Core for many years and from whom I have received so much valuable information in order to write this book. Many of them belong to a group called "Truth in American Education," that consists of the leaders fighting Common Core in their various States across the nation. Many of them are also State leaders in Eagle Forum. I receive e–mails and articles from them full of information of what is happening in this battle almost every day. Many of the articles and news reports are referenced in this book.

I would like to specifically thank Dr. Sandra Stotsky and Dr. James Milgram, who were on the validation committee for Common Core and refused to sign off on it. They have been tirelessly traveling across the nation speaking at various State hearings and events to let people know the truth about Common Core and why they said no to it.

Thank you to other experts whom I have had the pleasure to work with in this battle, such as: Attorney Brad Dacus from the Pacific Justice Institute, who wrote the opt out form for getting out children out of the Assessment test for Common Core; Lydia Gutierrez, a classroom teacher, who had the courage to run for Superintendent of Public Instruction with a strong anti-Common Core platform; Assemblyman Tim Donnelly, a candidate for Governor of California, also with a bold anti-Common Core platform; Angela Weinzinger, a member of the Travis Unified School

Board, who strongly opposes Common Core and started her own face book page, Parents and Educators Against Common Core that now has over 18,000 members; Bill Evers and Ze've Wurman who both served in the Federal Education Department and are outspoken critics of Common Core.

Thank you to my Eagle Forum Board members who have taken up the gantlet, have become experts themselves on Common Core and gone forth boldly speaking out against it in their own school districts and for other groups. They are: Jeanne Goodin, Gloria Pruyne, Bonnie O'Neil in Orange County; Darcy Brandon and Mary Baker in San Diego; Ann Durham, Marge Sorbi, Jennifer Delaney, James Bennett, Eileen Berber, Mary Wolbert in Sonoma County; Duane Wildie, Dave Scanlan, Karen Klinger in the Sacramento area; Heather Gass, Nina Pellegrini, Debbie Bacigalupi in the East Bay, Erin Ryan and Louise Gliatto in Redding and Siskiyou County.

Thank you to many Tea Party leaders and Republican Women Groups who heard me speak and have now gotten involved in the battle. Thanks to Mandy Morello, an old friend, and a new friend, Sandra Smith, who started Democrats Against Common Core. They both helped me put on a rally against Common Core on the side of the State Capitol in Sacramento April 30 that was attended by over 150 people, mostly parents with children.

Thank you to radio show hosts and Fox News who have spoken often about Common Core, specifically: Dr. Stan Montieth, Glenn Beck, Barbara Simpson, Sharon Hughes, Melanie Morgon, and a new team - the Evan /Miller Report, consisting of Jason Miller and Cory Evan, who have asked me to join them as a weekly contributing reporter talking about Common Core.

And thank you to the many parents and grandparents, who have been waking up to this important topic across California and our nation and have gotten involved fighting this battle. You are the ones who are really making a difference.

And lastly, many thanks to my tireless editor, Ann Durham, and my patient printer, Scott Hartley of www.ARCCopy.com for the many hours spent in producing and printing this book!

Contents

Introduction

The above picture is the Common Core logo in 2012 showing the 46 states that have signed on to it depicted in gold and the original States that had not yet signed on depicted in a darker rusty orange. They are Alaska, Texas, Virginia, Nebraska (hidden behind the logo), and partially Minnesota, which adopted the English Language Arts but not the math. However, some of these four States signed on to something similar called College and Career Readiness, and Alaska has joined the Smarter Balance Assessment Consortium, the testing arm for Common Core.

What is Common Core or College and Career Readiness? It is the federal education program that is being pushed on all the 46 States where the governors signed on to it (most of them in 2010). It was first promoted as a wonderful form of "commonality" so all

States could share the same set of common standards, curriculum and assessments. Supposedly, that will make education better, "more rigorous," and students will be better scholars and better prepared for "college and career." Education will now go deeper into important subjects. "Instead of a mile wide and an inch thick, it will be a mile deep and an inch wide." These are all the mantras that are being used to promote Common Core.

The official name is Common Core State Standards Initiative (CCSSI), but as this book will point out, the States had nothing to do with the creation of Common Core. It was written by a national cartel that is trying to give itself some legitimacy and get support for the program by pretending that it is State-written and State-led. It is copyrighted, and States will have little (only 15%) ability to do anything other than what is on the prescribed curriculum.

New Names: Many States are no longer using the term Common Core but instead calling it "College and Career Readiness" or some other new term. Why is this happening? Because of all the push back it is getting by parents and educators waking up to how bad this program really is. But, don't be deceived, it is still the same Common Core, just with a new name.

The Four Cs of Common Core (CC): There are many nice sounding, distinctive words that are being used to try to sell CC to the public that **all begin with the letter C**. The ones promoting it the most are called **"the Four Cs of Common Core - communication, collaboration, critical thinking, and creativity."**

The Three Cs of Common Core: In Florida schools, there are **"Three Cs: claim, claim evidence, and commentary."**

Other impressive C words used to promote it are: college-and-career-ready, commonality, compassion, comprehensive, computer-based, continuality, consensus, and constructivism. These words sound okay, but are we really being told the truth about what they really mean and their impact on education, the teachers, students, and their parents when Common Core is totally implemented?

This booklet will explain their real meaning and also give the dark side of the many **hidden C words** that are not spoken about or downplayed and the frightening direction they are leading our nation. They are words such as: **central-control.** How much easier it will be to have total control of what is taught and what is not allowed to be taught in our schools when all standards and curriculum are coming from one source – the federal government. There can then be total indoctrination of our students as in other totalitarian regimes.

You will read of the **cartel** that created Common Core and the **corporations such as the Bill and Malinda Gates Foundation** that are funding it and promoting it worldwide. They have given out millions and billions of dollars, but they stand to make enormous profits from the sale of the computers, the e-books, the tests, and the teacher training.

You will read how our children are being prepared to be **"cogs in a global workforce"** and **"citizens of the world"** as are children in other countries. Common Core is a global plan for the entire world and is already in place in many other countries. It is being promoted by the United Nations, UNESCO, and the Pearson Foundation publishing company that is publishing the majority of text books, e-books, and the tests for Common Core. They have offices in 70 other nations with 36,000 employees. It is also funded and promoted by the Bill and Malinda Gates Foundation.

You will read more about the **curriculum** of Common Core: the strange, complicated math, the insidious indoctrination that is coming into the classroom through the wide door of "informational text" in English/Language Arts, history, and social science; the inappropriate, explicit sexual literature that has been labeled "Common Core approved;" and the one-sided biased, pseudo-science that is being pushed in the "Next Generation Science Standards (NGSS)" that obviously has a political agenda.

You will learn more about the **collection of intrusive data through Common Core,** tracing and tracking the child from **"cradle to grave"** or from "womb to tomb," and that this data can be shared across State lines and sold to the highest bidder. Who knows where that data will end up and what it will be used for? Will it be used to choose the student's job in the global work force? Will his career choice no longer be his own, as in other totalitarian, central-controlled countries?

This book also contains **comments and testimonials** by courageous teachers, administrators, parents and students describing what Common Core and the assessment test is really like, and why they are so opposed to it.

You will read a **chronological brief history** of how we got to where we are. The reader will see that Common Core is nothing new, but just the frosting on the cake in the steps of the progressives in achieving their goal of total control of education, so we can be better prepared to be global citizens in their one-world government and New World Order.

You will read **what you as a concerned parent, grandparent, or citizen can do** to find out more and take a stand to try to stop Common Core before it has become too entrenched in your school and schools across our nation. It does not matter if the schools are public, private, charter schools or home schools, unless it can be stopped, they will all be affected and come under the influence of

CC. If the child is seeking to go on to college he will have to understand the CC standards and curriculum because all the college entrance tests are being aligned with Common Core.

And lastly you will read suggestions of **what we can replace Common Core with** – a system like we used to have when education in our nation was one of the best in the world - with true parental and local control in charge of our schools.

This book is a sequel to *Common Core, The Trojan Horse of Education Reform* (2012), also available from the same publisher.

The Hidden Cs of Common Core

Chapter I –

C-Words to Sell Common Core to the Public:

Commercials Promoting Common Core State Standards: As opposition is rising in grassroots groups across the nation, so are expensive commercials appearing on all the major television stations and on the internet. As you will discover there is much big corporate money behind Common Core paying for these ads – such as the Bill and Melinda Gates Foundation through the selling of the computers or iPads and other forms of technology for every child in every school across America, and corporations such as the Pearson Foundation, who are publishing all the new e-books and tests now required for Common Core.

This is a picture of a strange logo introducing the link to a new promotional website, www.thecommoncore.com, that appeared on the internet in April, 2014. As Wayne Harropson, a school board

member opposed to Common Core in Orange County, pointed out, "This looks like something off the Benghazi Embassy wall with strokes of red blood painted in the background." One wonders why such a logo would be chosen? To me, it shows the big hand in white of the federal government that is really behind Common Core. The words at the bottom read "LEARN MORE" (in white), "GO FURTHER" (in red). As one finds our more about Common Core, these words take on new meaning. Perhaps they really mean –

LEARN MORE and GO FURTHER towards SOCIALISM AND COMMUNISM because that is the direction Common Core is leading our nation.

All the nice sounding words that are repeated over and over promoting Common Core appear on www.thecommoncore.com website; the only problem is they are totally false as this book points out. The false statements are in bold:

> *The Common Core State Standards are a crucial first step.* **They raise the bar in our K-12 classrooms.**
>
> *The Common Core State Standards were* **developed by educators from across the country.** *Employers and higher education leaders helped determine how well our students must perform to be "***college and career ready.***" And over the course of two years governors and education chiefs from 45 states – and from both political parties –* **voluntarily adopted the Standards.**
>
> **The Standards are as high as the best standards in any individual state** *and* **comparable to those in the highest-performing nations around the world.** *And that's great news. It will mean our schools* **equip graduates with the skills they need to succeed.**
>
> *The future is in session in schools nationwide. Now we need to help give it a chance to succeed.*[1]

Rebuttal to the above paragraph: There were five education experts on the validation committee for Common Core who refused to sign off on the standards. Obviously, they did agree that the **"standards would raise the bar in our K-12 classrooms"**: These experts all held PhDs: Dr. Sandra Stotsky Professor Emerita University of Arkansas; Dr. James Milgram, math professor emeritus at Stanford; Dr. Alfino Flores, Hollowell Math Professor University of Delaware; Dr. Barry McGaw, Director of Melbourne Education Research Institute, University of Melbourne, former Education Director at OECD (Organization for Economic Cooperation and Development); and Dr. Dylan William, Deputy

Director, Institute of Education, University of London. None of the comments that they submitted of why they refused to sign off were allowed to be published. But both Drs. Stotsky and Milgram have become very outspoken critics since. Many of their statements you will read in this book.

The standards were not developed by educators from across the country. Those educators who were involved only submitted "suggestion box" input. The standards were created by a national cartel of various organizations, mainly Achieve.Inc., business leaders, a few governors, a few State School Superintendents. The five main writers had never had any K-12 teaching experience, which is obvious especially to teachers who try to decipher them, with their complicated and wordy language, especially for the younger grades.

According to Drs. Stotsky and Milgram, the standards will actually make our students less ready for college and career. They will only be ready for a junior college, not a four-year university. This is also what was admitted by Jason Zimba, himself, the main writer for the math standards.

At a hearing in Massachusetts of the Board of Secondary and Elementary Education, March 23, 2010, Zimba admitted that the CC math standards are not designed to prepare students for STEM (science, technology, engineering, and math) studies, but also that they're not designed to get a student into any selective college, even in a non-STEM discipline. See the actual video clip.[2]

Governors and Education Chiefs from 45 States signed onto the standards "voluntarily." No, they were coerced with a bribe, the possibility of winning part of $4.35 billion grant money, a waiver to get out of No Child Left Behind, and a threat that if they didn't sign on their Title I money would be taken away.

The Standards are as high as the best standards in any individual state and comparable to those in the highest-performing nations around the world. No, they are not as high as Massachusetts standards were, nor California's standards before Common Core. And they are not comparable to the highest-performing nations around the world. Sandra Stotsky points out that there is not a single nation anywhere that will testify that our standards are "internationally benchmarked." There are nations who looked at them, but they were not tested against other countries. In fact, they have not been field tested anywhere. Our children are the guinea pigs on which they are trying out the standards, the curriculum, and the assessments.

Our schools equip graduates with the skills they need to succeed. Before Common Core that was the case. With Common Core standards in place, our graduates will not be equipped with the knowledge or skills they will need to succeed. That will be greatly dumbed down.

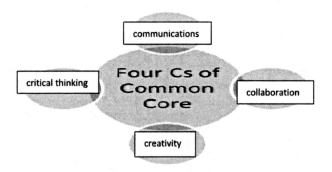

"The Four Cs of Common Core": These are nice-sounding words to make CC sound more appealing to parents and educators. The words are: "communication, collaboration, critical thinking skills, and creativity." They are defined in teacher training manuals as:

1. **Communication** - sharing thoughts, questions, ideas, and solutions.
2. **Collaboration** – working together to reach a goal, putting talent expertise and smarts to work.
3. **Critical thinking** – looking at a problem in a new way, linking learning across subjects and disciplines.
4. **Creativity** – trying new approaches to get things done – equals innovation and invention.[3]

12

Are the Four Cs Something New? Teachers are told if they are doing their CC program correctly then they will have their students incorporating the above terms each and every day. Is this something new? Were these traits not part of a good classroom for hundreds of years in our nation already?

As a speech, drama, debate and journalism teacher, my students were using communication skills, collaboration, critical thinking, and creativity each day without the school district having to pay for an expensive new program, with new computers, new e-books, new teacher training, etc.

Personally, I think Common Core and its "new and innovative teaching methods" is an insult to dedicated, good teachers who for generations have used innovative methods and have inspired and produced outstanding students in our nation – when teachers were left with the freedom to do so.

A Closer Look at the Four Cs – What they will mean When Common Core is Totally Implemented:

1. Communication will be limited between teachers and students when students are doing their CC assignments mainly on computers and then meeting with other students to do their group work. Teachers will become facilitators who are not supposed to stand in front of the classroom and teach. Teachers are already being told that the best teachers let the children construct their own meaning; the teacher is not supposed to tell them what that meaning is.

The teacher's communication with other teachers will also be limited as they become more fearful to state any opposition to CC, afraid of what the other teachers might report on them, which will then be written up on the evaluations and data collected on them.

13

2. Collaborative: Yes, students will have opportunity to collaborate with each other, since much of CC is group-learning as they work on assignments together. Students are told to "think, pair, and share" - to think on their own, then to pair up with another student and share their ideas. But is that the best way of learning? Usually, it is just certain bright, motivated students who do most of the group work, and the others just follow his/her lead, and yet all share in the credit and get the same grade. Is that fair to the one student who has done the most work, and do the others really learn from the assignment and the experience? If left on their own, would they even know what to do? What will happen to them in the assessment test when they no longer have the group leader telling them what to do? Or will there be a group project in the assessment test? What happens when they go out for a job interview and are on their own?

There is a very telling cartoon video of a girl applying for a job called "I Choose C." When the man interviewing her asks a question of her qualifications she is stumped and looks around for her team to help her. When the man asks what she is doing, she says she needs someone to help her "think, pair, and share." Sorry, all this group work is not preparing our students for real life experiences where they will be on their own.[4]

Collaboration between teachers is what is being promoted as a real plus with Common Core. According to *NEA Today*, the National Education Association magazine, Winter Issue, 2014, teachers, who teach different subjects, will collaborate their efforts so students will be studying one book in ELA, and another one in history, and another one in science, and all the books will complement each other. The writer of the article, Cindy Long gives examples of this: For ELA, the students are assigned to read *The Eleventh Plague*, a futuristic novel about a teenager's life in a post-apocalyptic world; for science the students could read *Silent Spring* by Rachel Carson [a book which many believe is based on false science [5]], and for history, they could read *Changes in the Land: Indians, Colonists, and the Ecology of New England,* which tells of the impact on the environment by early settlers.

Collaboration, obviously, is especially helpful when all the teachers are teaching the same "indoctrination" as with the above books. The three books are all telling how man has destroyed the environment, even those poor early settlers who were trying to just barely eke out an existence and survive – they were destroying the earth as well.[6] [There are many parents and grandparents who are concerned that their children and grandchildren are only getting a very biased view on the above issues, one that is based on pseudo-science, not real science. I am one of those. How much easier it will be to persuade children to just one way of thinking when they are getting a triple dose of indoctrination from all three teachers and subjects through "collaboration.]

Later when CC is fully implemented, collaboration will be limited. Teachers won't really have much need to collaborate. Their lesson plans will be laid out for them each and every day on the computer, all in alignment with the CC standards and teaching to the assessment that is going on in every classroom in every State across the nation. As you will read later, where Common Core is more fully entrenched, teachers are saying their lessons are "scripted, or canned," and they are not supposed to add any comments of their own.

Was Common Core a collaborative effort written by the States? We are told that the standards, the curriculum and the assessment have all been part of a **"collaborative effort,"** written by like-minded, concerned teachers from States across the nation. It is therefore "State-written and State-led."[7]

According to attorney Emmett McGroarty, director of the American Principles Project of Washington, D.C., and a strong opponent of CC, if teachers had anything to do with the writing of the lesson plans and standards, it was by conference calls and "suggestion-box input."[8] The standards were essentially already written before any input was called for from the States.

In other words, State school board members, superintendents, or teachers from various States who think that they had input and were part of the planning and writing were being deceived or "Delphied" into thinking they were part of it.

The Delphi technique was developed by the Rand Corporation back in the 1960s. It is a technique that uses a skilled facilitator to manipulate people so that they will think that they are part of the decision-making process and will thus be more supportive of the outcome. But really the outcome has already been long planned and decided. The participants are duped, deceived, and manipulated into thinking they are part of the process and are making a difference.

As you will read in the next chapter, the CC standards were written by a national/international cartel who referred to themselves as "the Chiefs." As McGroarty states:

> *The Chiefs started writing them [the standards] in July of 2009 and by March, 2010, they had the draft completed. This was quite fast, and I would submit to you **impossible if they were being written by 45 states.**[9]*

3. Critical thinking used to mean looking at both sides of an issue – both pros and cons, before making up one's mind as to what is really right, correct or true. I taught my debate students that a healthy debate is a wonderful way to develop critical thinking skills, to learn and present both sides of an issue. My students would do so each and every day. Sometimes they would be for the pro-side of an issue, sometimes the opposite side. The student whom they would be opposing one day would maybe be their debate partner the next day. Nobody was offended when they were on the opposite sides on issues; they all remained good friends.

It used to be that teachers could have a good healthy debate about a controversial subject and still come out friends. That does not seem to be the case anymore. Most teachers do not seem to be asked to look at the other side or to have an open mind on controversial issues. There seems to be only one viewpoint allowed, the liberal, progressive one that teachers have been indoctrinated into.

In faculty lounges when I have tried to present an opposite view on such subjects as "global warming," or whether there was really a "hole in the ozone layer," or most recently to give a different view on Common Core, I have had teachers leave the room, or leave the parking lot and tell me, "I refuse to talk to you. Goodbye."

Many teachers and administrators do not want to listen to any opposition to CC. It is almost sacrilegious if they do so. Perhaps they are fearful of someone spying on them when they are listening to the other side, for they are aware that data is being collected on them -- as well as their students.

From my personal experience, I believe "critical thinking" has now become "new-speak" language for what is having the "**proper, leftist, progressive-education attitude and thinking – known as "Disposition and Habits of Mind."**"[10]

This definition is echoed by Berit Kjos, author of *Brave New Schools*. She states:

> *Most parents and teachers still believe that critical thinking refers to factual, logical thinking. They have been misled. School fliers explain that it means teaching students "to think for themselves." It actually means the opposite; it's a psychological strategy for dismantling old beliefs and values and instilling new ones by limiting factual knowledge while encouraging myths, imagination, and group synthesis. Since it trades the traditional broad knowledge base for selected information that supports the new ideology, most students can easily be manipulated toward the preplanned outcomes [11]*

I am afraid, under the guise of "developing critical thinking skills," students will only be exposed, indoctrinated, and programmed to accept the politically-correct, progressive view point. They will follow the examples of their teachers, and their minds will be closed to accepting any other ideas or opinions.

Low-order Thinking Skills? When educators promote Common Core by saying it is teaching children "critical thinking," they often add another mantra of "higher order thinking skills." According to blogger Richard Day, Common Core is promoting just the opposite. He quotes a New York English teacher, Jeremiah Chafee:

> *If this author can be believed, **low-ordered thinking skills** dictated by Common Core "Exemplars" seem to undermine creative and critical thinking. Will we find ourselves five years from now wondering why such a great idea isn't working...and blaming teachers for the failure?[12]*

4. Creativity: Teachers who have been already teaching CC for some time as part of a pilot program say that their creativity to do new and innovative things is being stifled. They must do exactly what the CC guidelines tell them.

There are "master teachers" or "guides" that are assigned to supposedly help train the teachers, but many think they are really "master spies" to make sure that the teachers do all that they are assigned and do not deviate from the prescribed CC guidelines.

A teacher in Lake Arrowhead, California, who heard me speak about my first book on Common Core, told me afterwards that she had already had her own experience with a master teacher, who was assigned to her class for an entire week. Whenever the teacher was not following strictly the prescribed CC curriculum, the master teacher was scribbling down notes. Where did those notes end up and what happened to the teacher? Was she reprimanded for not following CC rigidly? Was that recorded in her data file?

Supposedly, States are allowed 15% flexibility to do their own creative thing different than the prescribed course, but they are being told that whatever they come up with in that 15% will not be on the Assessment test, and since there is little time to teach everything that will be on the test, why waste your time trying to come up with anything different if it won't be tested?

Common Core is too "Prescriptive," and "Standardization Drives out Creativity": Superintendent of Scarsdale, New York, Michael McGill, who will be retiring in the spring of 2014, said that "Common Core has laudable goals but is too prescriptive." He added that the English/language arts standards need not "downplay literature" as they "promote analytical reading of nonfiction." And New York's lesson plans for math are "so encompassing that they foster full curricula, not standards."

We understand the impulse to see quality raised across the board, but we don't think it's healthy to have everyone do the same thing the same way. Standardization can drive out creativity and innovation, which are what make education outstanding.[13]

"Three Cs of Common Core – Claim, Claim Evidence, and Commentary:" An illustration is given on the Achieve website of a teacher in a Florida Middle School, Christina Phillips, who had her 6th grade students read essays and identify whether the underlined text is "making a statement, presenting evidence, or expressing a fact-based opinion." The following conversation is then given from her classroom:

'OK, so let's start with blue first. Okay?' Phillips asked. 'The blue said, 'This pig made his house of bricks.' Is that factual evidence from the text? Or is that my opinion?
'That's evidence!' a student pops back.
'Textual evidence,' Phillps confirmed 'So, blue would represent?'
'Claim evidence,' the students said.
'Claim evidence. So circle it and tell me how you know,' she said, asking them to fill out their assignment.
   Phillips said Common Core meant big changes in her lessons. It's all designed to make sure kids are prepared for college-level or professional work by the time they graduate high school.
   'Four years ago, there wouldn't be any text in a writing assignment.' She said. 'It would simply be a prompt. And we would probably have kids writing a lot more anecdotes. Now, they have to use the text. 'You know, it's what's expected at the higher level.'[14]

This all sounds like a really good lesson the teacher is teaching, whether what a student is reading and writing about is making a statement, giving evidence or just an opinion. But that is not new, that is something I used to do with my English, speech and debate classes 40 years ago. One of the biggest differences is the low level of classical English literature in Common Core or none at all, and the boring or highly politicized "informational text" that students are given to read. Notice these students are in the 6th grade and are reading an essay about a pig making his house out of bricks; how stimulating is that? Isn't that what was read back in kindergarten or the first grade?

A big part of Common Core is teaching children to do lots of writing, even in math children are to explain and write about each step they are making in solving the problem. The best way to teach writing is by first teaching students to love reading. The best writers are avid readers. That is how you learn about different writing styles and build up your vocabulary to enrich your writing.

Students in elementary school used to have 80% of their reading coming from classical English literature, great books that have withstood the test of time. They would be reading exciting plots that show how characters grow and change and become wiser and better people as they meet and overcome obstacles. They would read beautiful, uplifting, memorable words that made reading enjoyable, something that they began to love. Reading was helping them to also be better people, learning about moral truths, about making wise decisions and choosing the difference between right and wrong.

What memorable experience are most children learning in schools today from reading the assigned literature or little booklets or "informational text on line"? Very little, if any could be called great works of Classical English literature. Only one play of Shakespeare is assigned – *Romeo and Juliet*. However, in Chapter V you will read of the inappropriate, shocking, pornographic sexual novels young teens are being assigned to read in middle school that are "Common Core aligned" and of the "politically correct" selections that they are being given obviously for indoctrination purposes.

[A list of great recommended Classical Literature that has withstood the test of time, from which young people can learn wisdom and moral truths is given in the last chapter.]

Content – According to English literature expert Sandra Stotsky, the most important C word is missing from the "Four Cs" or the "Three Cs of Common Core." That word is "content." Content is what education is supposed to be all about. Without important content knowledge that comes from time-honored great classics and historical novels, there is not much of substance on which to create or collaborate, communicate, and think critically. Surely there are more exciting subjects to claim, claim evidence or comment on than pigs making houses out of bricks?

Other Nice-Sounding C Words to Promote Common Core - but what they really mean: close-reading, closing the achievement gap, cold-reading, college-and-career ready, commonality, comprehensive, constructivism, consensus, compassion or social justice, continuality, computer-based, computerized-exams, computer facilitators.

Close Reading – is greatly emphasized in Common Core, not only in English/language arts, but also in math, history, science, whatever the child is reading. What does close reading actually mean? It is a new name for the Socratic method, where you ponder and ask questions as to what the text really mean – "paying close attention to individual words, syntax, and the order in which sentences and ideas unfold as they are read."[15]

Close Reading and Social Justice: To "level the playing field," a term that is often used with Common Core, the teacher is to not give the students any background information about the text they are reading. They are to find it all by themselves. According to David Coleman, the architect of the ELA standards, it is all about social justice, making sure not one child is "privileged above the other."

> *This close reading approach forces students to rely exclusively on the text instead of privileging background knowledge, and levels the playing field for all students.*

For example, in teaching the Gettysburg Address, the teacher is not allowed to enrich the assignment or make it more interesting for the students by giving any background information, what year it was, where President Lincoln was when he gave the speech - that they were in the middle of the bloody Civil War, and Gettysburg is where a terrible battle had just taken place, how many had lost their lives, what the Civil War was all about, etc.

Instead the students just have to read the text cold turkey without any knowledge of what was going on. If the teacher reads it to them, she is also to read it without any feeling or inflection in her voice, or that would maybe give some clue as to how the teacher feels about the text and would persuade the students to her viewpoint.

Again, according to Professor Dr. Sandra Stotsky, there is no evidence that would prove David Coleman's ideas are true. In fact, it is just the opposite:

> *Not only is there no research to suggest that in keeping the historical context for a historical document a secret, the teacher ensures equality in student effort to understand it, there is nothing to suggest that historical ignorance serves the cause of social justice. We have*

good reason to worry about the content of the proposed national history and social studies standards…if an animating idea behind Common Core's English language arts standards is that ignorance makes us equal.[16]

Close Reading will Better Prepare Students for Computerized Scoring on Essay Tests? It has been speculated by some that CC's obsession with "close reading" and requiring students to only look within the text for "evidence" rather than outside sources or teacher's giving any background information, is because the future plans is for the computers to do all the scoring on the assessment tests, including even the essays. Computerized scoring of written essays requires a controlled vocabulary.

Thus, students are being trained from early ages to rely solely on the text at hand when writing about a passage so that the same vocabulary will be in their essays, and the pre-programmed computer will recognize the words and give the student credit for using them. .[17]

Cold Readings: This term is often used interchangeably with close reading. Reading Anchor Standard 10 defines cold reading as: "The ability to read and comprehend complex literary and informational texts independently and proficiently."[18]

Sandra Stotsky states the following about her opposition to cold reading where the teacher is not allowed to give any historical background:

> *Two of the many bizarre ideas that the "chief architect" of Common Core's English language arts standards has mandated in our "national standards" or told teachers outright are the notion that teachers should do "cold" readings of historical documents like the Gettysburg Address and that doing so "levels the playing field." Both ideas suggest the thinking of someone who has never taught in K-12. Worse yet, they contribute to historical illiteracy.*

"Closing the Achievement Gap:" For some reason, high achievement by hard working students in our public schools is now no longer applauded; it is just the opposite. Under the new mantra of "social justice," all students are supposed to come out of our schools the same, without a wide gap between their achievement. The only way for that to happen is to lower the standards.

A teacher in the LA area, told me that she was told by her principal that if she did not stop demanding such high expectations of her students that her job was in jeopardy. She was making the other teacher look bad. She did not change her teaching or what she expected of her students, and sure enough, she lost her job.

Comments by Mary Graber, PhD, who is Fighting Common Core in Georgia – a Principal Praises CC because it "Closes the Achievement Gap":

Common Core encourages "close reading" of only short excerpts and encourages a lot of group work so that struggling readers get the material. The dumbed-down standards make the teachers look good. One principal at a hearing in Georgia said he liked CC because it closed the "achievement gap."

Why Would Educators want to Close the Achievement Gap? Mary Graber gives the real reason – a dumbed down, more malleable workforce, content to do menial jobs:

I noted it in one of my articles - If you dumb things down enough and spread out the work and grades you will close all kinds of gaps. Everyone does well. Teacher is happy. Principal is happy. Superintendent is happy. Chamber of Commerce is happy. Governor is happy. Voila! You have a ready workforce.[19]

College and Career Ready: These words are often used to promote Common Core, and as CC is getting less and less popular, these words are often used to replace it. What do they really mean? Are students going to be better prepared for college and career as CC implies? Actually, they will not, as you will see from the many statements made throughout this book.

Some people are afraid that what these words really mean is that Common Core is a two-tier system, similar to what Germany has, where early on, students will be classified as college-bound, or career-bound according to test scores and data collected on them.

The college-bound students will supposedly take more rigorous courses necessary for entrance into college. The career-bound will be steered towards just one certain career that will not demand more advanced classes.

This may sound good on the surface but it is against the tradition of freedoms and opportunities that Americans have had that they could be whatever they would like to be. Some students are late bloomers and do better the more mature they become. Under Common Core, their opportunities for growth would be limited. Some call it the **"Five Ls"**: **"limited learning for life-long labor."**

According to experts, the Common Core standards have been so dumbed down that even those students who are college bound are only going to be prepared for a junior college entry level, not a real university.

"Minimal College Readiness:" As was mentioned in the introduction to this chapter, even Jason Zimba, the leading writer of the math standards, admitted in a March 2010 meeting held before the Massachusetts Board of Education that Common Core math will only prepare students for *"minimal college readiness." "It will not be for STEM (science, technology, engineering, and mathematics), and it will not be for selective colleges like UC Berkeley."* His comments and the transcripts of his exact words are written in a report by Dr. Milgram and Sandra Scotsky, who were on the Common Core validation committee.[20] Mrs. Scotsky was present when Zimba made those statements and was also asking him questions. One can also view Jason Zimba saying those words in a documentary film that was released the end of March, 2014, "Building the Machine," which has made quite a stir and ruffled lots of feathers across the nation.[21]

Dr. James Milgram, PhD, professor emeritus of math at Stanford, was asked to be part of the validation committee for the Common Core math standards and turned out to be the only one of the 25-member committee who had a PhD math degree He refused to sign off approving the standards. He believes the standards to be

lowered, not higher. He said the teaching of algebra is being postponed from the 8th grade to the 9th, leaving no room for calculus in the senior year. Little memorization is asked for, and a confusing form of Geometry will be taught that was thrown out of the Soviet Union 50 years ago. Key topics of Euclidian Geometry, proofs, and deductive reasoning will no longer be taught.

Professor Milgram stated that the math standards were "a product of politics and special interest groups." "A number of these sources were mainly focused on things like making the standards as non-challenging as possible. Others were focused on making sure their favorite topics were present, and handled in the way they liked." He also said that it led to a number of "extremely serious failings in the Common Core that made it premature for any State hoping to improve math scores to implement them and that the Core Math standards were designed to reflect very low expectations."[22]

He also stated that "by the end of the 7th year, CC math is about two years behind the math of other high-achieving countries."[23] It also leaves students one or two years behind the National Mathematics Advisory Panel's recommendations and the requirements of some States.

Dr. Sandra Stotsky, PhD, is a former English teacher at the University of Arkansas, and one of the experts who helped Massachusetts achieve some of the highest standards in the nation. Stotsky was asked to be on the validation committee for the English, Language Arts Standards. She, like Milgram, refused to sign off on the standards believing they would be lowered. She said:

...opposition needs to start with the 'standards' themselves because they are so vulnerable. They will lower the academic level of what 70% of our kids study in school. That's part of the intention behind them.

As has been mentioned, Common Core lowers the amount of classical literature that is being taught from 80% in elementary down to 50%, and in high school down to 30%. It will be replaced with "informational text" so that students can better read non-fiction and on-line assignments.

Why is that so bad? Many great works of art won't be taught – classical literature teaches moral truths, skills in making wise decisions, how to be responsible citizens, the value of liberty, etc. One does not learn that from a computer manual or other on-line "informational texts."

Sandra Stotsky also states that the Common Core standards are not real standards but are **empty "skill sets."** They state such things as the students "will read closely," "they will analyze how and why." Such are skills that can be stated for any grade level and any subject. A real standard, according to Stotsky, must state the "literature or culture content." If the standard is well-written then it gives a true objective, the criteria for judging something. The curriculum follows with the actual study to reach the standard. The assessment test is also written according to the standards.[24]

Not College and Career ready: Stotsky argues that the lack of literary material required by the standards does "not ensure…sufficient literary and cultural knowledge for authentic college-level work."

Critique of the standards by other education professionals, policy analysts, and government officials:

1. **The standards are academically deficient.** Other education professionals agree with professors Millgram and Stotsky that the standards are not high but just the opposite.
2. **Standards are not really necessary for a good education.** Brookings Institute policy analyst Grover Whitehurst observes that "high academic standards and high student achievement are not connected." Statistics show that states with high academic standards score about the same on standardized assessments as states with low standards.
3. **There was coercion of governors to sign on to Common Core and the carrot and stick way of implementing them:** Randi Weingarten, president of the FTA, the second-largest teachers' union in America, and Diane Ravitch, professor at NYU, and an education historian who has pushed for national standards for years, both criticize the government's use of Race to the Top (RTTT) funding to coerce States into adopting and implementing the Common Core.
4. **Costs:** States will have a difficult time shouldering the enormous costs of implementing Common Core. Estimates range from $12 to $16 billion for the entire nation. Yet the federal government has given only $4.35 billion as the bribe to entice them to sign on.
5. **Federal Department of Education takeover of State's Authority:** Finally, members of Congress, U.S. senators, and the Republican National Committee oppose Common Core because it is essentially the usurpation by the federal government of education authority that is to be left to the States.

Lawmakers have raised concerns about the Department of Education's unilateral revision of FERPA (Family Education Rights Protection Act), its push for expanded state longitudinal data systems, its close involvement in Common Core implementation and in the assessment results.[25]

Commonality: One of the mantras that is used to promote Common Core is the "commonality" that such a program will bring - meaning if a student moves from one State to another, they will not have to have a whole new program. They will not find themselves struggling behind, nor will they be too far ahead. They will actually not miss a lesson. Using computers and e-books, all States will have the same program, the same lessons, the same instructions on the same day.[26]

Maybe that sounds like a good idea on the surface, but has commonality ever been the tradition of education in our nation? **No, our nation has operated under a system of competition not commonality.** Competition between schools motivates a lower performing school to want to improve and do better. When everything is all the same, there is no more competition and no incentive to improve or to become better. Everything sinks to the lowest common denominator.

Compassion or Social Justice: Compassion in one school district, Bennett Valley in Santa Rosa, CA, had gained such importance they included it along with the Four Cs mentioned at the beginning of Chapter One. So they now have Five Cs of Common Core.

Over time, the word compassion has morphed in its meaning to be just another word for **social justice,** which is running rampart through the entire Common Core standards and curriculum. No matter what subject, even math, social justice is being taught.

31

Social Justice in Math: This picture shows a logo from a conference for teachers showing how even in math social justice is being taught – "Creating balance in an unjust world." And how are math teachers supposed to do that? Perhaps the following will help answer that question:

I was a guest on a talk radio program for KID in Idaho Falls, April, 18, 2013. A man called into the show from Pocatello, a city about an hour east of Idaho Falls. He said that his wife had been selected to be one of the math teachers to be part of a committee to submit math questions for the Smarter Balance Assessment Consortium that was creating the Common Core test. His wife was told this was a great honor that she was selected.

She sat through a long meeting where the teachers on the committee were told what kind of math questions they could not submit. One of those was anything to do with a mortgage. Why? "Because that would be socially unjust." Not every child comes from a home where the parents have a mortgage. Many parents are just renting their homes. So, from now on no child may be taught about mortgages because that would be discriminatory against those who do not have one. Instead of teaching the child about home ownership and letting him aspire to someday own his own home, the whole subject will be dropped from the curriculum – all for the sake of social justice. The man calling in on the show said at this point, his wife was thoroughly disgusted with the whole thing and left the meeting and resigned from the committee.

"Fight for Social Justice": These are some of the quotes showing the emphasis on social justice by Arne Duncan, Obama's Secretary of Education:

*I believe that education is the civil rights issue of our generation. And if you care about promoting opportunity and reducing inequality, the classroom is the place to start. Great teaching is about so much more than education; **it is a daily fight for social justice.**"* – Arne Duncan, October 9, 2009 speech.[27]

*"The fight for quality education is about so much more than education. **It's a fight for social justice.**"* – IES research conference, 2009.

What does Social Justice Really Mean? From the teacher in Pocatello, Idaho, we learn that it means not only **no discrimination**, but **no aspiration** to anything better than anyone else. One writer, Dean Kalaha, states that "social justice is a euphemism for progressive/liberal power and ideology."[28]

The Foundational Philosophy Behind Common Core is a Social Justice Agenda: As one does more and more research in the background of Common Core and its creators, one discovers social justice is the uniting link that brought all sorts of progressives t the table and will continue to unite them. Education to them is exactly as Arne Duncan said, "A daily fight for social justice."

"Create Students Ready for Social Action:" The ultimate goal of Common Core is to bring about social justice through the students themselves. They will be totally indoctrinated into the progressive philosophy and will "force" the social-justice agenda through their own actions. This is described in an article by blogger Diane Rufino, May 11, 2013, where she states the following:

> *The foundational philosophy of Common Core is to create students ready for social action so they can force a social-justice agenda. Common Core is not about students who actually have a grasp of the intricate facts of a true set of ..."core knowledge." Common Core is about..."an obsession with race, class, gender, and sexuality as the forces of history and political identity."*
>
> *Nationalizing education via Common Core is about promoting an agenda of anti-capitalism, sustainability, white guilt, global citizenship, self-esteem, affective math, and culture sensitive spelling and language. This is done in the name of consciousness raising, moral relativity, fairness, diversity, and multiculturalism.*[29] [Note: in the chapter on Curriculum, one can read examples of how much of these "social justice" agendas are being taught.]

Social Justice is also all about "Redistribution of Wealth" – taking from those who have and giving to those who have not – so we can all be equal – equally poor that is. The elitists pushing this upon us will be the only ones with any wealth.

As I mention in my book, *Common Core, a Trojan Horse for Education Reform*, part of the plan is to "**take money from the suburban schools and give to the inner city schools**," which will eventually cause the wealthier schools to have to close down.[30]

And to achieve true social justice we must have all students the same – equally dumbed down. Stanley Kurz in his book, *Spreading the Wealth*, states that Common Core is designed to "artificially suppress achievement gaps" by "undercutting standards," "defining performance down" and "equalizing college readiness."[31]

Obama's U.S. Equity and Excellence Commission recently published a report called "For Each And Every Child" that is all about redistributing education and wealth. You will read the following phrases about what Obama's plans are:

...allocate resources to level the playing field across states; address disparities; advance national equity and excellence goals using a combination of incentives and enforcement.

Destroy Local Control: How can Obama achieve his social justice and equity plans? He recognizes that one of the biggest hindrances is local control of schools by school boards and city and county governments: In the report he stated, *"Historically, our approach to local control has often made it difficult to achieve funding adequacy and educational equity."*

This is one more of the deceptive, hidden goals of Common Core. As you destroy local control; you can have easier access to force redistribution of wealth, to take from the wealthier schools and give to the inner city schools, all through the process of consensus, making the people believe that this was done by the voice of the people. (Thanks to Rabbi Daniel Lapin and Christal Swazey for the above quotes about social justice found on Christal's website. She is one of the Three Moms Against Common Core in Utah.)[32]

Social Justice will be Incorporated into the SAT Test: David Coleman, the Chief Architect of the CC English Language Arts standards, and the President of the College Board, has announced that the SAT will be changed to "level the playing field" for high school students from a wider range of families.

Dean Kalahar, in an article for the American Thinker, questions this plan, "Wait a minute: the SAT was created to "level the playing field." That was how the SAT was originally sold to the American public. It was a test that would make it possible for any student, no matter how low his socio-economic background, his race, or gender, who worked hard enough to pass the test, could then be eligible to enter the finest universities. As Kalahar states, "a test by its very un-human nature does not have feelings, attitudes, or stereotypes."

Kalahar Calls the New Plan for the SAT "Stunning Hypocrisy":

> *...keep using the SAT testing system but change the test to get the discriminatory results they believe achieve "social justice," a euphemism for progressive/liberal power and ideology. That way you fool the public by using the SAT's good name and reputation but bias the test against academic excellence and college readiness.*
>
> *...to end inequality of results based on misperceived injustice and discrimination, some want to change the SAT so they can use discrimination and inequitable practices. That's just stunning hypocrisy and hubris.*[33]

Comprehensive: We are told that Common Core is to be "comprehensive" in its implementation.[34] What does that mean? According to Webster's dictionary, comprehensive means "all encompassing, a large scope, inclusive." That means those pushing CC want it to be for every school and every child, even those in private Christian schools and those who are home schooled.

They also want it to affect colleges and universities by having the college entrance tests, the ACT and the SAT, aligned to the Common Core standards. The GED, the high school equivalency test required for most jobs, will also be aligned to Common Core.

Common Core is not just supposed to be for the United States. It is meant to be world-wide, promoted by UNESCO and the United

Nations. Thus CC will be comprehensive all over the globe, no escaping it.

Consensus: We are told that Common Core was formed by its creators coming to a consensus on the many suggestions given. Many Americans are so used to hearing the word consensus that they are confused thinking that it is a good word, "that is how a democracy works, that decisions are made by consensus, by the majority rule."

Others believe that consensus is undermining our entire concept of what form of government we have. We are not a democracy; we are a Constitutional Republic, and we are not supposed to operate on consensus, or majority rule. We are to operate on the Rule of Law that protects the rights of all people, even the minorities.

One young Christian student in the public schools, Ashley Anderson, described consensus as following:

> *It's everyone coming together, realizing their differences, and putting them aside for the sake of the group. When this happens, all individuality, patriotism, and faith disappear.* ***You can't be part of the consensus process and keep your faith in God...people learn to compromise individual beliefs and ideas in order to work for "common goals."*** *Working together as a team, (soon) using the same currency and having the same leader(s), the same ideals, and the same minds, all over the world, is all part of the global government that the United Nations proposes.[35]*

Computer-based: Eventually, the goal is for every child to have a computer, which will be their primary source for learning. Students will be taught with e-books or on the internet, not only with their assignments but also with their testing. Text books will be a thing of the past.

This is touted as being modern, up to date, where children will be truly geared for the 21st century, where everything is computer-based. But will it really be so wonderful? According to a study done at Western Michigan University in 2012, only 27.7 % of students who were part of virtual schools (taught by computers all day long) met federally mandated academic goals compared to 52% of public schools where teachers still taught the classes.[36] It is obviously better to have a teacher in front of the class and interacting with students. The following is a comment by a teacher stating exactly that:

> *As much as I love technology I know that a computer program could never replace the relationship between a teacher and a student. In this day and age authentic interactions are harder to come by. That is one of a hundred reasons why a computer should not be allowed to replace a teacher. One teacher, 60 computers, 60 students is not authentic. It's a factory. Minds are not items on a conveyor belt. You can't mass produce intelligence, citizenship, compassion, or problem solving.* (Amber Henry response comments to an article entitled, "My Teacher the Computer" by Kelly Kovacic)[37]

Computers Make Possible "Flipped Classrooms": Schools across the nation are trying out a new program called "Flipped Classrooms." According to *the River Journal*, a newspaper that reports on several communities in upstate New York, eight teachers were selected at Irvington High School, to try out the Flipped Classroom program. The article describes it as:

> *Rather than students sitting for a lecture and then working on the material at home via homework, they watch an*

online video or Power point presentation at home that has been created by or voiced-over by their teacher, then come into the class to do their work.[38]

The idea originated in 2007 with two teachers in Woodland Park, Colorado, Jonathan Bergman and Aaron Sams, who wanted a way to pass lectures on to students who were sick and not able to attend class for a while. They discovered software to make power points of their lectures and posted them online for the students to look at while at home in their beds. According to a website promoting it, many schools are now using it. Students don't need to rely just on their own teacher's presentations. An organization called the Khan Academy has 2400 short video presentations that students can access to teach them in a wide range of subjects including arithmetic, physics, economics and history.[39]

Computerized Adaptive Testing (CAT): This is a program in which the computerized test adapts to the student's performance: As can be seen in the following illustration, if a child is doing well on the test, the questions will become more difficult. If the child is not doing well, the questions become easier.

Closing the Achievement Gap: As can be seen on the illustration on the next page, eventually, the test questions become too difficult for most advanced students, so they are now given easier ones that bring their scores down to the middle. The lower performing children, who are able to answer the easier questions, are raised up to the middle.

So, essentially, the higher performing students and the lower performing ones come out about the same. This is called "Closing the Achievement Gap," something social justice advocates have wanted to do for a long time. They do not want a wide gap between students who excel and those who do not. That is called "socially unjust." So let's bring them all down to the middle. That is why some people call Common Core and Obama's Race to the Top, really a "Race to the Middle."

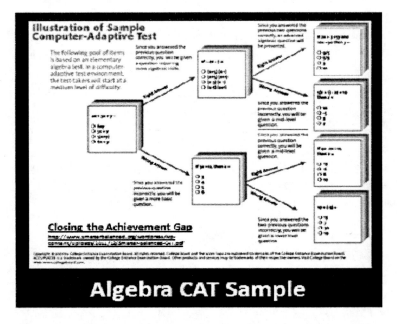

Computer Adaptive Testing used for Reprogramming: How much easier it will be to indoctrinate and change a child's attitude to a new way of thinking by making him keep repeating a question on a test until he gets the politically correct answer right. Even if the child knows from his conservative values and teachings at home that the answer is not correct, he will have to give the programmed answer or he cannot go on in the test. And with the data collection going on when a child takes the computerized test, will it be possible to use that answer against the child in his future?

Computer Waves - There is also a health risk of exposing children too much to the harmful electro-magnetic waves of computers as they sit in front of their computers for so many hours a day.

There is even a greater health risk from the RF waves of Wi-Fi, which probably will be in every classroom if every child has a computer, the ultimate goal of Common Core. Wi-Fi has been banned in public schools in New Zealand, Australia, and many nations in Europe because of the health risks to children whose skulls and bones are not developed enough to resist the harmful rays of Wi-Fi. These nations have their internet connection done through wires not wireless.[40]

Computer Facilitators: As has already been mentioned, eventually, the goal is that all lessons will be taught digitally by computers, with very little instruction or actual teaching from the teachers. Teachers are just going to become facilitators. How many teachers, who have spent four or five or even more years getting their college degrees and becoming experts in their subjects, relish the thought of just becoming computer facilitators, without any real opportunity to teach their subjects? If they don't like this idea – tough! Teachers are already being warned that if they try to go back to their old files or their old ways, their jobs will be in jeopardy. Being a tenured teacher does not seem to mean anything anymore as to job security.

Perhaps the day will come when teachers will no longer need to have college degrees or to be certified to teach in the classroom. After all, they will not be teachers, just computer lab technicians or facilitators. That would certainly save lots of money for a State strapped with trying to come up with the funds to bring in the new technology for Common Core. Non-certified facilitators do not get as high a salary as a certified teacher. So computers come in and the teachers go out.

Continuality: Common Core is designed to be permanent. It is to be revolutionary, with no turning back to traditional education. If all the States are locked into it, all having invested $millions and $billions for the new computers and software, e-books, and intensive teacher development, it will be very hard to go back to any other method. If all the States have made the enormous changes in methods and teaching, and if they are all dependent on some kind of grant money, or waiver, or Title I money from the federal government, it will be very hard to shake free the shackles of Common Core, which over the years will become even more tightly bound around them.

Constructivism: Teachers are being trained that the proper common core method is to let the children construct their own meaning, their own understanding, their own truths. (Actually, rarely, is the word truth even used. Students are taught that there are no absolute truths.) Even in math, the children are left to construct their own meaning.

Another name for constructivism is "funderstanding – or finding one's own understanding. The following is what is written on a "funderstanding" website:

> *The purpose of learning is for an individual to construct his or her own meaning, not just memorize the "right" answers and regurgitate someone else's meaning...*[41]

So, teachers are no longer to teach. As a teacher, I would not relish the idea of no longer be able to stand in front of a classroom and impart the great ideas, meaning, truths, and the correct and right answers that I spent so long acquiring.

What if education throughout the ages had always had this new "constructivism" philosophy? Would we have not learned from those who came before us? Would we have to redo the progress that has already been made? Would we have to go back and re-invent the wheel so we can proudly say that we "constructed our own meaning"?

Consensus and the Delphi Technique: The Delphi Technique is the method used to bring everyone to consensus, especially if they are a diverse group with different opinions.

It was developed by the Rand Corporation back in the 1950s and is defined by business as "a multistep method used to estimate future demand for a product or service whereby a special group of experts in economic forecasting exchange are drawn to consensus."

The name comes from an ancient Greek temple of Delphi, where kings would travel far to speak to the priestess there who supposedly had the gift of forecasting the future. However, she would skilfully word the forecast in such a way that whether the outcome was good or bad for the king, she could say, "See that is what I told you."

What the Delphi technique is really is a psychological method to manipulate a diverse group of people into thinking that they had some kind of input in a pre-conceived, and already developed outcome. That is what happened to anyone from a local State who thinks that they had any input into the Standards or the Assessment test. It did not matter how high up they were, whether an educator, or administrator, or State School board trustee, or governor, the Standards and assessments were already written by a cartel or consortium behind closed doors, as you will read in Chapter III and VI. Anyone who thinks differently was "delphied" or deceived into thinking they were a vital part of the whole process.[42]

"Curriculum has nothing to do with the standards." For some reason teachers are being taught to use this mantra when the Common Core standards are being criticized. Maybe it is to somehow make it appear that teachers still have some flexibility and can come up with their own curriculum? Or it is to make it appear that Common Core is not in violation of federal laws, since the curriculum and testing is to not be created or under the control of the federal government? Well, in reply to this statement, let us hear from the expert and Common Core's biggest benefactor, Bill Gates, himself. Many people even call Common Core, "Gates ed," since he is the one who has given millions to fund the cartel that created it and has given millions to help spread it across the nation and even worldwide. (See Chapter III for the exact numbers.)

Gates made the following statement about how the curriculum, the standards and the testing will all line up together at the National Conference of State Legislators July 21, 2009:

> *We'll know we've succeeded when the curriculum and the tests are aligned to these standards...To create just these kinds of tests—next-generation assessments aligned to the common core. When the tests are aligned to the common standards, the curriculum will line up as well.*

"Customers eager to buy products": Gates reveals perhaps a little too much about what is really behind this new education program called Common Core and why he has been so happily investing millions in it. It is all about making money. He will be getting $billions back as will many other people. Gates continues:

—and that will unleash powerful market forces in the service of better teaching. For the first time, there will be a large base of customers eager to buy products that can help every kid learn and every teacher get better...."[43]

Closer Look at the Standards - How Repetitive They Are, Without Meaningful Progression, "Fundamentally Flawed," Complex and Confusing: The following information comes from Allyson Williams, a member of the Truth in American Education network. She gives specific examples of the standards and her observations:

> *...one thing I notice when I look at the standards is how **they just repeat themselves over and over.** There are a few very basic skills like establishing a main idea and supporting ideas and there doesn't seem to be any meaningful progression. For example, I cut and pasted these standards from each grade level so you could compare them side by side. Is there really a difference between "clear" and "relevant" evidence and "strong" and "thorough" evidence?*

- **CCSS.ELA-Literacy.W.6.1** Write arguments to support claims with clear reasons and relevant evidence.
- **CCSS.ELA-Literacy.RL.7.1** Cite several pieces of textual evidence to support analysis of what the text says explicitly as well as inferences drawn from the text.

- **CCSS.ELA-Literacy.RL.8.1** Cite the textual evidence that most strongly supports an analysis of what the text says explicitly as well as inferences drawn from the text.
- **CCSS.ELA-Literacy.RL.9-10.1** Cite strong and thorough textual evidence to support analysis of what the text says explicitly as well as inferences drawn from the text.
- **CCSS.ELA-Literacy.RL.11-12.1** Cite strong and thorough textual evidence to support analysis of what the text says explicitly as well as inferences drawn from the text, including determining where the text leaves matters uncertain.

Williams explains more about the standards and their lexile text complexity and how flawed that is:

> *It seems the primary progression in CCSS is the lexile text complexity, and I think their theory is **fundamentally flawed**. Textual complexity is not synonymous with the complexity or importance of ideas. The greatest thoughts of civilizations as embodied in classic literature are often ranked below informational texts in lexile complexity when my own preference would be to increase the former as children mature.*

What does Lexile mean? For the average lay person who has not heard the latest educrat newspeak, the "Lexile® Framework for Reading is an approach to reading and text measurement. There are two Lexile measures - *the reader measure and the text measure*:

> *A Lexile reader measure represents a person's reading ability on the Lexile scale. A Lexile text measure represents a text's difficulty level on the Lexile scale. When used together, they can help a reader choose a book or other reading material that is at an appropriate difficulty level. The Lexile reader measure can also be*

used to monitor a reader's growth in reading ability over time.

A picture on the website shows that the higher up on the scale you go (all the way to 2000), the more difficult the book is. So if you want an easier book to read, you need to choose a book that is lower on the scale (which goes all the way down to 5).[44]

Comparison of the CC Standards with the Highly Acclaimed Standards of Sandra Stotsky for Massachusetts: Allyson Williams shows examples of the clear, direct standards coming from those written by Sandra Stotsky in Massachusetts and compares them with the complex, wordy, confusing CCSS standards: [Those of Stotsky are in bold and not italicized]

- **1.VC.1 Predict the meaning of a new word from its context when reading a text or listening to one read aloud.**
- *CCSS.ELA-Literacy.L.1.4* Determine or clarify the meaning of unknown and multiple-meaning words and phrases based on grade 1 reading and content, choosing flexibly from an array of strategies.
- *CCSS.ELA-Literacy.L.1.4a* Use sentence-level context as a clue to the meaning of a word or phrase.
- *CCSS.ELA-Literacy.L.1.4b* Use frequently occurring affixes as a clue to the meaning of a word.
- **1.VC.2 Demonstrate understanding of concepts by sorting written words and pictures into various categories (e.g., living things, animals, birds).**
- *CCSS.ELA-Literacy.L.1.5a* Sort words into categories (e.g., colors, clothing) to gain a sense of the concepts the categories represent.
- *CCSS.ELA-Literacy.L.1.5b* Define words by category and by one or more key attributes (e.g., a duck is a bird that swims; a tiger is a large cat with stripes).

- *CCSS.ELA-Literacy.L.1.5d* Distinguish shades of meaning among verbs differing in manner (e.g., look, peek, glance, stare, glare, scowl) and adjectives differing in intensity (e.g., large, gigantic) by defining or choosing them or by acting out the meanings.

Williams writes: *"I have a daughter about first grade age. I'm trying to picture how she would explain the difference between peek and glance or a glare and a scowl."*

- *CCSS.ELA-Literacy.L.1.6* Use words and phrases acquired through conversations, reading and being read to, and responding to texts, including using frequently occurring conjunctions to signal simple relationships (e.g., because).

Williams asks: *"...what does this last sentence mean? Isn't this just what people do? How else do people acquire language? Why not just write a standard about conjunctions?"*

Cursive-writing: We are being told that there will be no requirement for cursive writing to be taught.[45] However, in California, teachers are told you can go head and teach cursive if you want to under the 15% wiggle-room rule, but it won't be on the assessment test. Most teachers are very worried about that test since in many States their salary is tied to the test results, so they would rather not deviate from the prescribed Common Core material.

Chapter II –

Hidden C-Words that are not being Spoken about or are Downplayed that are Radically Transforming Education and our Once-Free Nation

This chapter gives in alphabetical order the many hidden C words that will help the reader understand what Common Core is really all about and the detrimental effect it is having on our nation.

Canned Script: Teachers are finding out that once CC is fully implemented, they no longer have the freedom to teach as they choose. Their every words are chosen for them. One teacher from

Delaware describes it as a canned script. "I was given a curriculum and told by my administration to teach it "word-for-word." In a meeting with my administration, I was reprimanded with "Don't forget, standards drive our instruction." The teacher's entire letter was published in the *Washington Post*, Nov. 13, 2013. Excerpts from it can be read in chapter IX.

Canned On-line Videos Suggested by Bill Gates to Teach Students: In the same talk that Bill Gates gave to State legislators mentioned at the end of Chapter I, July 21, 2009, he also recommended videos to be used in the teaching of Common Core. That way teachers won't have to really do the teaching – just play the video and have the "master teacher" take over the class. Of course, these videos will make it so much easier to indoctrinate the children to the new philosophies and methods of Common Core. Even if the teacher does not agree, what can she possibly do about it? She no longer is really teaching the class:

> *There can also be—and there should be —online videos of every required course, taught by master teachers, and made available free of charge...They are phenomenal tools that can help every student in the country—if we get the common standards that will encourage people to make them.*[46]

A Year's Worth of Canned Classroom-Ready Lesson Plans by the NEA: Dennis Van Roekel, the President of the National Education Association, the largest teacher union in the nation, suggested that the NEA should create "a year's worth of classroom-ready lesson plans aligned to Common Core and available for teachers free." Surprisingly, this suggestion came just after the NEA had received almost $4 million from Bill Gates in July of 2013. This was the same month that the NEA formerly indorsed the standards. [47]

Capital (human): This is the new definition of our children. To the elite behind Common Core, our children are not unique individuals, created by a loving Heavenly Father, with unique gifts and talents; they are nothing more than human capital to be used and exploited in their global workforce – to be marched through the factory schools and come out with the same one-size-fits-all, cookie-cutter design, and, above all, have the same politically correct socialist mindset and thinking.

Cartel-Written: We are being told that Common Core is "States-written and States-led," but that is not true. As you will read in Chapter III, it was a very large cartel who wrote the standards and there were no teachers representing different States among them. Maybe they were able to submit ideas, but it was a "suggestion box" format, with five main people actually doing the writing, and none of those had any K-12 teaching experience.

Centralization – Common Core puts all the control of education, the development of its standards and testing under the control of the federal Department of Education. This has been happening gradually, but under Obama and Common Core, it is now on fast track. Central control is the same thing as socialism or nationalism.

Has this made education better in our country? No, just the opposite. As our education system has become more and more socialized (more controlled by the federal government, less controlled by the States and the people) the quality of education has declined. Socialism is killing the quality of education in the United States, in spite of the fact that we spend more money on education than any other nation in the world.

Centralization and Its Effect on State and Local School Boards: As has already been mentioned, one of the goals of Common Core and its education reform is to destroy local representation. As we are seeing with regionalization, where counties and city governments are being placed under the jurisdiction of large regional governments, that have unelected commissioners ruling over them, experts are saying that is the plan for education as well. One would think the local school boards and superintendents would be realizing this and come out strongly opposed to Common Core. Some of them are highly paid for what they do. Their jobs and salaries are going to be eliminated.

Sandra Stotsky was asked if the goal was to not only eliminate local school boards and superintendents, but also State boards? Her answer was:

> *I don't think it's much of a leap to think the state boards will be out of jobs shortly after the local boards. Unless they sign on to become "state-assigned" or "redistributed" to regional nodes of supervision under the federal U. S. Department of Education. Makes you wonder if any of them realize yet they have backed the wrong horse?*

That explains why the data that is collected on the children already bypasses local and State school boards and goes to the consortium, then, to the Federal Department of education – then who knows where?

Central Control and Indoctrination: Every totalitarian State has central control over education. That way they can ensure that the students will only hear the prescribed indoctrination and propaganda to make them be faithful and obedient servants to the supreme dictator. It was Vladimir Lenin, former leader for the Soviet Union, who said, *"Give me four years to teach the children and the seed I have sown will never be uprooted."*

"Change": Remember Obama's promise in 2008 to achieve the "fundamental transformation of our society?" If Common Core is totally implemented that goal would be accomplished. How much easier it will be when education is under one central control "big brother" to bring in to the schools and into the minds of the youth and future leaders of our nation whatever socialist philosophy big brother believes in.

Remember Obama's mantra in 2008 of "Hope and Change?" Change has long been the word used for socialist government transformation, starting with the plans of one of Obama's heroes - Franklin Delenore Roosevelt, FDR, to continue to bring us closer and closer to the desired socialist government that progressives are striving to create. FDR even had an acronym for it. It was called "The Politics of Change (TPOC) in Local Government Reform." Along with that acronym, FDR created a National Resource Planning Board (NRPB). Its sole purpose was to restructure our form of government and turn the States into nine large regional governments. Why would he want to do that? The States had always been a pain in the neck to a president and his cohorts who want to execute law without anyone holding them back. Just as the three branches of government – executive, legislative, and judicial - are to provide a check and balance so not any one branch becomes too large and powerful, **the States are like a fourth branch of government, to also provide a fourth check**. Certain rights and powers are to be left to the States and not to be infringed on by the big federal government.

How could a president get around that fourth check? Just abolish the States and turn them into large regions that would no longer have the power that States have. FDR was following the advice of his good buddy Joseph Stalin, the dictator of the Soviet Union, who wrote in his book, *Marxism and the National Question* (published in 1943):

> *Divide the world into regional groups as a transitional stage to total world government. Later the regional*

groups can be brought all the way into single world dictatorship."[48]

FDR even had a map drawn up showing the USA divided into ten large regions (districts) and it was on the cover of a cereal box so that children and their parents could get used to the idea of regional government. The map is shown on page 125 of the book I wrote in 2010 called *By Stealth and Deception*. Little did I know then how far the plans for changing our form of government into regions and regional control had already progressed.[49]

Change Agents: This has become the accepted name now for teachers, administrators, and school psychologists who are all about changing children's attitudes. Another name for them is facilitators.

Change the Name: When people begin to find out just how bad a program is, the progressives have a great solution – just give it a new title and go right on with the new program. That is also what is happening with Common Core. Iowa is calling it Iowa Core; Utah is calling it Utah Core; Florida is calling it "Next Generation Sunshine State Standards; Indiana which has supposedly gotten rid of it is using the name "College and Career Readiness Standards. Nevada is calling it Nevada Academic Content Standards. Arizona Governor Jan Brewer recently signed an executive order to erase the name "Common Core" for their new math and reading standards, and Louisiana lawmakers are mulling a name change as well.[50]

The former governor of Arkansas, Mike Huckabee, was serving as the governor in charge of the National Governors Association in 2006, when Common Core was first being presented to them, and he believes that he is one of those who helped create it. [If that is the case, he was probably "Delphied" into thinking that he had a significant part in creating something that had more or less already been created by Achieve. Achieve skillfully convinced many that they were in on ground zero in this plan when it was already planned. This is called the Delphi Technique, created by the Rand Corporation in the 1960s. Skilled facilitators are trained to persuade a group of people to adopt a preconceived and already planned program , by making the people think it is their own idea.]

Huckabee is still a big Common Core supporter, but according to *Fox News*, at a February, 2014 meeting of the Council of Chief State School Officers, which helped draft the standards, Huckabee told State education leaders that they should be urged to ditch the "Common Core" name, because it had become "toxic." **"Rebrand it, refocus it, but don't retreat,"** Huckabee said.[51]

Earlier in December, 2013, he said the following about Common Core on a facebook posting that makes it sound like he had changed his mind about CC and no longer supported it: [This also makes it sound like the States can do whatever they want to it to change it. But that is also not correct. States are only supposed to be able to change it within 15%, and since those changes won't be on the assessment test, most States are not bothering about it.]

> *...I don't support what Common Core has become in many states or school districts. I'm dead set against the federal government creating a uniform curriculum for any subject; I oppose the collection of personal data on students that would identify them and track them and any effort to give that personal information to the federal government. I am steadfast in my belief that parents should ultimately decide the best venue for their children's education, whether public schools, private schools, religious schools or home-schools. I believe education is a local or state function — not a federal one...[52]*

Department of Education no longer Calling it Common Core: One of the opponents of Common Core who is part of the nationwide network of Truth in American Education reported that she heard Deborah Delisle from the Federal Department of Education talk March 20, 2014, on "The Federal Education Perspective: Where We Are and Where We Are Going."

Delisle talked about the 5 pillars of the DOE's efforts: pre-K, K-12 reform, college affordability, school climate, and the equity initiative. She used the phrase "college and career ready" but never once mention the words "Common Core."

Changing Attitudes - this is what Common Core is all about and what education goals have been centered on for many years. For example, Dr. Bertrand Raven, professor in the Psychology Department at the University of California, Los Angeles, was in the process of building a computer-based device for "changing attitudes" back in the 1960s. This was discovered by Betsy Kraus, a Catholic researcher and writer:

> *This device will work on the principle that students' attitudes could be changed effectively by using the Socratic method of asking an appropriate series of leading questions designed to right the balance between appropriate attitudes and those deemed less acceptable. For instance, after first determining a student's constellation of attitudes through appropriate testing procedures, the machine would calculate which attitudes are "out of phase" and which of these are amenable to change.*[53]

Charter Schools: Why are Charter Schools included in the hidden Cs of Common Core? Aren't charter schools a solution to the problem of education? Does that not make things better to have school choice? That is what I used to think as well. Then I found out that in the majority of cases, when a school becomes a Charter School, they no longer come under the auspices of the elected school board, so no longer under the control of the voters in that district. They are usually run by a private corporation, a local charter board, or come directly under a State-appointed Charter Commission. However, they still receive tax paying dollars to help fund them.

If parents have complaints, who do they go to? If there is no longer an elected official over the school, there is no accountability to the parents. We again have **education without representation.**

In the Race to the Top funding, the 46 governors who were competing for the grant money to usher in Common Core actually received more points for the number of charter schools they had in their States, rather than public schools. In other words, charter schools are being encouraged and are made to sound really good – above public schools. Why?

If you want to usher in socialism, as the Obama administration has made great strides in doing, one of the main objectives is to destroy local control and representative government – what every good socialist country has done.

Charter Schools are Designed to Help Usher in a Soviet System: According to Charlotte Iserbyt who has written and spoken much against Charter Schools: "Charter Schools are the Trojan horse to change our form of government to the unelected council system – the Soviet system."[54] This is by design; it is not happening by chance. A socialist, totalitarian ruler does not want representative government. He wants government by appointed commissioners who will only answer to him, not the people.

Charter Schools may be Illegal: In a December 2013 summary judgment ruling in Washington State in regards to the Cesar Chavez Charter School, the courts ruled that if education is to be open and "common" for all students, then perhaps Charter schools are in violation of State laws:

> *A charter school cannot be defined as a common school because it is not under the control of the voters of the school district. The statutes places control under a private non-profit organization, a local charter board/or the Charter Commission.*
>
> *The system must be uniform in that every child shall have the same advantages and be subject to the same discipline as every other child...to summarize, a common school within the meaning of the Constitution is one that is common to all children...free, and subject to and under the control of the qualified voters of the district.* [55]

Cheating by Teachers and Administrators Has Increased: Because of the high-stakes testing that was ushered in by No Child Left Behind and will be made worse by Common Core, the salaries of the teachers are tied to their students' test scores. In fact, the future of the school is determined by those scores. If the school fails to raise the scores after three years, it can be on a probation list and even terminated. This has caused teachers to be tempted to cheat on the test scores of their students, to change the wrong answers to correct ones and to change grades. And it has caused principals and administrators to insist that teachers change grades. Fs and Ds must be raised to Cs.

At the Loudoun Valley High School in northern Virginia, an attorney was hired to investigate allegations by teachers and their formal complaints against the principal, assistant principal and the Special Education supervisor, who they say were harassing and threatening teachers with "negative consequences" if they did not raise the grades of their students. In some cases, the grades that were sent in by the teachers were actually changed by the administrators.[56] More is written on this in Chapter VII under testimonies of teachers.

In my book, *Common Core, A Trojan Horse for Education Reform,* I devote three pages to the subject of cheating. It appears that it is much more widespread than thought. Two writers, after studying seven years of scores in Chicago, estimate that teachers in 3-6% of the classrooms were tampering with scores. In California, it is estimated that in two years, 459 classrooms turned in suspicious looking scores, showing erasure marks from teachers.[57] These studies were ten years ago. One can only imagine that the high-stakes testing has only gotten worse and the temptations to cheat has increased.

Chemistry dumbed down or no longer taught: The Next Generation Science Standards (NGSS) are the new name for the Common Core science. According to Sandra Stotsky, chemistry will no longer be taught or will have a dumbed down version.

> ... *the main problem with NGSS is that it eliminates high school chemistry and, in effect, physics (since the math for it isn't there). It is science for dummies.*[58]

Children Indoctrination, the Earlier the Better: The government wants to get your children out of the home and away from the influence of parents even in infancy – actually from "birth" on. That is why so many early learning government programs have been started over the years to do so. Common Core is no exception.

Choice or Tax Credits or Voucher Programs: These are all various ways for parents to have funding to take their children to a school of their choice and thereby give their children a better education. The same taxes that would pay for a child to be in a public or charter school would be given to the parents in the form of a tax credit or a voucher so they can take their child to a school of their choice.

These programs all sound really good as a way to give parents choice and keep competition alive and well in schools. However, if all the future plans go into effect, "choice" will be contributing to more charter schools being created, the demise of the public schools, and thereby causing the end of representative government having any influence over education.

Christianity-not: Even Catholic Schools that had first adopted Common Core en masse across the nation are recognizing that Common Core is not consistent with true Christian teachings and are turning against it. They are realizing a one-size fits all, mandated script, "with only one form of thought allowed" is far from Christ's teachings of freedom and free choice. Christianity is not a gospel of force, nor one that limits a person's potential, nor one that teaches moral relativism and no absolute truth, or that children get to "construct" their own truth.

History of how Catholic Schools got Involved in Common Core: In 1984, Robert Mueller, wrote the World Core Curriculum for UNESCO, the United Nations' Education, Science, Culture Organization. Mueller is Catholic, but also is heavily involved in the New Age movement and a high ranking officer in the United Nations. He was the special guest speaker at a Catholic convention in 1985 in St. Louis, Missouri, and convinced the majority there of his "citizens of the world" viewpoint. This is reported by a Catholic researcher and writer, Betsy Kraus, who attended the conference herself and has written several publications revealing her concern for the transformation that has happened in Catholic schools.

The Goal of the World Core Curriculum*: to bring all educational standards under **one common roof** of compliance and global academic philosophical and religious sameness.*

The Gates Foundation gave more than $100,000 to the National Catholic Educational Association (NCEA) in September, 2013, to "support teacher training and materials on implementing the Common Core" in Catholic schools, as first reported byThe Cardinal Newman Society.

The NCEA defended the grant by assuring Catholics that the Common Core State Standards "are not a curriculum." Cardinal Newman Society President Patrick Reilly noted that the NCEA statement *"ignores the fact that the Common Core standards are intended to guide the development of curricula and testing in schools nationwide, which is a clear goal of the Gates Foundation."*

Catholic Common Core Identity Initiative (CCCII) was promoted by the NCEA to "share information, resources, tools and strategies that Catholic educators can use to develop standards-based, gospel values-based curriculum for their dioceses and schools" in compliance with the Common Core.

However, the Cardinal Newman Society reported that the CCCII website was riddled with problems which required the NCEA to correct the first-grade unit plan by removing three resources which celebrated families headed by same-sex or divorced couples.[59]

Dr. Andrew Seeley, executive director of the Institute for Catholic Liberal Education and a tutor at Thomas Aquinas College in Santa Paula, Calif., warned fellow Catholics of the dangers of Common Core in a five-page "Issue Bulletin" written Dec. 31, 2013. It is entitled "The Common Core vs. the Classical Roots of Catholic Education" and appeared on the Cardinal Newman Society website. Dr. Seeley stated many strong arguments against Common Core that every Christian parent should be aware of:

- *"The goals and methods of CC are at odds with the discovery of truth and an authentically Catholic education."* He states that even though much of Catholic education has been "compromised by State standards and new theories of education," it still maintained some key elements of a classical education, especially in regards to the study of religion, history and literature. "

- Common Core tries to instill "critical thinking" in children much too young for it. Up until age 11, children cannot make those decisions. But they are ready to "trustingly" accept whatever is presented to them in an orderly, engaging manner." [This is a perfect age for indoctrination – as those behind Common Core realize. The children will trust the information their teachers present to them, because they have no background on which to evaluate if this is really true or not.]

- CC *"curricular materials are likely to usher in a secular orthodoxy...a dictatorship of relativism."* This will be the result of the teaching of "mutual understanding" and "openness to a wide variety of cultures." [As many Christian teachers have discovered in the public schools, the teaching of "multi-culturalism" really means that there is no one culture that is any better than any other culture. Thus, the American culture is put down and taught as nothing special. In turn, the Christian culture is also put down, while "secular humanism, which is really atheism, is praised, and Islam is praised above Christianity, as the "true religion of peace."]

- *"The true believer is in real danger"* **from such secular education:** Dr. Seeley quotes from Alan Bloom, the author of *Closing the American Mind*, who gives evidence of how children who were once strong Christians cannot withstand the constant bombardment of secular humanism in their classrooms.
- *Common Core seeks to "educate for life," but their highest goals only concern "career success" and being productive "global citizen":* [There is nothing about developing strong moral character or learning great truths to prepare them to make wise decision and to better understand American history and culture so we can better preserve our form of government. These are the things that Catholic schools used to teach to prepare students to be "life-long learners."]
- **And How will this Affect Catholic Teachers?** Dr. Seeley writes, because of the obsession with preparing students for the assessments, implementation of CCSSI will mean "much *harassment for teachers and much less time to actively work with students.*

Dr. Seeley gives good suggestions for Catholic schools to use instead of Common Core, which are listed in the last chapter. He closes his article with the following hope for Catholic educators:

> *Ironically, it may be the Common Core State Standard Initiative that will awaken all Catholic educators to reject encroaching secular content and methods, and rediscover the riches of their own tradition.* **Given the unique, supernatural beauty of the Catholic faith, they should be decidedly skeptical of anything that bills itself as "common."**[60]

Pope Francis Speaks out against Any Form of Education Experimentation with One-Form of Thought: In a speech made on April 14, 2014, at the Vatican in Rome, that was mainly addressing and condemning clerical sexual abuse, he also spoke about the rights of parents to "decide the moral and religious education of their children" and added the following:

*And in this regard I would like to express my rejection of **any kind of educational experimentation with children.** We cannot experiment with children and young people. The horrors of the manipulation of education that we experienced in the great genocidal dictatorships of twentieth century have not disappeared; they have retained a current relevance under various guises and proposals and, with the pretense of modernity, push children and young people to walk on the dictatorial path of 'only one form of thought.' A week ago a great teacher said to me... 'with these education projects I don't know if we're sending the kids to school or to a **re-education camp'..."***

[It is good that the Pope did not name the "education experimentation" and "one form of thought" as Common Core, because he probably has heard that it is already going through many name changes, and it would already has different names in different countries of the world anyway.]

A Warning against the Culture and the Media: In his same speech, the Holy Father also warned against the dangers "posed by contemporary culture and widespread mentality propagated by the mass media."[61] [As you will notice in Chapter IV, there is much propaganda supporting Common Core on national media funded by big corporations and written by the Chamber of Commerce, who received many millions of dollars to write and promote the ads.]

This is the motto that is found on the front page of the Cardinal Newman Society website along with the words, "Promoting and Defending Faithful Catholic Education." This is their motto for standing up against Common Core.

"Christ is our Only Core": This is the statement by the principal, staff, and teachers of a large private Christian school in Santa Rosa, CA. the Rincon Valley Christian School, which is run by the Santa Rosa Bible Church. This school adamantly refuses to teach Common Core and continues on with its same high standards and high quality of education based on the truths of the Bible. Let us hope that many other Christian schools are following their example and that Christian parents fighting Common Core can use that motto as well.

Christianity is Degraded and Islam Praised: Due to the fact that there is much funding coming from big oil in Muslim countries that is being used to influence or buy education publishing companies, world history text books now used in American schools have a pro-Islam slant. Over the years the words in the textbooks have been changed to whitewash the true history of Islam and write about it only in glowing terms. They have also changed the true history of Christianity and either ignore all the good that Christianity has done or write about it disparagingly.

As a substitute teacher, I had to teach a two-week course on Islam in the 7th grade at a middle school in Healdsburg, CA in 2002. I was shocked as I witnessed firsthand the pro-Islam bias and the anti-Christian slurs in the text book. I was also amazed at the suggestions that I was to do as a teacher – such as have the students make a prayer rug, memorize scriptures from the Koran, come dressed in Muslim attire, have a Muslim name, and memorize the Five Pillars of Islam.

I thought to myself? "What ever happened to the 1962 Supreme Court ruling of "Separation of Church and State" that took Bible reading and prayer out of our public schools? The Islam teaching is putting it right back in, but not with the Bible, the Quran. How can this teaching of Islam even be allowed?" I found out that those behind the indoctrination of Islam in our schools try to pass it off as teaching a culture. Teachers are told, "You're not really teaching a religion, you're teaching the culture of Islam. That is perfectly legal."

What did I do? As a devout Christian, I chose not to do any of the suggestions given for the teacher. I thought to myself, "Well, if I now get to teach a religion or "religious culture," I think I will teach the religion of my choice," and I brought in as much as I could about the "cousins of the Muslims," which the text book does start off talking about under the seed of Abraham. The book suggests that the teacher write *Abraham* at the top of the chalk board and write *Isaac* and *Ishmael* under Abraham, and put Mohammad under Ishmael and Bible prophets under Isaac, so that is what I did.

I asked the students "Can any of you name some of the prophets in the Bible who might have been descendants from Isaac? One of the boys mentioned Moses. I answered, "Very good! Would you like to know something more about Moses? It is a fascinating story of a little boy who is found floating in a basket and is raised by the Queen of Egypt!" "But before I can tell you about Moses, I first have to tell you about how millions of Children of Isarel, the descendants of Abraham ended up as slaves in Egypt. I will have to first tell you the story of Joseph who was sold into Egypt to be a slave when he was about your age." That was such a fascinating story it took up the whole period. Other days were similar.

When I had to teach the Five Pillars of Islam, I gave each of the students a copy of the Ten Commandments, the creed that the Jews and Christians live by and had them compare the two side by side. Of course, the only creed that matches is the first one, "Thou shalt have no other Gods before me" the first of The Ten Commandments and "There is no other god but Allah," the first of the Five Pillars."

The text book I was teaching from in 2002 was called *Through the Centuries*. A few years later I had to teach from one called *World History, Medieval and Modern Times* that was even worse in its pro-Islam bias. Here is a direct quote from it about what is written concerning the Crusades.

> *Another legacy of the Crusades was rising Christian hostility toward Jews...More and more Christians believed that non-Christians were their enemy. Muslims, however, allowed Jews and Christians to live in peace in most cases. Many Crusaders who stayed in Palestine came to respect Muslims, but Christian intolerance toward Jews continued. (p.330)*

Notice that the whole story is twisted. It sounds like Christians were in Jerusalem fighting to rid the city of the Jews, not to stop the invasion of Muslims across Africa and the Middle East that soon would be spreading into Europe if not stopped.

The Muslim invasions were not happy, peaceful events as the textbook portrays them. "*The caliphs showed tolerance to the people they conquered...The conquered people welcomed the Muslim armies as liberators...Muslims let conquered people keep their own religion if they wished to do so.* (pp. 98, 100, 101)

The truth was the Muslim armies were pillaging, plundering, killing the men and putting women and children into slavery where ever they went. Those who survived were forced to become Muslims and worship Allah or were killed by the sword, exactly as the Quran tells them to do. *"I will cast terror in the hearts of those who disbelieve. Therefore, strike off their heads and strike off every fingertip of them.* (Quran 8:12)

Under Common Core, a Christian Teacher would Have no Freedom to Deviate from the Lesson: Under Common Core, the entire pro-Islam lesson would have been scripted for me. There could be no deviation, even if the teacher knows that the lesson is full of false information, she/he must teach it as written.

That is what the teachers in Texas were experiencing with the CSCOPE method, their digital education program, which was also written by Linda Darling Hammond and another very liberal writer of education books, Lucy Calkins.[62] (More is written about CSCOPE at the end of this chapter.)

Clandestine: So much of Common Core was done behind closed doors: the writing of it; asking for a gag order on those involved with it -- even the validation committee had to sign a statement they would not talk about it; the bypassing of Congress; the bypassing of State legislators; bypassing local school districts; especially not wanting parents to know about it until it was a done deal and already implemented and then it would be very hard to get rid of it. I call it education by stealth and deception.

Classical English Literature Being Replaced by "Informational Text" is a Detriment to Students: This will not improve but lower students' college and career readiness: Dr. Sandra Stotsky, the ELA expert, who refused to sign off on the Common Core standards, and Mark Bauerlein, an Emory College English professor wrote a paper together that stated: *"...the analytical and critical-thinking skills developed by a deep study of literature will prepare students for college more effectively than reading informational texts."*

Class Divide: These two scholars also write that they think there is going to be a big distinction between private schools and public schools. *"Private schools and public schools in affluent suburbs will teach a literature-rich curriculum, while most public school students will suffer from a "literature deficit."*

According to Charles Chieppo and Jamie Gass of the Pioneer Institute, Mark Twain's *Huckleberry Finn* isn't included in Massachusetts' new Common Cored curriculum. It's not banned either. It's just not mentioned. *"These new English standards include less than half as much classic literature and poetry than the Massachusetts standards they will replace."*

This will, of course, widen the achievement gap, but only between elite schools and the Common Core schools that will all be sufficiently dumbed down the same. Could that be what the elite special people behind Common Core want? Of the cartel that wrote Common Core, how many send their children to private, elite schools, where they are educated in much rich, classical English literature, traditional math, etc.[63]

Climate Change: A big part of the science standards for Common Core is about "global warming." The Next Generation Science Standards is the official name for the standards. They recommend that global warming and climate change be included in every subject not just the science classroom.

Coercion for the Entire Common Core Program: We are told that the governors of the 46 States and District of Columbia who signed onto Common Core happily "volunteered" to sign on. That is not the case. The governors were coerced into doing so because of three reasons: a bribe, a waiver, and a threat. The bribe was the possibility of winning a share of $4.35 billion grant money that the governors could compete for if they signed onto Common Core sight unseen. The waiver was to let them get out of the rigid requirements of No Child Left Behind, that no one liked and the governors were happy to get out of. Lastly there was the threat of governors losing their Title I money if they did not sign on. Title I is a large grant of $14.5 billion that the governors all share that they use to pay for the costs of their underprivileged children and for special ed. Of course, they could not give up that money, so it was one more incentive for the governors to say yes to Common Core. [64]

In an interview with PBS, March 28, 2014, expert Dianne Ravitch was asked about the way the governors signed on to Common Core. She agreed that they were "bought or coerced." This was not voluntary.[65]

Coercion of Teachers to Support Common Core: This is a statement from Mary Graber, PhD Teacher and Writer in Georgia: In answer to the question "Why teachers love Common Core," she replied:

> *As I discovered through an open records request, teachers are strongly encouraged (pressured?) to support Common Core by principals and superintendents.* [66]

More is written about this pressure in Chapter IV and what teachers are saying in opposition to Common Core.

Coerced Early Learning with Race to the Top Grant Money: Of course, as with all aspects of the program, there is grant money set up to entice the governors of the various States to sign on. It is called "Race to the Top-Early Challenge Competition." What is the grant money to be used for? According to an *Associated Press* article, December 19, 2013, that announced the six new winning States, the grant money is to be used "to improve early learning programs for **babies, toddlers and preschoolers.**"

The FDOE and Health and Human Services Department jointly share the program and issue the grant money. It is set up in three different stages of competition. So if your State did not get the money the first time, they can try, try again. There are 14 States who have already won grant money and signed on.

Some Call this Race to the Trough!

Costs of Early Challenge Competition: How much money was used to bribe the States with? The new winners will share in $280 million. The total combined for all 20 States now signed on is $1 billion. Who are the new winners in what many are calling the "race to the trough" as one by one the States sell their souls for money? The winning States in the Race to the Top-Early Challenge competition were Georgia, Kentucky, Michigan, New Jersey, Pennsylvania and Vermont.

According to the AP article, the winning States must show their plans for children not just in preschool, but from birth to age 5!

The winning states must show a willingness to carry out comprehensive improvements to programs focused on children from birth to age 5. 'This investment is a down payment to support and implement high-quality early learning programs across the country,' Education Secretary Arne Duncan said in a statement. 'There is still a lot more work for us to do.'

The article states how Obama wants to raise cigarette taxes to help fund "universal preschool for 4-year olds." They are also planning to "require lower-performing Head Start Programs to compete for funding as part of an effort to improve the quality of Head Start programs."[67] Did you notice the word "require." They won't even have the choice if they want to compete for funding or not?

Cog in the Wheel of the Government Workforce: As with other countries that have central control over education, the careers for the children are essentially chosen for them. They are given the limited learning that they will need to fill the niche that the government wants them to fill in the planned economy and government workforce.

Cognitive Development: This was a theory developed by Jean Piaget that used to be taught to all future teachers in their university education courses, that "children's brains develop in stages." That is why so much of Common Core is way over the head of beginning elementary students. Anyone who had actually had experience teaching in a K-12 classroom would have known this and would have created the standards and suggested curriculum differently.[68]

Cognitive Dissonance: This is a psychological method used to slowly change and mold children's beliefs and attitudes. Conflicting materials are presented that are in direct opposition of children's moral and religious beliefs. They are presented in such a way that results in mental confusion. The children are asked to discuss and try to defend their opposing beliefs and values, and then synthesize them to attain "consensus and commonality" with those of the others in the classroom. Slowly, the child's original beliefs and attitudes give way to accept the new "group think." "Each conflict which becomes consensus is another step towards the ultimate 'unity of mankind."[69]

Collectivism / Common Good: Both of these terms promote the socialist/communist mindset, where we are not to think of ourselves as individuals but as part of the collective or the common good. Teachers are to promote more collective thinking and equity, not rewards for individual excellence.

In other words, who cares about the individual child and his intrinsic worth and making education exciting and motivating for him? **Common Core is all about the child's worth to the common good, to the collective**, his contribution to America's success and competition in the global economy.

Common Core–lite: When a State first starts the implementation, those in control try to get the teachers to go along by not being too demanding at first. It is called "the drip system" or incrementally bringing in the big changes. So the teachers at first think this is not so bad. "I can live with this. It is not too different than what I have done before." However, as you have read at the beginning of this chapter, after a while, the tough policies begin to come in, and the canned scripts and the teachers discover they can no longer have the freedom to be the kind of teacher they used to be.

Common Sense-not: There is so much about Common Core that does not seem to make much common sense at all, unless one sees the enormous profit margin big corporations promoting it are going to be making from it such as the Bill Gates and the Pearson Foundations. Then it makes perfectly good sense. They will be making billions from the computers coming into the classrooms and the e-books that Pearson is publishing. Gates and Pearson have also formed a partnership to do the teacher training which will also rake in many more millions of dollars.

Communitarianism: One of the experts who has been researching and writing about this term for many years is Keven Eggers who lives in Napa, California and writes an opt ed column for the Napa Valley Register. Here is how he defines it:

> *Communitarianism is the idea that the community (often called community rights) is supreme over the individual – individual rights don't exist within the community. It is what is driving our city policies today. The Napa County General Plan calls for "balancing the rights of the individual with the rights of the community and the needs of the environment."*
>
> *This sounds good until you ask who gets to do the balancing and what are the rights of the community? My sheriff told me, 'When you live in the community, you have to surrender some of your rights.' I found out that means essentially the total absence of individual rights."[70]*

Communitarian Collectivism: According to *the World Book Dictionary*, communitarian means a member of a communistic community and a supporter of its principles. Collectivism is another name for communism which is defined as "a political and economic system in which the means of production of goods and services and the distribution of wealth are controlled by the people as a group or by the government. This takes away the importance of the individual and makes the "common good" take precedent over all else.

Communitarian Law: Most people have no idea that such a term exists. That was by design, to keep us in the dark as our laws are being transformed to a communistic system. According to Kevin Eggers, *"Communitarian Law is the global to local community plan for the world."*

The blogger and former talk show host Marti Oakley defines it as "reinventing government:"

> *Communitarian Law is the new legal system used by regional and local governments affiliated with the emerging global government. This new law circumvents national law via a program of "balancing," often implemented by a small group of self-appointed elites who achieve consensus (not voting). For Americans, the adoption of these evolving principles transports us from a constitutional system where we expect clearly defined basic rights (like due process and legal searches) to a more "moral" way of enforcing "social justice" that only a few upper level academics can define.*

Moral is the chosen word for how the Communists describe their tactics and methods for ushering in a one-world global government. Of course, it is just the opposite of what *moral* means to most Americans. The Communist *moral* has nothing to do with God or religion.

Communitarian Law limits individual rights and property rights:

> *Communitarian law is the precedent that requires the courts to rule in favor of the self-defined "community" against individuals protected by constitutional law. It limits the property rights of individuals in all member nations.[71]*

One of the most well-known communitarian law decisions was the U.S. Supreme Court decision in Kelo v. The City of New London, which made it possible for a city to usher in much broader eminent domain tactics for development to raise taxes.

Communitarian: "A member of a communistic community and supporter of communistic principles." World Book Encyclopedia." Communists prefer calling themselves "communitarians" rather than communists, because it sounds better.[72]

Community: According to Noah Webster's 1828 Dictionary, a community was "A society of people having common rights and privileges, or common interests, civil, political, or ecclesiastical."[73]

According to Kevin Eggers, that has changed. The community is now city government - all the boards, the committees, the elected and non-elected city officials that run the city government and think of themselves as so powerful that the individual must give up his rights to them. Notice how much closer we are getting to the following definition:

Community – Communistic: The term community is defined according to the *World Book Encyclopedia, 1984,* as:

> *One that is defined, constructed, and controlled by a communitarian government elite which exercises autocratic, despotic, totalitarian government control over production, labor, and distribution, culture, and the thought, behavior, and emotional life of all community members. The ruling elite makes the rules of the community universal and binding on all and enforces obedience upon everyone."*

Community Education (CE): the UN's communistic plan to control all of us from birth through death through the school becoming the center of education. Regionalism, sustainable development, community policing, faith-based initiatives, school-based clinics, etc., etc. come under community education (re-education, ed). This report covers in great detail: definition of community education (C.E.) UN/UNESCO, Change Agents in C.E., Strategies in C.E., Individually Guided Education in C.E., History of C.E., International C.E., Blueprint for Community-Centered Schools, Future of Education.

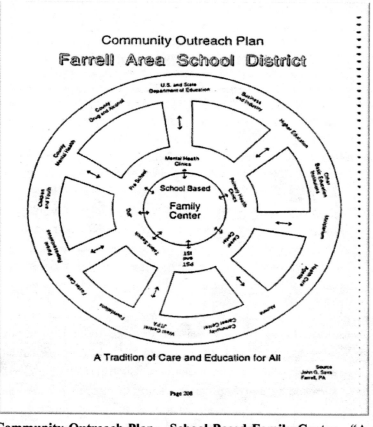

Community Outreach Plan – School Based Family Center - "A Tradition of Care and Education for all: The above circle plan comes from Farrell, Pennsylvania. This is the design for how the Community Education will work. Notice that "parent representative" is on the outside of the circle – they don't get to play a very big role at all.

This was created back in 1995 and appeared in a book by Anita Hoge, *Womb to Tomb, the Managed Economy, The merging of Education-Healthcare-Labor*. She writes the following explaining the chart and tells what the book contains:

> ...*This is the partnership that parent engagement and parental responsibility and involvement mean. Partnership is defined as equal ownership. FAMILY is re-defined: "Any person or persons that have a common bond, of shared responsibility for each other and/or children in their care. The book tells:*
>
> *How Governments will use Schools to create new Capital; Why OBE (outcome Based Education) was needed to identify and track individuals; Focuses on the Use of Technology to Track and Remediate Children towards Political Correctness; Focuses on the use of Electronic Portfolios which will include entire medical histories as well as psychological dossiers; Aligns Cradle to Grave Plans in Community Based Health Care Centers that used to be Neighborhood Schools."*[74]

Communist-Like: When you read all that is written in the preceding pages, the Marxist background of the key players behind Common Core, the Marxist background of President Obama and those surrounding him who are promoting Common Core, and the Marxist sounding Community Education System, the entire program begins to appear very communist-like. It is top-down, central-controlled over all aspects of education, from national standards, to the curriculum, to the testing, to the enormous data collection over all children and teachers just like the Soviet Union and Communist China.

Remember the speech by the former president of the USSR, Nikita Krushev back in September 29, 1959, when he took off his shoe and pounded on the lectern with it and made the following statement:

> *Your children's children will live under communism. You Americans are so gullible. No, you won't accept communism outright, but we will keep feeding you small doses of socialism until you wake up and find out you already have communism. We won't have to fight you; we will so weaken your economy, until you fall like over ripe fruit into our hands.*[75]

Common Core will make this Communist goal so much easier, for the exact same system of education will be in place in our nation so total indoctrination can be brought into the schools without any hindrance on the part of conservative educators who believe differently. Most of those will have already resigned in disgust, as we see already happening, or they will have been gotten rid of by other means.

Competence–not: As the famous economist Milton Friedman wrote 50 years ago, public education is a great example of socialism in the United States. "Socialism, instead of rewarding competence, rewards incompetence."

Competition-not: Common Core will destroy competition. What has helped to make America a great country, a land of the free, that others wanted to come to, was not commonality, but the free enterprise system, freedom to compete - what makes one company or business better than another and attracts people to its doors. This is no different with schools. When one school is better than another, it attracts parents who send their children there in place of a poorer school. Competition inspires the lower performing school to want to do better. Without competition, where is the incentive to do better? All schools will sink to the lowest common denominator.

Compliant Children and Teachers: Compliance to the new Common Core will become more and more demanding. To achieve this compliance, don't be too shocked if we see the rate of medication increase in those students who just might be labeled hyper or ADHD, so they can be calmed down and perform better on tests and not be a distraction to others. As a *New York Times* author reports, "teachers will have quieter classrooms, school districts will receive more funding" (for more students labeled as ADHD) "and it's a win all around – except for the child who is drugged into submission."[76]

Complicated? Teachers and parents are being told that Common Core is not complicated, that it is going to simplify education, to make concepts more understandable. Just look at the following, complicated design of Race to the Top and Common Core on this flow chart. It is a mass of confusion.

The red lines show all the funding mechanisms for Common Core; the blue lines show all the organizations and government laws and policies leading up to it; the green lines show the enormous amount of groups and organizations involved in the data collection – 16 listed, more than any other part of the chart; and the yellow lines – only 3 show anything to do with the teachers. Obviously, teachers don't have a lot of priority if they are just going to be facilitators in the massive scheme. Thanks to Restore Oklahoma Public Education (ROPE) who created the chart. On their website, you can read their full document entitled "<u>Common Core State Standards and Race To the Top, an Introduction to Marxism 101.</u>"[77]

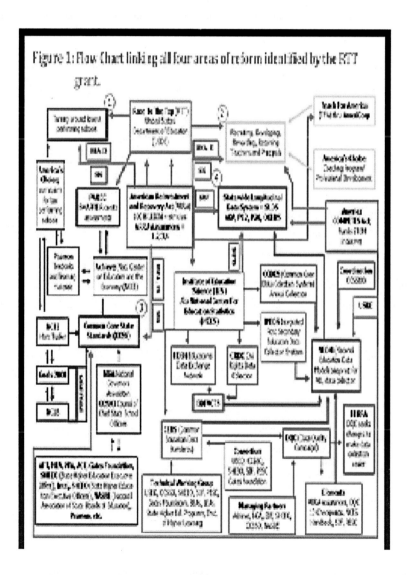

Complicity: When one considers how many people had to be complicit in this plan of Common Core and had to keep it quiet for how many years, it is quite mind boggling. Their goal was to have it more entrenched and already implemented before parents really found out about it. That way it would be very hard to stop it.

Copyrighted: Common Core State Standards Initiative is copyrighted by the NGA (National Governors Association) and CCSSO (Council on Chief State School Officers). If something were truly created by the States and State-led, why is there a copyright on it held by two private, lobbying groups in Washington D.C.? As you will read in the copyright, States are free to use it "without royalties," but they can't change it in any way to better fit the needs of their State. Again, how can that be called State-led or a State initiative? Here is how the copyright reads:

> THE COMMON CORE STATE STANDARDS ARE PROVIDED UNDER TERMS OF THIS PUBLIC LICENSE. THE COMMON CORE STATE STANDARDS ARE PROTECTED BY COPYRIGHT AND OTHER APPLICABLE LAW. ANY USE OF THE COMMON CORE STATE STANDARDS OTHER THAN AS AUTHORIZED UNDER THIS LICENSE OR COPYRIGHT LAW IS PROHIBITED.
>
> ANY PERSON WHO EXCERCISES ANY RIGHTS TO THE COMMON CORE STATE STANDARDS THEREBY ACCEPTS AND AGREES TO BE BOUND BY THE TERMS OF THE LICENSE. THE RIGHTS CONTAINED HEREIN ARE GRANTED IN ACCEPTANCE OF SUCH TERMS AND CONDITIONS.
>
> License Grant:
> The NGA Center for Best Practices (NGA Center) and the Council of Chief State School Officers (CCSSO) hereby grant a limited, non-exclusive, royalty-free license to copy, publish, distribute, and display the Common Core State Standards for purposes that support the Common

Core State Standards initiative. These uses may involve the Common Core State Standards as a whole or selected excerpts or portions.[78]

Compulsory: When every teacher is now forced to do the same thing, to use the same Common Core materials and standards at peril of their jobs, that sounds like this is pretty well compulsory, with no wiggle room to get out of it.

Commodity, Cogs, and Capital - the new definition of our children. To the mighty corporations funding and pushing Common Core into our schools, our children are nothing more than a commodity to be used to enhance their profit margin, a cog to fit into the wheel of the global workforce, and human capital to be used and controlled for lifelong labor.

This has been made possible by public private partnerships where corporation and governments have combined. You now have public (tax paying) money helping to fund the corporation, and big business is dictating the rules. This process has been accelerated by a systems managed world, aided and abetted by technology, with both entities – government and business - factoring a digitized humanity into the planned, programmed, budgeted society.

Who is losing out in this equation? We are: humanity, individuals and especially our children who are to become pawns to do exactly what corporate business declares and government enforces.

Competition-Not: One of the things that has helped America to be a great nation is competition and a free-enterprise system where people would be given many choices and the freedom to choose what they wanted. That was also in the school system. If one school was doing better than another, parents would take their children out of the poorer performing school and put them in the better school. That would motivate the administration of the lower performing poorer school to try to do better. With Common Core there is no more competition since all schools are to be the same with the exact same standards, same scripted lessons, same curriculum. That will cause all schools to sink to the lowest common denominator, not raise them higher.

Computer Lock-In: The CC curriculum and assessments are locked into classroom education through computer management. It was originally called PPBS (Planning, Programming, Budgeting System), later called MBO (Management by Objectives), later called TQM (Total Quality Management). Whatever it is now called, it is much more comprehensive, with all of the additional interconnectedness, upgrading, and cybernation add-ons. As researcher Betsy Kraus writes, there will be no way for a child to escape the computer lock-in and "mind control" techniques to change a child's incorrect attitude:

> *The child is subjected to predetermined goals, objectives, performance indicators, and metrics, and then assessed to show how well he/she is performing according to criteria. The results are all processed, sorted, and data-banked by computers. If the child does not perform correctly, he/she will not advance from one learning step to the next.*
>
> *The advancement from one step to the next can be assisted by an individual learning technique called scaffolding (a concept of Lev Vyotsky, Soviet, Marxist psychologist). If, in the scaffolding (staircase) process, the students do not display the proper, processed attitudes and "parrot" the predetermined information, they will be recycled via the computer for more instruction and assessments until they display the given outcome. It's a loop system and there is no way to escape it.[79]*

Conditioned Responses: Behaviorist John B. Watson was an influential spokesman for spreading the idea that human behavior was nothing more than a set of "conditioned responses." A child could be conditioned and programmed to fill any cog that was needed in the government work force.

Conditioning: This is the psychological process of giving rewards and punishments to train a child to perform on command such as a lab rat. This will be much easier to do now with the use of computers. If the child performs well on the assignment, an immediate reward pops up: bells and whistles, etc. If the child does not perform well, a frowning face appears; the child cannot go onto the next level.

Confusing: The logo of Common Core shows half circles that cannot quite meet to get their act together. That is a perfect depiction of the confusion of Common Core.

Many parents are complaining about the confusing math that their children are now asked to do. Children who used to love math and were really good at it, now are doing poorly and do not like it at all. My own son, who is a very successful CPA, grew up loving math in school. When told about the new Common Core math, where he would have to go through so many "regrouping" processes to finally get the answer to a simple addition, subtraction, or multiplication problem, and then write an essay about what he did, said he probably would have hated math and would never have chosen to become a CPA.

Consortia-written Assessment: A consortia is a fancier sounding name but essentially means the same thing as a cartel. The consortia consists of two groups that the different States belong to and are supposed to be giving their input into the creation of the test. More is written about the consortia and the assessments in Chapter VII.

Conformity: From Germany to Communist China to Russia to the USA today, to actually all 70 countries where the Pearson Foundation has their offices, the elites behind Common Core have a common goal – "conformity *uber alles*" – conformity above all else. That used to be hard to achieve – people could read and research and think for themselves, but now with big business, big government and big education having formed a partnership, conformity is going to be much easier.

There will be no more "thinking outside of the box." Everything will be coming from and conformed to the big-central-controlled box. Our children will be locked inside the box until they are sufficiently indoctrinated and programmed to come forth shaped into the correct cog for the global workforce.

Who are those involved in the big conformity box, the partnership of big business, big government and big education? Along with all those listed earlier in the chapter who are part of the cartel that created it, there are the big businesses of the Gates Foundation, Intel, Microsoft, and the Pearson Foundation, the largest education publishing company in the world, joined by the Federal Department of Education who funded the Consortia, the creators of the assessment testing. And spreading Common Core worldwide is UNESCO, the United Nations Education, Science, and Culture Organization. More corporations are listed who are part of the conformity box in the next chapter.

The following picture and quote on the next page are great illustrations of the conformity being asked for with Common Core and how impossible and unfair it is, for just as different animals were created with different abilities, strengths and weaknesses, so are our children unique and special with their own talents and gifts.

Instead of being encouraged and motivated to reach their full worth and high potential, their own "genius," they will all be required to go through the same factory school to come out with the same cookie cutter design.

Contract or MOU (Memorandum of Understanding) that Each of the 46 States Signed for RTT Funding: Thanks to some amazing researchers, the MOUs for each of the States are showing up and, low and behold, they are all the same. This is more evidence that CC was **not** State-initiated or State led. There are so many requirements for each State to go through – pages and pages of hoops that they have to jump through. Here is the one that Colorado signed on to, but they are similar for every State.[80]

The States had to sign their life away – agreeing to so many regulations and giving back so much information to get the points that would make them eligible for the money, which most of them did not win. The following is just a small sample of some of what was required. There is more under the chapter on data collection:

Each year, the State has to submit a report to the Secretary of Education that describes: "the use of the funds; how they were distributed; the number of jobs that were saved or created; the State's progress in reducing inequities in the distribution of highly qualified teachers [They don't want highly qualified teachers all in one good school. They will have to be sent somewhere else. Do the teachers have any say in this?]; implementing a State Longitudinal Data System; developing and implementing assessments for limited

English proficiency students and students with disabilities; a description of modernization, renovation, or repairs approved and project costs. And there is even a statement on **"closing the achievement gap"**:

> *The State will cooperate with any U.S. comptroller General evaluation of the use of funds ...on the progress towards closing the achievement gaps. (ARRA Division H, Section 14009) page 6*

Cooperation not Competition: This has been the mantra of education for many years now. Common Core promotes this even more. It has become a gender and racial issue. Propaganda, given to the teachers, states that girls and minorities learn best by cooperation - not competition; and by a sense of "community" not by the white male's sense of "individuality" with his "linear" thinking and deductive reasoning.

Cooperative Learning: This is the kind of education we have seen becoming more common in the classrooms ever since the 1990s, where children learn and work in groups, and where usually one bright child ends up doing all the work for all the others and they all get the same grade. It became the adopted math curriculum nationwide during the 1990's (with no proof of its methods) as districts and states were offered multimillions of dollars from the National Science Foundation to adopt the "new" reform materials. These would bring "equity" to the math classroom, and administrators couldn't wait to adopt them. Common Core will be using group learning more and more.

Corporate Fellows: This is the program promoted by the National Governors Association, NGA, to bring in corporations and form partnerships with them. Their "corporate fellows' brochure" includes as its byline, "partnering for solutions." The program "promotes the exchange of knowledge and expertise between the private sector and governors on public policy issues affecting issues and states." To become a "Corporate Fellow" one only has to pay the membership dues of $20,000 per year. In the next chapter, one can see the many corporate members and their funding of Common Core.

Conformity: As can be seen in the following cartoon, conformity in education, making all children fit a one-size fits all blueprint, is not a good thing, greatly dumbs down education and destroys any hope or motivation that a child can become exceptional or gifted.

Our Education System

"Everybody is a genius. But if you judge a fish by its ability to climb a tree, it will live its whole life believing that it is stupid."

- Albert Einstein

Costly: Common Core is going to cost an estimated $16 billion for all of the States and individually States will have to pay hundreds of millions - if not billions. The estimate for California according to the State Department of Education is $1.36 billion to $1.56 billion, which is very close to Fordham Institute's estimate at $1.6 billion.[81]

Of course, that did not include the costs of the assessment test which is to be implemented in the school year 2014 2015, which will be an estimated $1.2 billion. California's costs for the STAR test which we have had since 1999 was only $13 per student. That cost could rise to $200 per student with the Common Core Assessment.

Why is it so expensive? The biggest expenses are the costs of new technology, computers, and software; other expenses are teacher training and e-books with everything taught and tested on line. A huge cost for the assessment will be the grading. Thirty per cent of the test is to be projects and essays with open-ended questions. That will require people to grade them, not just computers.

Creativity-not: Teachers and administrators, who are in support of Common Core, say that it will bring more creativity into the classroom. Others say just the opposite. It only stands to reason that if you have a national system that is coming from top-down, that is to be the same for all schools and all States across the nation, how could there be any room for individual creativity?

Innovation, deviation, and the freedom of a teacher to do what she knows best will also be gone. One teacher told me that she was told by the administrator that if she dared to use her old files and did not switch totally to the new Common Core materials that her job was in jeopardy, even though she was a tenured teacher. She said it does not mean very much to be tenured anymore.

Another teacher told me that she has had a visit from a "master teacher" who sat in her classroom for a whole week and took notes. If the teacher dared to deviate from the prescribed common core curriculum, the master teacher took much more notes about her. She was afraid to deviate in any way.

Credits (either vouchers or tax credits): I used to think credits were a good thing. Then parents would be able to send their children to any private or charter school of their choice, thinking they would get a better education, and it wouldn't cost the parents anything, because it would be paid for by taxes coming from the public just like public schools. However, after doing much research and hearing the opinions of experts like: Charlotte Iserbyt, who served in the Department of Education under Ronald Reagan and wrote a book about it called *The Deliberate Dumbing Down of America,* and Betsy Kraus, an expert on Catholic Education, I have changed my mind about credits.

Five Objections to Credits: The following is from Betsy Kraus, written in her documentary report "Catholic Education in America, to Deceive the Elect," October, 2013

1. **Credits take away accountability,** because private and most charter schools are no longer under the jurisdiction of an elected school board. Thus you have education without representation.
2. **"Social Justice" will be diminished:** Social Justice is the big mantra of Common Core, which essentially means all students and schools are to be treated equal, or redistribution of wealth, but if more students who come from fairly wealthy families leave the public schools and have the means to travel to the suburbs to take advantage of private or charter schools, that will leave only the poor students in the inner city schools and less

money will be there for them, because so much will have been taken away to fund private or charter schools.

3. **Private schools will lose their autonomy and freedom** and will be subjected to the same "regulations, coercions, co-optations, and financial dependence as public schools."

4. **Thus private and charter schools will become exactly like the public schools**, except they will have no elected official over them with no accountability. How do you get rid of bad policies without any elected official to vote out of office?

5. **Credits will open the school for data collection or "checkups":** A privately owned and run school can say no to the federal government's seeking to collect data on children, but when that private school now receives tax credits, it must go along with what the government is asking or lose the money, and then the school could be closed down. This is a statement made by Luther Olsen, the Republican Chairman of the Education Committee in Wisconsin: *"No matter if you're a public school, a charter school or a choice school, if you get a check, you're going to get a checkup."*[82]

"Critical Thinking Skills" is Just a Ploy to Sell Common Core – True Analytical Thinking is not New: The big issue that pro-CC advocates always seem to fall back on in a debate is their claim that the main difference between old and new standards is "critical thinking." This is what Sandra Stotsky says on the subject:

> *In a non-political sense, [critical thinking] meant simply analytical thinking/writing/reading. That's what formal schooling has been trying to inculcate for thousands of years.*
>
> *The best you can do in a debate format is ask for an example of a real lesson in any subject that this board member thinks develops critical thinking. If she can't come up with one good example of how a student learned*

to be more analytical about something, then she's talking through her hat.

The point is that the school curriculum by high school years has always tried to teach students to analyze something. It wasn't "added" by CC to their standards. They just added the words to their sales pitch. Analysis of a text, a chemical experiment, a math problem, whatever, has always been what a K-12 curriculum aimed for, and it can't take place in the absence of content knowledge.

CC has added the words as if to sprinkle magic on its content-free ELA standards. CC does not foster literary/historical knowledge in the ELA curriculum and by definition, can't develop critical thinking. One can't think critically or analytically about anything with an intellectual vacuum in your head.[83]

Critical Thinking or Higher Order Thinking and the Dialectic: According to one author, both critical thinking and higher order thinking are based on the Socratic method of thinking, which is designed to bring the student "to a dialectic method of consensus." They are a form of "values clarification" to change students' values. One young Christian girl, Ashley Andersen, describes the process as following:

Every day your child is in school their mind is molded to conform more with the group, and they are trained to defend their new family. There is no such thing as individuality in public schools; everyone is part of the "herd"...individuality gives way into what is called the "community" or group experience.

A process called "critical thinking" accomplishes this. In every lesson, and in every subject, we had "critical thinking" questions in public school. My paradigm or worldview was not the same as what is being taught in public school. The things modeled for me at home – like Christian values, and faith, were mocked...when the

93

students receive challenges to their belief system, the message comes across loud and clear: "Your parents have nothing of value to say to you; leave their world behind you; you don't need them." Public school is the frying pan where your children's brains are scrambled. Think about it. It's no longer about the facts, i.e., two plus two equals four, but about the manipulations."[84]

CSCOPE – Still Alive and Well in Texas but under a new Name: As you read in the introduction, Texas was one of the four States where the governor, State superintendent, and State School Board chose not to sign on to Common Core. They didn't need it in Texas since they already had their own form of a top-down, central-controlled, one-size-fits-all system called CSCOPE. In fact, it is a much more intrusive, regimented form that many believe is the forerunner for Common Core, created by some of the same people behind the scenes such as Linda Darling Hammond, who is the leader for the Common Core SBAC test.

I wrote about CSCOPE in my first book, *Common Core, The Trojan Horse for Education Reform* and told how it had been in Texas since 2007. Some of the similarities between it and Common Core are: with both systems all the lessons are done by computers; the lessons are already planned and scripted for the teacher - whether she likes them or not, and whether the information is accurate or not; the lessons are geared for the children to do part on the computer and then meet in groups and do group work with constructivism; the teachers become facilitators and no longer really teach; the curriculum is very one-sided, liberal and biased.

How CSCOPE is much more regimented is that the teachers have to sign a "gag order" when they are hired that they will not say anything about the program to parents. Nor can parents see the actual program, only a "parent-friendly" version. The children have no homework because the creators of CSCOPE do not want parents seeing what the children are learning.

Texas teachers opposed to CSCOPE began to resign so that they could finally reveal the truth about what was really going on. These teachers told how the lessons were a one-size-fits-all system, had an anti-American, anti-Christian, anti-Jewish, pro-Islam bent. They were using group-teaching, constructivism methods with the teacher as the facilitator. [85] Doesn't that sound just like Common Core?

Thanks to groups like Texas Eagle Forum and the Glenn Beck show enough national attention was drawn to CSOPE, that in May of 2013, the State School Board voted to 'supposedly' throw it out of Texas.

But like all evil, liberal concoctions, they just can't seem to really die. They keep reappearing but with a new name. It is now called **"Teks Resource System"** and according to one website, "its nasty fingers are still squeezing the life out of Texas schools."

The following is a statement made by one of the teachers who is still teaching under the CSCOPE / Teks Resource System. As one can see her comments sound very similar to what teachers are saying about Common Core:

I have gone from being a teacher having the confidence that I could accomplish anything in the classroom to a teacher that no longer knows which end is up.
Metaphors are our mantra..."a ship without a rudder, a kite without a string, a compass without a needle."

How sad that education in our district wears the mask of deceit. I just wish that sanity could return to our classrooms.[86]

Chapter III

Cartel-Written

Common Core was not written by States and is Not States Driven; Who Were the Members of the Cartel who wrote it; Their Connections and their Objectives?

We are told that the standards were State-written, State-led and State-driven, but that is not true. They were written by a cartel of mostly test and curriculum developers who were hired by three private Washington, D.C., organizations: Achieve Inc., the National Governors Association (NGA), Council for Chief State School Officers (CCSSO), and funded by a fourth private entity, the Bill and Melinda Gates Foundation.[87]

Achieve - the Leader of the Cartel and the Main Proponent of National Standards: The main architect of Common Core was a group founded by corporation heads and governors back in 1996 called Achieve Inc., who invited other groups to join with them: the NGA, the CCSSO, members of the Obama administration, the Federal Department of Education (FDOE), teacher labor unions – the Federal Teachers Association (FTA), American College Testing (ACT), and the College Board - now under the leadership of David Coleman, the main writer of the Common Core English Language Arts Standards. Other left-leaning organizations that were part of the cartel were: the Apollo Alliance, heavily funded by George Soros through his Tides Foundation, the Alliance for Excellent Education, and the Hunt Institute, a project of former NC Governor, James Hunt Jr.

Before we examine the step by step process of how Common Core was created by the cartel, let us first learn more about Achieve, the leader of the cartel. It was created back in 1996 when a few governors were invited to meet with corporate leaders such as IBM and form an organization to improve education by creating a series of national standards. According to Achieve's website, this handful of governors and corporate leaders was somehow expanded to include all of them: (Emphasis added.)

> *Created in 1996 by **the nation's governors and corporate leaders**, Achieve is an independent, bipartisan, non-profit education reform organization based in Washington, DC that helps states raise academic standards and graduation requirements, improve assessments and strengthen accountability so all students graduate ready for college, work and citizenship.*

Achieve Furthers Progressives' Goal of Central Control over Education: As reporter Alex Newman writes, Achieve gave a major boost to the progressives' longtime objective of "smashing State and local sovereignty over education, while centralizing control over schools at the federal level." They did this by forming a "public-private partnership (PPP) over education."[88]

What is a Public Private Partnershp? This is when business (the private sector) and government (the public sector) form a partnership, something that used to always be frowned on in our nation. Big business used to be able to serve as a sort of "check and balance" on big government and help reign in its power. If business

has now formed a partnership with government, there is nothing to stop the abuse of power by both big business and big government. Another name for a PPP is fascism, where private ownership of property is allowed but with total government control.

One of Achieve's Goals - Get Rid of Local School Districts:

Louis Gerstner Jr., former IBM CEO, who co-chaired Achieve from its beginning until 2002, spoke about education reform for the CEO Council at the *Wall Street Journal* in November, 2008, and told them that to fix the nation's schools they should be run more efficiently, like a business, like he ran IBM: "The nation's 16,000 school districts need to be abolished."[89] This certainly reveals the high regard Achieve and Common Core have for elected representative government and local control of education – let's abolish it totally!

Gerstner wrote an article that was published in *the Wall Street Journal,* December 1, 2008, which restated his shocking proposal:

> *Abolish all local school districts, save 70 (50 states; 20 largest cities).* **Some states may choose to leave some of the rest as community service organizations, but they would have no direct involvement in the critical task of establishing standards, selecting teachers, and developing curricula.**[90]

As has already been mentioned, one of the goals of the Obama administration and other socialist leaders, such as FDR, is to destroy local control and representative government. If you want a big, powerful, socialist federal government, State and local control are a real hindrance. They need to be abolished or their power and authority limited or usurped through setting up regional governments with unelected commissioners to rule over them. The power and authority of local school districts can also be weakened by changing public schools into charter schools that in most States no longer have elected school boards running them. California is the exception to that rule.

Other Objectives: Gerstner gave other objectives for education reform in his *Wall Street Journal* article which (except for a few) all seem to be incorporated into Common Core – so much for CCSSI being "written by States and being State led." Gerstner recommended President-elect Obama convene a meeting of our nation's governors and seek agreement to the following:

1) National Standards: *"Establish a set of national standards for a core curriculum. I would suggest we start with four subjects: reading, math, science and social studies."* [Earlier in the article he had called for a "rigorous" curriculum. Is this where the idea came to use "rigorous" whenever supporters speak about Common Core?]
2) Higher Compensation for Teachers*: "Greatly improve the quality of teaching in our classrooms, supported by substantially higher compensation for our best teachers...*He recommends *"$100,000 to be measured by student learning."* [So teachers' salaries will be determined by how well the students do on their tests that measure student learning. This is called "merit pay" or "high stake testing," which is going on in many States and is causing wide-scale cheating by teachers and even administrators. In California, it was estimated teachers in 123 schools were suspected of cheating in 2007.[91] More is written about this under "cheating." Such high salaries would certainly keep some teachers tied to supporting Common Core, even though they really don't like it.]
3) *"Allow school leaders to remove underperforming teachers.* [Teachers have told me that they were threatened with losing their jobs if they dared to use their old files and not go along totally with all the new, innovative Common Core ideas or if they expressed opposition to Common Core.]

4) Teaching Certification and Regular Re-evaluations: *"Establish national standards for teacher certification and require regular re-evaluations of teacher skills."*

5) Constant Tests and Evaluations: *"Measure student and teacher performance on a systematic basis, supported by tests and assessments. Establish a National Skills Day on which every third, sixth, ninth and 12th-grader would be tested against the national standards. Results would be published nationwide for every school in America."*

6) Extend the school day and the school year *to effectively add 20 more days of schooling for all K-12 students. Increase "time on task" for all students; this means more time in school each day, and a longer school year.*[92]

Longer School Days and a Longer School Year: In case, the last suggestion seems like a radical, leftist idea where students will be part of the education/indoctrination system for a much longer time each day and year, guess what? The same ideas have been promoted by Republicans, such as Senator Lamar Alexander, the former governor of Tennessee, who served as Secretary of Education for President George Bush Sr. from 1991 to 1993. In a speech that Alexander gave to the 1989 Governor's Education Summit held in Kansas, he suggested extending the time in the classroom from 6 a.m. to 6 p.m., six days a week, and having a year round school. He proposed having the school as the "center of the community," where children would be taken from 3 months old to age 18. It would include prenatal care for the mother (essentially womb to tomb), with a team of teachers to follow the child from age 3 months to the 8th grade.[93]

Chris Christie, also a Republican Governor, agrees with Lamar Alexander, President Obama and his Secretary of Education, Arne Duncan, that children should have longer days at school (even serving dinner, along with lunch and breakfast), having more preschools, and having an extension of schools days in the summer by at least 20 days.[94]

Three Questions about Gerstner's Suggestions for Education Reform: Gerstner predicted that three questions would be raised about his suggestions:

1) National Standards vs Local School Autonomy? He seems to think that the strong tradition of local school autonomy is outdated now and polls show that most Americans want national standards. [He, however, does not site any polls to back up his statement.]

2) Long Length of Time to Implement? Gerstner says that it can go quickly *"if we follow a focused, pragmatic approach."* Even if not all 50 States have signed on, *"we can get started with 30. The rest will be driven to abandon their "see no evil" blinders by their citizens as the original group achieves momentum and success."* We won't have to start from scratch but draw *"on existing domestic and foreign programs."*

3) How do we pay for all of this? Gerstner thinks that billions will be saved by consolidating the operations of 15,000 school districts and that *"the U.S. Department of Education can direct all of its discretionary funds to this effort."*[95]

Background Information on Michael Cohen, President of

Achieve, Inc. since 2003. Has the liberal philosophy of Achieve changed any under Cohen's leadership? No, it is just more closely aligned now with the NGA and the FDOE because of Cohen's education background, while under Gerstner's leadership, Achieve was more aligned with the corporate part of the partnership.

Cohen has been a career-long federal education officer, serving as the Director of Education Policy at the NGA (1985-90) and Director of Planning and Policy

Development at the National Association of State Boards of Education (1983-1985). During the Clinton Administration he served as Assistant Secretary for Elementary and Secondary Education, Special Assistant to President Clinton for Education Policy, and Senior Advisor to U.S. Secretary of Education Richard Riley. Achieve's website tells more of the accomplishments with Michael Cohen as president:

> Under Mike's leadership, Achieve launched the American Diploma Project Network, formed the Partnership for the Assessment of College and Career Readiness (PARCC) – one of two multi-state consortia developing common assessments – and helped develop the Common Core State Standards.[96]

President Cohen Serves as Project Managers for PAARC:: It is amazing to see how intertwined Achieve and Cohen are in every aspect of Common Core and the link to the Federal Department of Education. Cohen went from a career in the U.S. Department of Education to leading Achieve, the national-standards group that wrote the CCSS, to then working for the national standards' testing arm, PARCC, as its project manager, thus writing the tests for those standards which his group had written, that now will be federally directed and overseen by the Department he long worked for.[97]

The tests will "signal whether students are on track to graduate ready for college and the workplace" as defined by that small D.C. group. How have they been able to have such power and influence and achieve so much in such a short time? Much has been possible through the generous funding of Bill Gates, who has given them **$56,297,699.**

Other Contributors: Achieve proudly lists on their website all the other businesses and foundations that support them. So, of course, these all would be supporting Common Core as well – Achieve's biggest accomplishment. They are:

AT&T Foundation
The Battelle Foundation
Bill & Melinda Gates Foundation
The Boeing Company
Brookhill Foundation
Carnegie Corporation of New York
Chevron
The Cisco Foundation
DuPont
The GE Foundation
IBM Corporation
Intel Foundation
JP Morgan Chase Foundation
The Joyce Foundation
The Leona & Harry B. Helmsley Charitable Trust
Lumina Foundation
MetLife Foundation
Microsoft
Nationwide
Noyce Foundation
The Prudential Foundation
Sandler Foundation
State Farm Insurance Companies
Travelers Foundation
The William and Flora Hewlett Foundation[98]

"Change State Policies and Practices": These are the words that Achieve has on their website. What if the States don't think that their policies and practices need to be changed? Tough! That is what Achieve and Common Core are all about. The website also boasts that their work is the **"pre-cursor to Common Core."**

> Our work doesn't stop with the publication of reports; *we have developed tools that help states change policies and practices.* Chief among these are benchmark expectations

– model K-12 academic standards – in mathematics and English…which served as a pre-cursor to the Common Core State Standards." [99]

Achieve was using the words "Common Core" back in 2008 before the cartel had been organized. They issued a report called "Out of Many, One: Toward Rigorous Common Core Standards from the Ground Up." According to their website, they "partnered with the NGA and CCSSO on the Initiative and a number of Achieve staff and consultants served on the writing and review teams."[100]

"State-Led?" Most Common Core opponents believe that the partnership with the NGA and CCSSO was formed because Achieve needed to give their Common Core dream some State-led "legitimacy" to abide by U.S. Constitutional law? According to three federal laws and the 10th Amendment, education policy is to originate with and be left up to the States,[101] thus they had to make some pretense that the States were involved in its creation. By making it appear that the governors and their chief State Superintendents were on board then it could be labeled "State-written and State-led."

NGA - National Governors Association: Here is the logo for the NGA. The next picture shows Bill Gates speaking before the NGA in November of 2010 just two months after the majority of governors had signed on to Common Core, sight unseen.

What is the NGA? Founded in 1908, it is a Washington D.C.-based trade, lobbying, and networking association that calls itself "the collective voice of the nation's governors and is one of Washington D.C.'s most highly respected public policy organizations."[102]

All governors are invited to join, but not all do. The governors do not really represent their States in any national policy decisions because they were not elected to do so. They were only elected to represent us in our own States.

Council of Chief State School Officers: They are also a Washington D.C.-based, unelected lobbying association and trade group of state superintendents of schools and other state and local education administrators that lobby Congress and government agencies. Again, like the NGA, not all superintendents belong and, thus, not all States are represented.

Important Facts about the NGA and CCSSO: They are both NGOs - non-governmental organizations. Their names sound very impressive, but they are not governmental organizations and only some governors, some State superintendents, and State school board members attend them, not all of them. Membership is supposedly voluntary, but according to an NGA spokesperson Jode Omear, all the governors belong from all 50 States and 5 territories, whether they pay dues or not and whether they want to belong or not.

The Membership is Very Expensive: For the NGA, membership dues range from $22,000 - $176,000 a year depending on how large the State is and what "services" the State is receiving back from the NGA. What services do they receive? According to Omear, the States receive, *"technical assistance from NGA staff; grants from the federal government and foundations that are managed by NGA; and policy academies that share best practices among states where travel and attendance of state employees are funded by NGA."*

Omear believes "the states get more value from membership than what they pay in dues." She said that the NGA provides many services to the states that are valuable as they deal with many similar issues.

However, the Governor of Maine, Paul Le Page, dropped his membership believing that he received no value from it.

> *I get no value out of those meetings. They are too politically correct and everybody is lovey-dovey and no decisions are ever made. There are some tough decisions that need to be made in this country, and we need to start making them.*[103]

Is the NGA the Place for Making Tough Policy Decisions? Good for Governor Le Page for dropping his membership in the NGA, but does he really believe a costly, trade, networking, NGO association is the place to make tough policy decisions? Isn't that why we have elected representatives in Congress and our State legislators? Obviously, the governors and State superintendents who belong to the NGA and CCSSO have conveniently forgotten that Congress and State legislators even exist. They were completely bypassed when governors and State School Boards signed onto Common Core bringing it into their States.

For the governors and State superintendents who do actively belong to the NGA and CCSSO and are participating in designing policy for the nation such as Common Core standards, the question should be asked of them, **who gave you that right and authority**? We did not elect you to do such things. We elected you to govern our own State - that is all.

NGA and CCSSO have a copyright and hold the trademark on CCSSI: Not only did the NGA and CCSSO (under the direction and with the help of Achieve) take over the creation of the CC standards, but they went a step farther to ensure that any State that signed on could not change them. At the NGA website, one can read *"Attribution; Copyright Notice: NGA Center/CCSSO shall be acknowledged as the sole owners and developers of the Common Core State Standards, and no claims to the contrary shall be made."* http://www.corestandards.org/.

Why is this information about the copyright and trademark important? Proponents of Common Core try to pass off the NGA and CCSSO as official government agencies to give CC the appearance of having been written by someone having to do with State government. But a copyright is not allowed by a governmental organization. The copyright also makes it almost impossible for a State to legally do any changing of the CC Standards to make them "fit" their State.[104]

So much for the 15% innovations the States have been told they can have? Those innovations will not be on the national assessment test, standardized to be the same for all States, so why would teachers be told to teach anything else or take the time to do so when it will not be on the test?

The NGA and CCSSO hold their meetings behind closed doors, which would be illegal for any official governmental organization. NGOs are not subject to a FOIA (Freedom of Information Act) request. That is why it is difficult to really know all that went on behind the scenes in writing the CC Standards.

Cartel's History – How Common Core was Created: Thanks to many good researchers and from leaks that have come forth from people actually involved inside the cartel, here is the timeline of the creation of Common Core.

Before we begin, let us make clear that **there were only a handful of elected officials that were involved**, a few governors and a few State Superintendents, in spite of the claim that all States were represented. Hunt's press release and a paper describing how Common Core came into existence written by Dane Linn, the NGA education director, tell of the endorsement and involvement of only a few elected officials, not someone from every State.[105]

Timeline for the Creation of Common Core:

- **2007 commission of 15 people,** headed by two former governors, had recommended national standards.
- **June 2008 Hunt Institute Education Forum:** The NGA first directly involved the governors in nationalizing education standards when it co-hosted an education forum with the Hunt Institute, a project of former N.C. Governor. James Hunt Jr.

- **December 2008 - Report Released Calling for National Education Standards:** Achieve, the NGA, and the CCSSO released the report calling for national standards. The report recommended "a strong state-federal partnership" to accomplish this goal.
- **June 1, 2009 – Report Issued that 46 States Had Joined a "State-led Process to Develop a Common Core of Standards:** The report does not explain what "joining" entailed or how it could be called "State-led."
- **June 15, 2009 - "National Standards and a Federal-State Partnership":** Two weeks later, the NGA-Hunt education forum featured "national standards advocacy" to the 21 governors and staff who attended. The new U.S. Education Secretary Arne Duncan spoke of "national standards as a federal-state partnership."

"[M]y job is to help you succeed" in adopting "common national standards," Duncan told the assembly. He said States initiated Common Core because a 2007 commission of 15 people, headed by two former governors, had recommended national standards. Who was the commission funded by? None other than the Bill and Melinda Gates Foundation.

Duncan also said that the federal government "empowers states to decide what kids need to learn and how to measure it." One of the ways it would do that was by funding national Common Core tests.

Committees to Write and Give Feedback on Common Core Standards: By July 1, 2009, NGA and CCSSO had formed three committees:

1. First, there were two work groups, with about a dozen members in each who wrote the math and English standards. These groups had no K-12 teachers, but did include a few professors.

2. Second were two feedback groups, who were supposed to provide research and advice to the writers. Those had 18 members each, who were mostly professors but did include one high school math teacher.

3. Third was the 29-member validation committee, announced in September 2009, which acted as the final gate for Common Core. Their job was to "ensure [the standards] are research and evidence-based." As has been already reported in Chapter One, five of those members, all who have PhDs, refused to sign off that they were research or evidence-based or that they were higher or better standards. Two of those are outspoken critics of Common Core, Sandra Stotsky and James Milgram.

Influence Coming from Classroom Teachers? Was Common Core really written by teachers from the various States as proponents are saying? While many people sat on these various committees, only one in sixty was a classroom teacher, according to teaching coach and blogger Anthony Cody.

Dane Linn says only six States sent in teacher and staff feedback, but according to Mark Bauerlein, an Emory University professor who sat on a feedback committee, committee members weren't sure what effect their advice or suggestions had, or if they were even used.

I have no idea how much influence committee members had on final product. Some of the things I advised made their way into the standards. Some of them didn't. I'm not sure why or how.

Several people on the validation committee said the same: They had no idea what happened to their comments once they submitted them.

Gag Orders or Confidentiality Agreements: All of the various groups involved in the standards writing, discussions, and in the validations were sealed by confidentiality agreements that were to be held in private.

Achieve Formed a partnership with the US Education Delivery Institute (USEDI) for Leadership Training of Common Core: Since Achieve was involved in every other aspect in writing and developing Common Core, it would, of course, be involved in the training of leaders, to make sure CC is done properly.

What is USEDI? It was founded in May, 2010, and is led by its director, Sir Michael Barber, a British subject, who was knighted by Queen Elizabeth for his education reform in Great Britain. [No one seems to ask how does a British citizen start a U.S. Institute?]

Sir Barber has written a book that helps in his leadership training called *Deliverology 101*. He is also the leader for the PARCC consortium, one of the two groups writing the assessment test and has produced a power point presentation about it. (See Chapter VII)

If you go to the US Education Delivery Institute website and click on funding, you see the following wealthy corporations that have given large donations to Barber's Institute: Of course, Bill and Melinda Gates Foundation is mentioned first; then Carnegie Foundation, Harold K.L Castle Foundation of Hawaii, and William and Flora Hewlett Foundation (of Hewlett and Packer - HP computers).[106]

Sir Michael Barber is so left leaning in his views that he is even leaning to his left in the picture of him. He is an atheist and a globalist who does not believe in borders or the sovereignty of nations and believes children are to be taught to think of themselves as "global citizens." He brings in the international aspect of Common Core and is helping to spread it worldwide as he serves as the Chief Education Officer for **Pearson Foundation**, the largest publishing company in the world and the one that will be doing most of the e-books for Common Core. Pearson has offices in 70 other nations and 36,000 employees. If you go to their website, they proudly show a map that reveals the location of their offices on every continent of the world.[107] They have taken over 100 other education publishing companies. However, Pearson lets them keep their own name, so no one knows just how large Pearson is. The following are some of the foremost names: Scott Foresman, Prentice Hall, Addison-Wesley, Allyn and Bacon, Benjamin Cummings and Longman.[108]

The Five Lead Writers: The only ones who would know how much influence the committee members or suggestions coming from teachers had on the final product were the lead writers of the standards: David Coleman and Susan Pimentel in English, and Jason Zimba, Phil Daro, and William McCallum in math. How were they selected? It appears that the link to all of them was Bill Gates. He knew all of them through their backgrounds in technology. Was he allowed to do the selection because of the $millions he had already put into Common Core?

The Lead Writers Were all Inexperienced as Teachers: None of the writers had any previous experience in the classroom as K-12 teachers. Could this explain why so many teachers, especially in the younger grades, are saying the standards sound so strange and are difficult to understand? Here is more information and pictures of three of the top team members who wrote the standards:

David Coleman: Coleman led the team of five writers who gathered all the information from the other members of the cartel and produced the standards. He is, therefore, given the title of being **"the architect of Common Core."** His main job was writing the English Language Arts Standards. He was assisted by Sue Pimental, who also had no background as a classroom teacher.

David grew up as the only child in a left-leaning, intellectual home with a psychologist for a father and his mother, Liz Coleman is the president of a small liberal arts college in Vermont called Bennington College. Coleman comes by his left-leaning ideology mainly from his mother. She is a big proponent of big government and top-down, federal education with Marxist ideology.

David's liberal beliefs were further molded by attending Yale University, where he received a BA in philosophy, a second BA in English literature, and an MA in Greek philosophy, which he received as a Rhodes Scholar in England. [Maybe that explains why the standards sound like "Greek" to the average teachers who are trying to decipher them.]

Coleman's Education Philosophy – Standards Should be "Fewer, Clearer, and Higher": While working on the Grow Network, Coleman discovered that the standards the tests were trying to measure "were so vast and vague, it was hard to make high-quality assessments." After he and Zimba formed Student Achievement Partners, that now helps States implement the Common Core standards, they wrote a seminal paper in 2008 calling for "math and science standards that are fewer, clearer, and higher." Coleman also believes that "every child should be a smart thinker, a deep thinker, someone who's analytical and probing."[109]

But what about those children who aren't smart or deep thinkers, who are not analytical and probing? Being the mother of six children, I know that each child is different; each child comes to this earth with varying gifts and talents. Some may enjoy being analytical and curious, others not. Some are great scholars, writers and orators. Others are gifted in music or art. To try to force them all to be the same, the same cookie-cutter design is not right; to force their teachers to have to teach the exact same way is not right either; and to mandate that each school be the same, like a factory producing an army of mechanical robots is not right either.

Coleman also Believes Common Core will Help Overcome Social Justice and Inequality: Coleman says it is worth it because too many students, especially poor minority children, aren't being challenged. "These standards are the most serious attempt this country has yet made to come to grips with those early sources of inequality," he says.[110]

As you will read later, Coleman also believes that he, as President of the College Board, must make changes to the SAT to make it more socially just and not so difficult for under privileged students. Does that not sound like it will be dumbed down?

How Was Coleman Selected to Write the Standards? With no background as a teacher, having never written standards before, why was David Coleman "the chosen one" to write the English standards for all teachers? Was it because of his background – having already worked with Obama, Arne Duncan, and Bill Ayers in Chicago? Or was it because he had already worked with Achieve; or was he the chosen one of Bill Gates, who is the great funder for the cartel and the various organizations being represented on it?

Many educators resent the fact that someone so inexperienced is telling them how to run their English classrooms. One of those is Dianne Ravitch, a professor at New York University, a popular education blogger and a strong critic of Common Core. She believes that Coleman's personal disdain for reading fiction and "imaginative writing" is why the CC English standards were so written, with all teachers having to now follow his personal bias. Is that fair? Coleman's ELA Standards have reduced reading fiction and classical English literature from 80% to 50% in elementary school and all the way down to 30% in high school and replaced it with "informational text" – all because of David Coleman's own personal bias? Here is what Ravitch writes on her blog:

> *I don't like the idea that some disembodied national agency tells teachers to cut back on the novels, poetry, and short stories and focus on informational text. That shows not only a hostility to imaginative literature but a disregard for teachers' professionalism. I mean, he can have his opinion but why foist it on the nation?* [111]

Coleman's past jobs were running his own education data and assessment company, so he knows all about collecting data on students which Common Core calls for. He now runs his own education consulting firm.[112] In October of 2012, Coleman was also appointed as the head of the College Board and announced that he would make sure that the SAT and the ACT, college entrance exams, will be compliant with Common Core.

Susan Pimentel was David Coleman's assistant in writing the English Language Arts Standards. She has no teaching background either, but received an advanced degree from Cornell University and worked as a senior policy advisor to Maryland Governor William Donald Schaefer, and as special counsel to Superintendent of Schools John Murphy in Prince George's County, MD.

Susan was a chief architect of the American Diploma Project Benchmarks (part of Achieve), designed to close the gap between high school demands and postsecondary expectations. (See next page) Since 2007, Susan has served on the National Assessment Governing Board, an independent, bipartisan board that sets policy for the national assessment. In addition to several articles, Susan is co-author with Denis P. Doyle of the book and CD-ROM, *Raising the Standard: An Eight-Step Action Guide For Schools and Communities.* She now serves with David Coleman and Jason Zimba of Student Achievement Partners in supporting the faithful implementation of the Common Core.

The following is what is written about the American Diploma Project Benchmarks on the Achieve website (emphasis added):

> *When they were released in 2004, the ADP Benchmarks reflected an unprecedented convergence in what employers and postsecondary faculty say are needed for new employees and for freshmen entering credit-bearing coursework to be successful.* ***Today, they stand as the precursor to the Common Core State Standards.***[113]

According to Sandra Stotsky, even though Susan Pimental had never been a classroom teacher, she did have some prior experience developing K-12 standards. Sandra had worked with her in 2008 developing the Texas ELA standards. Susan was under contract with an organization called "Standards Work" that had a contract with the Texas Board of Education.[114]

Jason Zimba was David Coleman's chief partner in writing the Common Core math standards. He is an astrophysicist, has a Ph.D.

in mathematical physics, which he teaches at Bennington College, the same college that David Coleman's mother is president of. Zimba also has no background as a K-12 teacher.

Coleman and Zimba are childhood friends and the co-founders of **Student Achievement Partners,** "which assembles leading thinkers and researchers to design actions that will improve student achievement. The group integrates policy analysis, research, and design to focus on the most significant outcomes for students."[115] This organization played a leading role in developing the Common Core standards and actively supports States and school districts in implementing them.

Zimba Caught on a Video Clip Admitting the Low Epectations of his Math Standards: As was mentioned in Chapter I, Zimba was recorded speaking before the Massachusetts Department of Education, in March, 2010, with Sandra Stotsksy asking him questions, and he admitted that his creation, the Common Core math standards would only prepare students for a minimum junior college level, not for "selective" colleges such as Berkeley and also not for STEM (Science, Technology, Engineering and Math) [116]

Two Other Members of the Math Team: Serving with Jason

Zimba were William McCallum, a math professor at the University of Arizona and Phil Daro, the only member of the team with K-12 teaching experience. However, he had majored in English as an undergraduate and had never had any experience teaching or developing math standards. He also had served on the staff of the NCEE (National Center for Education and the Economy). None had ever developed K-12 mathematics standards before.[117]

Coleman and Zimba are part of a group called **Students First**, where Coleman serves as the treasurer. According to Dianne Ravitch, Students First is an organization that most teachers would not agree with. She believes it seem to have a "contempt for experienced teachers." It is against seniority and tenure; against unions and collective bargaining; and supports basing evaluations on test scores, and supports efforts to privatize public education.[118]

Privatized education means that we would no longer have public schools as we know them. They would be privately owned and operated like charter schools, but still with tax paying dollars funding them. Why is that so bad? Because most privately owned and operated schools no longer come under the auspices of elected school boards. They thus become education without representation, and those running the schools are no longer accountable to the parents. If parents don't like what is going on in the school – tough! They have no say, no one to represent them. Un-elected officials running schools are what most socialist, dictator-run countries have.

Coleman's Yearly Salary as Head of the College Board: It sounds like the more teachers find out about David Coleman and his views, the more they are wondering how he was ever chosen to head up the powerful and highly paid position of the College Board? Coleman will have a yearly salary of $550,000 and total compensation of $750,000.[119]

What are Coleman's Plans for the Future of College Entrance Testing? Coleman is aligning the SAT and ACT, the college entrance tests to the Common Core standards, as well as the GED, the high school equivalency test. So a student coming from a private Christian school or one who is home schooled will have to understand and be trained in Common Core if they want to pass the tests to be able to get into college.

Replace the Tests: According to the *New York Times*, Coleman's ultimate goal is that the Common Core Assessment tests that students would take leaving high school would someday replace the college entrance tests, because the Assessments would be the same for all States. Therefore, making another standardized college entrance test no longer necessary. [120]

Effect on Home Schoolers? This would also make it very hard for home schooled children to be able to enter college. There would be no ACT or SAT for them to take. Would this force them to have to go back to public schools or at least force them to have to be taught in the Common Core curriculum and to take the CC assessment?

The Background of Coleman and Zimba and their Connection to Bill Ayers and Obama: Prior to Student Achievement Partners, Coleman and Zimba were co-founders of an organization in New York called the Grow Network started in 2000. Grow is an Internet-based program that analyzes data and test scores for teachers and parents and provides suggestions to both on what to do next. They especially were busy trying to explain the testing data of No Child Left Behind to teachers. Grow soon became a "leader in assessment reporting and customized instructional material."[121]

The Grow Network was given a $2.2 million contract to produce data studies for the Chicago Annenberg Challenge (CAC). That is what brought Coleman and Zimba to Chicago.[122] At that time,

Obama was sitting on the CAC Board (recruited by Bill Ayers) which paid for the contract, and Obama's U.S. Secretary of Education, Arne Duncan, was Chicago's Superintendent of Schools.

Less than a year later, the **Chicago Public Education Fund [known as "the Fund"]** began negotiating a contract with Grow Network on behalf of Chicago Public Schools. That is how Coleman and Zimba worked closely with Arne Duncan. Thus all the influential players were together in Chicago pushing their dreams of progressive (socialized or communist) education – now embodied in Common Core. The Grow Network was later sold to the McGraw-Hill Company in 2004.[123]

More About the "The Fund" and the CAC: The Fund was created in 1998 by the Chicago Annenberg Challenge (CAC), which was created primarily to raise funds to "reform" the Chicago public schools. In what direction would the schools be reformed? With the co-founder of the CAC being avowed Communist **Bill Ayers**, one can only guess what his intentions were for the Chicago schools. Ayers hired Barrack Obama to serve as the first chairmen for the CAC, with Ayers as the co-chairman. They served together for eight years. (Yet, Obama pretended he hardly knew Ayers when he was first running for president in 2008.)

Bill Ayers Radical, Violent Past, Communist Views, and his Influence on Education: The reader may wonder why the next few pages are devoted to giving the Communist background and radical views of Bill Ayers. It is because the younger generation knows very little about him, his profound influence on education philosophy today and his strong connections to and continued beliefs in Communism. Most of our younger generation also know very little about the evils of Communism. In fact, in most schools and universities today, it is being taught as "the best form of government, but just has a hard time being implemented."

Bill Ayers' radical, anti-American, pro-Communist views are certainly permeating anything that he still has influence on such as Common Core. He also has close ties and shares the same radical leftist, Marxist views as Linda Darling Hammond, the leader for the Smarter Balance Assessment Consortium.

In his college days at the University of Michigan, Ayers was a member of SDS - Students for a Democratic Society, a radical, Marxist group. But it was not radical enough for Ayers, so he co-founded and lead the communist anti-Vietnam War group called the "Weather Underground," which created and exploded bombs from 1969 to 1975 in over 30 locations. The bombs went off in various police buildings in San Francisco, Berkeley, Detroit, Michigan, New York City, and the National Guard building in Washington, D.C. They also went off in bigger government structures such as the Pentagon and the U.S. Capitol building. Fortunately, there were not many deaths, but lots of injuries, and millions of dollars in damages to buildings.

However, the bombing of the San Francisco police station in February 16, 1970, killed Police Sergeant Brian McDonnell, who died days later from the metal staples that were blasted through his body by the home-made bomb. Eight other officers were also injured. Another bomb meant to blow up some army barracks in New Jersey accidentally exploded in 1970 in the Greenwich Village townhouse where it was being made, killing three members of the Weather Underground themselves, including Diana Oughton, Ayers' girlfriend at the time.

Why the bombings? Ayers wrote a small book, published in 1974, which is his sort of radical "manifesto" to the world, called *Prairie*

Fire - The politics of revolutionary anti-imperialism. He dedicated the book to 100 "political prisoners" including Sirhan Sirhan, who shot and killed Bobby Kennedy. In the book, he proudly declares his communist affiliation and "bloody" intentions. By the many bombings, Bill Ayers and the other members of the Weather Underground were attempting to bring about a revolution against the evil Empire of America, against war, but also against capitalism, which he felt was the root of all evil:

> *We are a guerilla organization. We are communist men and women, underground in the United States for more than four years...We need a revolutionary communist party in order to lead the struggle, give coherence and direction to the fight, seize power and build the new society...Our intention is to disrupt the empire, to incapacitate it, to put pressure on the cracks, to make it hard to carry out its bloody functioning against the people of the world, to join the world struggle, to attack from the inside.*

Ayers and his new girlfriend Bernadine Dorhn (now his wife) went into hiding, with various false identities, while raising two children. The bombings continued. In 1981 they turned themselves in, and most charges were dropped against Ayers because of what he testified was "extreme governmental misconduct" during the long search for him. Many people think he was really let go because of his father's "extreme" power and wealthy influence. His father, Thomas Ayers, served as the CEO and President of Chicago's electric power company Commonwealth Edison and had great influence over many people in New York and Chicago.

Bernadine Dorhn had to serve seven months in a NYC federal jail in 1983 for her refusal to testify before a grand jury concerning the 1979 job she had working for a baby boutique called Broadway

Baby, where stolen customer IDs were used to rent trucks that were later used in a series of violent armed robberies bringing in stolen goods worth $2 million. The robberies were being performed by Black Panthers and former Weather Underground members.

Ayers and His Wife Today: With the help of Ayers father, the couple eventually found themselves with respectable professions in Chicago. Bill Ayers became the head of several non-profit "charity" boards, such as the Woods Fund and the previously mentioned Chicago Annenberg Challenge, where Obama served with Ayers for many years. Ayers later also became a professor of education and an elementary "education theorist" at the University of Illinois at Chicago. In 2008, he was elected Vice President of Curriculum studies by the American Educational Research Association.

Sol Stern, a former radical himself, who is now an author and fellow with the conservative Manhattan Institute and a contributing editor for their magazine, *City Journal*, is a harsh critic of Bill Ayers and his work in education. Stern stated:

> *Calling Bill Ayers a school reformer is a bit like calling Joseph Stalin an agricultural reformer. The media mainstreaming of a figure like Mr. Ayers could have terrible consequences for the country's politics and public schools.*[124]

Bernadine became a clerk and later an associate at the Chicago Law Firm of Sidley and Austin, where Michelle Obama worked with her, and Obama later joined the firm as a summer intern.

Bernadine later became an associate professor of law at North-western University.

Incidentally, neither Bill or Bernadine ever apologized for their former lives as terrorists and bombers. They are actually proud of

what they did. This picture shows Bill Ayers in 2001, defiantly stomping on the American flag, where he displays his continued disrespect and disdain for this "evil" country.[125]

It is amazing where fugitives from the law end up these days, especially if they have the right connections and seem to be far-left Marxists. One can only imagine what kind of Marxist teachings university students under their tutelage received.

According to Phyllis Schlafly, author, columnist and expert on Communism, Ayers continues to teach students "rebellion against American capitalism and imperialism."[126]

The Purpose of the Chicago Annenberg Challenge, CAC, and the Fund: The Fund existed and still exists to carry on the work of the Chicago Annenberg Challenge, the "reform" dream of Bill Ayers, to indoctrinates students in States and districts nationwide with a **"Marxist-Communist political and social ideology."**

The program focused on individual schools built around specific political themes to push students to "confront issues of inequity, war, and violence." The teacher education programs served as **"sites of resistance"** to an oppressive system. The point, said Ayers in his "Teaching Toward Freedom," is to "teach against oppression, against America's history of evil and racism, thereby forcing social transformation."[127]

Bill Ayers Influence on Obama Furthering His Marxist Ideology: Much has been written about the Communist party affiliations of Obama's mother, Ann Dunham, and his grandparents, Stanley and Madelyn Dunham, who raised him in his high school years, and their close ties with the Communist journalist and poet Frank Marshal Davis, who Obama refers to as his "mentor" and even calls him "Pop" in his book *Dreams of My Father*.[128]

In Chicago, Obama came under the tutelage and influence of Communist Bill Ayers as his co-chairman for eight years as he served with him on the CAC board. Many authorities believe that it was actually Ayers who wrote Obama's book *Dreams of My Father*. It has his style and imagery. And Obama had never written a book before. We actually have no record of his writings anywhere to compare one to another. All Obama's past has been sealed.

Obama Endorsed Bill Ayers' Book: When Obama was first running for the presidential election of 2008, his supporters tried to downplay the relation-ship that Obama and Ayers had. They thought having such a close friendship with a former terrorist and avid Communist might hurt Obama in the election. So, even though Obama launched his campaign in the home of Ayers and his wife, he, himself, tried to say that he hardly knew the Ayers family. They were just people in his neighborhood.

Barack Obama
State senator
A Kind and Just Parent: The
Children of Juvenile Court
by William Ayers
(Beacon Press)
"A searing and timely
account of the juvenile
court system, and the courageous individuals who
rescue hope from despair."

This picture of Obama appeared in the Chicago Tribune in 1997 when he was a State Senator. It is a write up of him praising a book written by Bill Ayers entitled *A Kind and Just Parent: Children of the Juvenile Court.* Obama wrote, *"A searing and timely account of the juvenile court system, and the courageous individuals who rescue hope from despair."*

Did CAC improve the Chicago Schools? What did Ayers and Obama accomplish in those 8 years running the CAC? Were the schools improved with higher test results? No, not at all, but $110 million dollars went through their hands ($60 from public funds) with no discernible results. How much of that money might have been used to grease the wheels of a political career for Obama?[129]

Important Question to Ask about the Cartel who Created Common Core Standards: Now that we understand more of the background, the Marxist influence and ideology of the two key players and writers of the cartel, David Coleman and Jason Zimba, and their connections to Marxist Ayers and Obama, Joy Pullman, Research Fellow of the Heartland Institute, asks the following question that is written on a small booklet that the Heartland Institute gives out, *The Common Core, A Bad Choice for America:* "Why should central-controlled, tax-payer funded, unaccountable to the public committees have the power to define what every school child should learn?"[130]

The answer is – they should not have such power. It certainly was not given to them by the American people. We did not elect our governors, nor our State superintendents to go to Washington to serve on some big cartel that created a national, top-down education program to take away State's rights – the very rights governors are supposed to be protecting. But most of us did not even know this was going on.

Constitutionality of the Cartel and the Involvement of the FDOE - Federal Department of Education - in Common Core?

The Obama administration and the FDOE know that legally they are not allowed to create or push through a federal education program on the States. There are three federal laws that forbid it: The Department of Education Organizational Act (1979); The General Education Provisions Act and The Elementary and Secondary Act (1965) most recently amended by the No Child Left Behind Act of 2001. They each essentially say the same thing:

> *The Federal Department of Education shall not be involved in developing, supervising or controlling instructional materials or curriculum.*

The Tenth Amendment also states that whatever is not written in the Constitution is to be left up to the States and local control. That is why traditionally each State has had jurisdiction over its own education program.

So, to get around these laws, the FDOE paid others to do what they are forbidden to do. But since tax paying dollars helped pay for the meetings and bribed the State governors to sign on, does that not make CCSSI federal, which is illegal?

Chapter IV

Common Core is Corporation-Driven and Funded with Hopes for a Big Cash-Cow in Profits

Cash Flow from and To Big Corporations: The more one learns about Common Core, the more one learns that not only is this all about control, but it is all about cash. There are billions to be made by the corporations that are backing it and promoting it. In this chapter you will learn of some of the biggest corporations that have given much money to the writing, development, and implementation of Common Core and will be getting much money back:

Common Core is Really "Gates Ed": Bill and Malinda Gates Foundation gave close to $150 million for the development of Common Core, and $50 million to various groups to help promote it, and $75 million to spreading it worldwide. According to information from March, 2014, the cost of what Gates has given to promote CC is now closer to $2.3 billion.[131]

Similarities Between the Gates Headquarters in Seattle, WA, and the Common Core Logo: For those of us who were wondering where the idea came from for the dizzy-looking logo for Common Core, that looks like it's been spliced in two and can't quite get its sides together, take a look at the Bill and Melinda Gates Foundation Center in Seattle. It looks just the logo. Do you think Gates had something to do with choosing the logo? With all the money he has invested in Common Core, that just might be a possibility.

Bill Gates Bought NGA, CCSSO, Achieve Inc., and Student Achievement Partners: As has already been mentioned, Common Core is not State led as we are being told; it is "Gates ed and Gates led." Gates paid for it, "lock, stock and barrel" – from its creators to its implementers and promoters. As Mercedes Schneider writes, "How foolish it is to believe that the man with the large checkbook is not calling the CCSS shots."

The four principal organizations associated with the creation of CCSS, the NGA, CCSSO, Achieve Inc, and Student Achievement

Partners all accepted millions from Bill Gates, both before and after the completion of the standards.

Below is a summary of the Gates funding, not only to the above mentioned groups but to various other groups to make sure they continue their loyal support of Common Core:

Dates	Organization	Amount	Purpose
1996-2008	Achieve Inc.	$23,500,000	Help Launch CCSS
2009	Achieve Inc.	$13,200,000	Building Alliances And Promoting CCSS
2010	Achieve Inc.	$9,300,000	Continued Support
2002-08	NGA	$23,600,000	High School Redesign And "Small Schools"
2009	NGA	$2,100,000	Implementation of CCSS
2011	NGA	$1,598,477	Rethinking Teacher Effectiveness
2002-07	CCSSO	$47,100,000	Data Access/ Data Driven Decisions
March 07	CCSSO	$21,642,317	Phase II National Education Data Partnership/Transparency/Accessibility
June 2009	CCSSO	$31,900,000	CCSS Implementation and Assessment/ Data Acquisition/ Control
July 2009	CCSSO	$9,961,842	Increase Leadership, Focus on Standards, Assessment, Data, Educator Development, Student Learning
Nov. 2009	CCSSO	$3,185,750	Partner with Federal, State, Public, Private Interests for Longitudinal Data Systems
June 2011	CCSSO	$9,388,911	Support CCSS Work
Oct. 2012	CCSSO	$1,100,000	Support Strategic Planning for CCSS and the Assessment Consortia
Nov. 2012	CCSSO	$1,277.648	Help States build Data Inoperability, Capability and IT Leadership Capability
July 2013	CCSSO	$4,000,000	Development of Assessments
June 2012	ADP Network	$9,297,699	Build National and Statewide Alliances/Engage with key Stakeholders
June 2012	Student AP	$6,500,000	Promote CCSS
	Total	$147.900,000	

In total, the four organizations primarily responsible for CCSS – NGA, CCSSO, Achieve, and Student Achievement Partners – have received close to **$150 million** from Bill Gates.

Other Major Education Organizations and Think Tanks That Have Taken Millions from Gates to Advance Common Core: For most of the organizations below, Gates has funded other reform-related efforts, including those related to charter schools, small schools, teacher evaluation, and data systems.

Name of Organization	Amount of Money	Purpose of Money
American Enterprise Institute:	$1,068,788	Promote CC
American Federation of Teachers:	$5,400,000	Promote CC and Teacher Development
Association for Supervision and Curriculum Development	$3,269,428.	Promote CC
Council of Great City Schools:	$5,010,988	Promote CC
Education Trust	$2,039,526	Promote CC
National Congress of Parents and Teachers	$499,962	Promote CC
National Education Association	$3,982,597	Promote CC
Thomas B. Fordham Institute:	$1,961,116 & $1,002,000	Track State Progress
NEA	$6,300,000 & $2,426,500	Affiliates as They Support CCSS
NEA Master Teachers	$3,882,600	Support Master Teachers in Math and ELA
*CGCS (Council of Great City Schools)	$4,910,988 & $100,000	Draft idea for Pilot Testing

*Gates paid CGCS $100,000 to propose a pilot study of CCSS in 2010 - not to actually conduct a pilot study– just to draft the idea of a pilot. Fifteen months later, there is no mention of a "proposal" much less of a pilot study materializing. Instead Gates paid CGCS to "just go ahead" and "coordinate successful implementation" of the untested CCSS. CCSS was never field tested anywhere before it was implemented.

Thanks to Mercedes Schneider for the above information that was written in the Huffington Post. She adds:

So much Gates cash, and so many hands willing to accept it. Bill Gates likes Common Core. So, he is purchasing it. In doing so, Gates demonstrates (sadly so) that when one has enough money, one can purchase fundamentally democratic institutions. Can Bill Gates buy a foundational democratic institution? Will America allow it? The fate of CCSS will provide crucial answers to those looming questions. [132]

Other Influential Groups who Received Millions from Gates to Promote Common Core: *The Washington Post* in May, 2013, listed other additional groups across the nation that Gates has given large contributions to over several years – to gain their support for Common Core. The purpose given for all of them is listed as "College-Ready US Program." The following list includes those that have received close to a million or more. Notice the many departments of educations from the various States and the number of universities. Of course, they are going to have to be supportive of Common Core or lose their large cash cow. Fordham Institute again is mentioned with another large sum:

Aspen Institute	$3,615,655
Achievement net	$3,002,252
University of Arizona	$3,416,901
MIT (Mass. Institute of Technology	$2,889,132
Scholastic Inc.	$4,463,541
Rockefeller Philanthropy	$4,618,652
Khan Academy Inc. (trading)	$4,079,361
Louisiana Department of Ed.	$7,351,708
Kentucky Department of Ed.	$9,125,277
National Writing Project	$3,095,593
New Vision for Public Schools Inc.	$8,149,935
James B. Hunt Inst. for Ed. Leadership	$5,549,352
Research for Action Inc.	$1,309,409
Purdue University	$1,453,832
Meta Metrics, Inc.	$3,468,005
New Visions for Public Schools, Inc.	$8,149,935
Kentucky Department of Education	$1,000,000
Georgia Department of Education	$1,980,892

Alliance for Excellent Education, Inc.	$3,200,004
Louisiana Department of Education	$7,351,708
Colorado Legacy Foundation 2011	$9,707,210
AFT Educational Foundation 2011	$1,000,000
AFT Educational Foundation 2012	$4,400,000
Kentucky Department of Education 2012	$1,903,089
Colorado Legacy Foundation 2012	$1,748,337
Fund for Public Schools Inc. 2012	$1,815,810
Assoc. Supervision/ Curriculum Development	$3,024,695
National Assoc. of State Boards of Education	$1,077,960
Thomas B. Fordham Institute	$959,116[133]
Thomas B. Fordham Institute 2014	$3,461,116[134]
Mark Tucker's NCEE 2009	$1,500,000

Fordham Institute's Conflict of Interest: The last figure showing over $3 million that Fordham has received by Bill Gates, is written about in an article by Jamie Gass of the Pioneer Institute. He tells how Fordham, after taking Gates money, conducted a study to evaluate and compare Common Core Standards to those of the States' prior standards. Do you think that could possibly be a fair or objective study? Of course not; Fordham made it appear that Common Core was better than all the other State standards.

Taking money from the Gates Foundation to both evaluate and promote standards that Gates financed is a conflict of interest; one that at the very least causes an objective observer to apply a higher level of scrutiny – even deep skepticism – to anything Fordham has to say about Common Core and the limits on federal authority.[135]

More Information on the Fordham Institute, which still Pretends to be a Conservative Organization: Its president Chester Finn published a book in 1991 called *We Must Take Charge.* The following is what Amazon has written about the book:

Fin proposes radical changes which he insists must be championed by all Americans if this atrophy is to be reversed. First and most importantly, he calls on us to reorganize education in relation to the results we want from it. This means establishing a clear cut standard of intellectual achievement that we will oblige all of our schools to enforce and our children to meet. To define this standard, we will need to rebuild instruction around, a national curriculum of core subjects - history, science, geography, math, literature and writing. And we must demand a more detailed flow of useful information, including reliable testing, about how our children are performing in relation to this standard.

For Finn, the implementation of these radical measures is essential to produce not only a knowledgeable twenty-first century work force that will keep our nation competitive, but an informed and reasoning citizenry capable of participating fully in a democracy. Challenging and candid, this book will point the way for all those insisting on the best that our schools can offer."[emphasis added][136]

Pat Richardson who sent this information about Fin and his book added these comments:

I appreciate that he [Finn] is concerned about democracy, but that is pretty invalid when you are breaking federal law in the first place by creating national curriculum. What's crazy is that he wrote this in 1991! And now, 23 years later, he's finally one step closer to his "radical" solution!

Colorado Department of Education Received $22 million from Gates for Support of Common Core: They are one of the largest Gates recipients in the nation: This money, of course, was offered during a time when funding for Colorado classrooms was slashed. Here is how the money was divided up:

CDE's Colorado Legacy Foundation received $9.7 million in Gates money in 2011, and $1.4 million in a second grant that year. CDE received another $6 million in 2012. In 2012, and 2010, CDE received $1.74 million each. In 2013, $828,000 was received.[137]

Other Groups who Receive Millions of Dollars to Promote CC in Colorado. The following is written by Jack Hassard, researcher and Professor Emeritus at Georgia State:

- **The Aspen Institute,** a very liberal group which does much of the training for leaders in Common Core and, "has spearheaded programs that look to break teachers' unions," received nearly $4 million in 2009, and $3.6 million and $1.5 million in 2013.
- **Colorado Children's Campaign,** a group whose mission appears to be "pushing charter schools and vouchers," has received $8.7 million. It's former head, Barbara O'Brien now sits on the Denver Public School Board. Hassard states, "This underscores the deep conflicts of interest causes by the massive Gates giving. Critics say the only programs getting attention in DPS are those funded by Gates."
- **Stand for Children,** a lobbying organization that has lobbied on behalf of Common Core. It received $3.4 million in 2010, $3.2 million in 2012 and $3.2 million and $900,000 in 2013.
- **The Fund for Colorado's Future** took in $1.6 million in 2009 and prior years.
- **The Colorado League of Charter Schools** brought in $800,000 in 2011.
- The **Rose Community Foundation** received $350,000 in 2013.
- **Colorado Succeeds**, a group led by a Republican political operative, netted $400,000 in 2013.
- **Jeffco Schools** received $5.2 million in 2013.
- **Mapleton Public Schools** received $2.7 million in 2009 and prior. This is from where Colorado State Senator

Mike Johnston hails. Johnston was the prime mover behind **SB191**, the bill which destroyed teacher tenure in Colorado.

A Colorado bill to halt the implementation of Common Core was killed by Democrats in the Colorado legislature early in 2014. Is it any wonder it was killed with all the money being poured into the State by Gates?

Hassard also claims that Gates has spent $2.3 billion pushing Common Core and that more than 1800 grants went to organizations from teachers unions to state departments of education to political groups like the National Governor's Association "with little transparency and next to no public review." Hassard states:

> *The Common Core now represents a de facto and de jure national school curriculum, something theoretically prohibited by federal law. ..the Common Core comes with common high-stakes tests and common textbooks, making the standards more than standards...the standards are inappropriate developmentally, pushing young children into material they aren't ready for.* [138]

Why all the Billions of Dollars in Charitable Giving? Are Bill and Melinda Gates just kind philanthropists who want to improve education, or do they have other motives? When every child has a computer in the schools, as is the Common Core plan, with all the software that will take, don't you think that Microsoft and the Gates Foundation will be raking in billions of dollars back in their coffers?

Even if the child does not end up with a Microsoft computer, Bill Gates owns part of the software for just about every computer. He will benefit nicely from Common Core.

Gate's Agenda is the Nation's Agenda: As has been mentioned, Gates has given much money to what used to be known as a "conservative think tank," the Thomas B. Fordham Institute for their support for Common Core. Michael B. Petrilli, Executive Vice President of Fordham, told the *Puget Sound Business Journal* in 2009 that **"The Gates Foundation's agenda has become the country's agenda in education."**[139]

Other Big Corporations Contributing to Common Core: **The General Electric Foundation** gave $33 million to Common Core. Will they also benefit back when the schools all have a bigger electrical bill from so many more children using computers?

GE Foundation Gave $240,000 to the National PTA to Promote CC in Feb. 2013: What will the PTA specifically do with that money? They will create State-specific assessment guides for every State that has adopted the Common Core State Standards. Betsy Landers, national PTA president, said:

> *"As the largest child advocacy organization in the country, National PTA has played a leading role in educating families and communities about the Common Core State Standards for years, creating a groundswell of support for this historic reform.*

PTA's Assessment Guides: The guides are written in "parent-friendly language" and modeled after the "Kentucky Parent's Guide to Assessments." They contain background information on the standards, the State-specific assessment consortium, testing timelines, sample test questions, impacts on students, new accountability systems and ways for parents to get involved and support their child's learning at home.

National PTA has Educated and Trained Millions in Support of CC: Since it began its work [indoctrination] on CC in 2009, the PTA proudly boasts of the huge numbers its "hard-working volunteers nationwide have educated." They have trained more than 2.8 million people electronically or in print and more than 38,000 people in advocacy and through educational trainings. [140]

The Pearson Foundation Wins Support for Common Core with all-expense Paid Trips for Educators and Prominent People: Pearson, the largest education-publishing company in the world, that is publishing most of the e-books and assessment tests, and also has formed a partnership with the Gates Foundation to do the teacher training for Common Core, did not give huge donations to its development, but is spending much money sending educators and prominent people on expense-paid, overseas vacations, hoping to win their support for Common Core.

"Since 2008, State education officials have been treated to trips to London, Helsinki, Finland, Singapore, and Rio de Janeiro." Were those vacations attached to "endorsements and support" for Common Core? The Pearson Foundation is expected to give much money in support of New York Governor Cuomo in his run for President in 2016, in return for his support of CC.[141]

Just as the Gates Foundation will be raking in billions through the sales of computers, the Pearson Foundation will be making billions through the sales of the e-books. Pearson has also formed a partnership with the Gates Foundation to do the teacher training in Common Core. So they will both be making much money through the costly training.

InBloom: As if that was not enough, **The Gates Foundation, the Carnegie Foundation, and Rupert Murdoch of News Corps (Fox News)** have funded and developed the database system. They turned it over to a nonprofit corporation called **inBloom**, established for the purpose of controlling the information.[142] Here are the companies which have heavily invested in inBloom:

> The Bill & Melinda Gates Foundation
> Carnegie Corporation of New York
> Fund for Educational Excellence
> The Joyce Foundation
> Laura and John Arnold Foundation
> Michael and Susan Dell Foundation
> National Alliance for Public Charter Schools
> Nellie Mae Education Foundation
> US Department of Education
> Walton Family Foundation
> Rupert Murdock's News Corp
> Anonymous

More is written about inBloom and the data collection in chapter V. As you will see, thanks to some diligent parents, inBloom had a short existence. One State after another began to drop out of it.

Business Roundtable: John Engler, the head of the Business Roundtable and former governor of Michigan, was interviewed on Mike Huckabee's radio program May, 2013, and highly praised Common Core.[143] Gates has funded Philanthropy Roundtable $1.6 million since 2005, with most of it being paid from 2009-12 for operating support.[144]

U.S. Chamber of Commerce: There are many articles showing the fierce support for Common Core by the Chamber of Commerce and especially by their national president, Tom Donohue.[145]

Ads by the Chamber and Business Roundtable to Promote Common Core: Donohue and the Business Roundtable have created ads to go out over various stations including conservative ones like FOX to promote Common Core. The Chamber even has a pledge for people to sign that they support it. One wonders if that will be a litmus test for future employees? Will they have to sign such a pledge? [146]

One also wonders if Donohue's support for Common Core has perhaps a little something to do with the fact that Bill Gates has given the chamber so many millions of dollars? They received $2.6 million to gain the support of big business in 2009, as Common Core was just getting started.[147] Later they received another $18 million in grant money for the Chamber's continued support, and, as you will read below, in 2014, they received an additional $1.38 million for ads to promote Common Core.

U. S. Chamber of Commerce Released "Puff Piece" on Common Core - Takes $1.38 million from Bill Gates (4/4/14) by Donna Garner, Texas educator and blogger:

> *The U. S. Chamber of Commerce released its "puff piece" video entitled "It's Time for Common Core State Standards." What the U. S. Chamber of Commerce does not bother to mention is that they have received a $1.38 million grant from the Bill and Melinda Gates Foundation -- "to lead the effort to engage and educate state and local chambers to support Common Core State Standards."[148]*
>
> *The U. S. Chamber of Commerce video is clearly a puff piece relying upon all 7 of the oft-used propaganda techniques - bandwagon, name calling, transfer, loaded words, plain folk, glittering generalities, and testimonials.*
>
> *What they did not include in this video is any actual peer-reviewed, replicated, independent research to prove that Common Core Standards will raise academic*

achievement. The reason none of this research is included is that no such research exists. The Common Core Standards are not internationally benchmarked and have no research to prove their academic excellence. They were written mainly by a handful of people, some of whom have never even taught a day in their lives in K-12.

The Common Core Standards are the worst, most destructive, and most expensive education fad our country has ever seen. [149]

Corporate Fellows and Corporate Takeover of Education: In Chapter II you briefly read of the many Corporate Fellows that pay enormous dues to belong to the NGA (National Governors' Association). In an article written by Dianne Ravitch, she states that such "opportunities" should not happen. She calls it "the corporate takeover of public education," and such an allegiance "ought not to be" for the following reasons:

- **NGA is part owner** of the Common Core State Standards (CCSS).
- NGA **is pushing** an entire spectrum of reforms that benefits corporate America. CCSS is only one component.
- For education corporations, CCSS alone is a potential cash cow: Curriculum, teacher and administrator professional development, student preparation (including tutoring and test prep), assessment writing, administration, and scoring. **Pots on top of pots of gold.**
- Add to that the corporate promise of online schools, charter schools, vouchers, turnaround companies, teacher evaluations, teacher remediation, alternative certification, data collection, data storage, and data sales.
- **For at least $20,000**, a corporation can purchase influence over NGA decisions. As noted in the **June 2012 *Republic Report*:**
- *The NGA's website says that **members give an annual contribution to the organization of $20,000, but this may obscure the true amount** of money that these corporations are giving NGA.*

- *Its conferences are also sponsored by corporations, with the National Journal reporting that as **many as 147 different corporate sponsors "ponied up" contributions** to be featured at the NGA's Winter Meeting in 2012.*

The following are some of NGA's corporate listing with corporate names that hold particular meaning in the current **corporate-friendly, education reform atmosphere:** *ACT, Amplify, Apple, College Board, Educational Testing Service, ExxonMobil, General Electric, McKinsey and Company, Microsoft, Pearson, Scholastic, and Walmart.* Why do they have particular meaning? Notice how all of them will be profiting by the Common Core State Standards (CCSS).

ACT and College Board were on the CCSS insider work group. David Coleman is now president of the College Board. Amplify is run by former NYC Chancellor Joel Klein and is connected to the CCSS assessment consortium, Smarter Balanced. Apple is involved in the Los Angeles Unified School District iPad fiasco, [where millions of dollars were spent on iPads for the students in the huge district, but the students were using them to play video games and access pornography, in spite of supposed safeguards placed on them. They also discovered that the money used to buy the iPads came from money raised in a bond measure that was to be used only for construction purposes.]

LAUSD Superintendent John Deasy owns Apple stock. Educational Testing Service (ETS) is connected to both CCSS testing consortia (PARCC and Smarter Balanced). ExxonMobil has taken a vocal stand for CCSS. General Electric donated $4 million to David Coleman's Student Achievement Partners in 2010. McKinsey and Company is the former employer of David Coleman. Microsoft is Bill Gates' company. It just abandoned the destructive employee evaluation methods that Gates is trying to impose upon public school teachers. Pearson is also involved in the LAUSD iPad fiasco. Pearson is also connected to both CCSS testing consortia.

Scholastic and Gates released partial results of a survey that notes (surprise, surprise) teachers are fine with CCSS. And finally, Walmart is owned by the Waltons, who are anti-union and pro-charter and spend millions on education privatization.

These companies are working hard to ensure that they benefit from their education reform. Their mantra is: **"Profits matter. Not students; Not teachers; Not schools; Not communities, just Profits."**[150]

As time goes by, we are probably going to see more and more corruption charges in regards to the corporations behind the scenes making lots of money from Common Core. The following is what appeared in the *New York Times*, December 13, 2013, revealing a ruling that was made against the Pearson Foundation because it was illegally using its non-profit status to promote and advance the Pearson Corporation's "profit-making arm."

According to the story by Javier Hernandez, the New York State Attorney General found that the foundation had helped develop products for its corporate parent, including course materials and software. The investigation also showed that the foundation had helped woo clients to Pearson's business side by paying their way to education conferences that were attended by its employees.

Partnership of Pearson and Gates to create online books: In April of 2011, the Pearson Foundation and the Gates Foundation formed a partnership to create 24 new online reading and math courses aligned with the Common Core. They would be getting millions back when the books are sold to teachers across the nation.

Foundation announced they would work together to create 24 new online reading and math courses aligned with the Common Core. "

> *Pearson executives believed the courses could later be sold commercially, and predicted potential profits of tens of millions of dollars. After Mr. Schneiderman's office began its investigation, the Pearson Foundation sold the courses to Pearson for $15.1 million.*

New York State's attorney general Eric T. Schneiderman won an agreement from the Pearson Foundation that they must pay back $7.7 million in fines.

> *The case shed a light on the competitive world of educational testing and technology, which Pearson has come to dominate. As federal and state leaders work to overhaul struggling schools by raising academic standards, educational companies are rushing to secure lucrative contracts in testing, textbooks and software.*
>
> *The attorney general's office also examined a series of education conferences sponsored by the Pearson Foundation, which paid for school officials to meet their foreign counterparts in places like Helsinki and Singapore.....*[151]

A Few Wealthy Individuals Override all Decisions in Education:
In an article by Myra Blackmon, a columnist for *the Banner-Herald*, March 8, 2014, written after she attended a large Network for Public Education national conference, and later after witnessing a 3-hour Georgia House Education Committee meeting on Common Core, she concluded that the battle for or against Common Core is not in the standards or the testing. They are systematic of a bigger problem.

The real problem is a systemic, far-reaching one that can be stopped only by a revolt among parents and educators. The real problem is that a very few, very wealthy individuals override the voices of thousands upon thousands of experienced educators and parents.

Blackmon lists a few of those wealthy individuals:, Bill Gates, the Walton Family and the Broad Foundation, who all carry more weight and influence than their millions of customers, their thousands of employees and much more than the 15,000 elected school boards in this country. She writes the following about the Pearson Foundation:

The huge education companies, with Pearson at the head of the pack, have a hugely profitable lock on the education system. They write the tests, which favor their own textbooks and packaged teacher training. They administer and score the hundreds of thousands of tests administered each year. They pour huge amounts of money into the coffers of politicians and so-called "reform" organizations.

A Corporate Takeover of American Education Driven by Profit, not Student Achievement:

Friends, this is, pure and simple, a corporate takeover of American public education. When the education companies have more say-so in developing standards than experienced educators, we are out of whack. When education decisions are driven by profit instead of real student achievement, we have utterly surrendered control of what happens to our children in public schools.

Federal Department of Education Guilty of a Travesty of Injustice: It produces "inequitable funding schemes like Race to the Top." And instead of "getting our own tax dollars into our own schools," they are tied "to corporate-driven, untested and unreliable processes."

Parents are Left Out: We are the losing voice in how our children are educated. When the Congress of the United States lets the DOE get away with such a travesty of justice and wisdom, it makes the problem even more intractable.

State Legislators Follow Suite: All this happens on a national scale, and then state legislatures get into it.

Often, as is the case ... in Georgia, they tie the hands of school boards, principals and teachers who know what to do if we will just let them do it... standards will become political and ideological, having little or no bearing on good education.. [152]

The Hidden Cs of Common Core

Chapter V –

Curriculum for Common Core –

Fair and Balanced - or Indoctrination, Propaganda, Developmentally and Age <u>Inappropriate</u>?

"Corrupt the young, get them away from religion. Get them interested in sex. Make them superficial, and destroy their ruggedness. Get control of all means of publicity, and thereby get the peoples' mind off their government by focusing their attention on athletics, sexy books and plays, and other trivialities. Divide the people into hostile groups by constantly harping on controversial matters of no importance." --Vladimir Ilyich Lenin – Former Dictator of the Soviet Union

Why did Lenin make such a statement and what would he hope to accomplish by achieving these goals? He knew that to conquer a nation and to change it from one that is free and independent to a totalitarian State, one must destroy a nation's morality. Moral people with strong religious ethics and principles that guide their lives are the ones who are more willing to stand up for liberty. They value liberty as a God-given gift, and something worth fighting for.

Lenin knew the best way to destroy morals was to get to the young, to destroy their religious beliefs, to get them involved in sex at an early age and all the sad things that follow: sexually transmitted diseases, unwanted pregnancy, abortion, feelings of guilt and remorse that often lead to drugs, alcohol, suicide. People in such a condition could care less what is going on with their government.

Hitler did the same thing in Germany and Austria before he totally took over and became the supreme *fuhrer*. He also changed the nation's morality by taking over and changing the curriculum in the public schools. A great personal testimony to that change in education is given by Kitty Werthmann, who now lives in South Dakota and serves as the Eagle Forum State President there. She was born in Austria in 1926 before Hitler took over and experienced personally the transformation of her country and the schools after Austria voted to be annexed with Germany under Hitler. Kitty was in the sixth grade. She states the change in her school just after the election:

> *I walked into my schoolroom to find the crucifix replaced by Hitler's picture hanging next to a Nazi flag. Our teacher, a very devout woman, stood up and told the class we wouldn't pray or have religion anymore.*

Hitler had the children go to school seven days a week. Sunday was compulsory "Youth Day" - a day full of fun activities, where they would participate in all sorts of sports with fancy, new equipment. There was no time (and soon no desire) to go to church. If the parents did not send the children to the Sunday youth day, the first time they would be given a warning, the second time a visit from the police and the third time they would be jailed.

The teachers were trained to turn the children against their parents, telling them that they were old fashioned, "old foggies; only Hitler understood us, not our parents."

Fortunately, Kitty's mother recognized early on the danger signs and pulled Kitty out and put her in a private Catholic school, so she got a good education and escaped the transformation happening to the other children. Kitty, at first was upset with her mother, but later became very grateful. She could see the changes in her old friends who had become only interested in the fun and games they were experiencing, and with emphasis on sex, many young girls ended up pregnant. Hitler wanted lots of babies born so he could have more soldiers in his army. It became "a badge of honor" to have a baby for Hitler. Students became oblivious to the changes taking place in their country – exactly what Hitler desired.[153]

The statement by Lenin at the beginning of this chapter has become a very accurate description of the youth of America today. The majority no longer are interested in religion or attending Church. They are inundated with sex, in movies, television shows, video games, and in sex education in our public schools, and, as you will see, in assigned reading material.

This chapter will make you aware of some of the most egregious new books that are replacing the great classics; e-books, on-line learning, surveys that are all part of the "approved" Common Core curriculum and "aligned" with the standards.

Percentage of Required Classical English Literature Lowered and Replaced with Informational Text: What used to be 80% in elementary school for classical English literature reading has been lowered to 50% with Common Core. In high school it is even less – down to 30%. That leaves much more room in the curriculum in every classroom for the reading of what is called "informational text." However, concerned parents are finding out that informational text just seems to be another term for "indoctrination." The door is now opened wide for greater time in the classroom to expose the children to indoctrination, propaganda and inappropriate material with a very biased slant to the left.

What about True Classical English Literature that is still listed on the Recommended Reading List? The selections are still listed, so parents will think all is well. But for those books that are read in class or assigned reading, it is just segments of the books, or summaries of them that students are reading. It is "English literature lite," rather than the full course. Teachers have no time for the full course because the time has been taken up with the reading of "informational text."

Common Core vs Great Literature: According to a *New York Daily News* article, "Common Core vs Great Literature," written by an English professor at Emory College, Mark Bauerline, "*the standards risked crowding out high-quality fiction, poetry, theater and other imaginative texts. They overemphasized nonfictional, information-rich prose, and required no British literature except one play by Shakespeare.*" That play was "Romeo and Juliet." [For a list of recommended great Classical English literature that has withstood the test of time go to Chapter XI.]

Bauerline, who served on the ELA "Feedback Committee" for the CCSSO was told this was not supposed to happen - "*the push for informational texts was not supposed to displace outstanding literary texts.*" It was supposed to give "*more general background knowledge, more broad familiarity with history, science, art and ideas — all of which would, among other things, enhance literary study.*"

Bauerline was told that the Common Core standards were supposed to "*set a higher bar of literary history.*" One of the ELA standards states that students will "*demonstrate knowledge of eighteenth-, nineteenth-, and early-twentieth-century foundational works of American literature.*" But according to the units rolled out so far by New York City's Education Department, the amount of classical English Literature is so minimal, Bauerline states, "*It is as if that standard doesn't even exist.*"[154]

What is so bad about Having Less Classical English Literature?
The quote that I have in my first book by Emmit McGrourty, an attorney with the American's Principles Project in Washington D.C. answers that question. He states:

> *Classical literature is the foundation of our nation. It teaches children to: investigate their surroundings; to make wise decisions; to have empathy; to exercise their liberties. You don't learn that from a computer manual.* [155]

Do you think that might be the main reason for less true classical literature? The proponents pushing Common Core do not want our children to be able to make wise decisions, to have discernment, to know good from evil, to have high morals and principles to guide their lives and to base their actions upon; to know how to stand up for liberty or to even know what liberty is? You can't create a good little global socialist, totally dependent on government, if a child has too much knowledge and can make wise decisions on his own. Instead, let us teach the children such books as the following:

Controversial Books that are Racist and Pornographic that are "Common Core aligned" and on the "recommended reading" lists.

***The Jacket* Teaches Racism and "White Privilege":** A two-week lesson plan is based on a book called *The Jacket* published by Zaner-Bloser. The story centers around a young white boy named Phil who wrongly accuses an African-American student of stealing his brother's jacket. The book is all about racism and "white privilege," teaching that the values of American society are racist and designed to benefit only white people.

A Book about the Life of Obama, Suggests that all White Voters are Racist: The website *BeforeItsNews.com* reported that children at Bluffview Elementary School, in Dupo, Illinois, were assigned to read the book that Obama is holding in the following picture. It is entitled *Barack Obama,* published by Lerner Publications and a part of Scholastic's "Reading Counts" program. On page 40 are the words that imply that white Voters are racist:

But some people said Americans weren't ready for that much change. Sure Barack was a nice fellow, they said. But white voters would never vote for a black president.

The book, approved for children as young as seven years old, mentions controversial comments made by President Obama's former pastor Jeremiah Wright, while also claiming that the president has worked to bring whites and blacks together.

President Obama Holding the Children's Book about himself:

This book is blatantly indoctrinating our youth into thinking that every white American who votes is racist. Should that not have Americans everywhere a little bit worried?

The book's comments were brought to the attention of the "Moms Against Duncan" Facebook page, a group of parents and education activists who are opposed to U.S. Secretary of Education Arne Duncan, who recently claimed that "white suburban moms" are only opposed to Common Core because it showed that their children weren't as smart as they thought. These moms believe that was an attempt by Duncan to paint the nation-wide backlash against the curriculum as "a race-based issue."

The book about Obama appears to follow the viewpoint that all opposition to the president is based purely on race, which the Moms against Duncan believe has reached near-comedic levels in its absurdity.[156]

Sexually Inappropriate Books and Posters – All Common Core Approved: The next few pages tell of reading assignments that parents have discovered that have graphic language describing sexual intercourse, rape scenes, etc. that not even newspapers would print, but students are expected to read – sometimes out loud in class.

The Bluest Eyes **by Black Author Toni Morrison** is among Common Core's "exemplar" texts for 11th graders. Supposedly, "it aligns with the standards and meets the course objectives and needs of students." What insidious objectives and needs could possibly be met by reading a book that is as sexually explicit, pornographic, and perverted as this one is and definitely not age appropriate?

The book tells the story of Pecola Breedlove, a young black girl, who prays every day for blond hair and blue eyes that she believes will allow her to fit in and be accepted by society. The book is full of sexually graphic descriptions and foul language as poor Pecola is raped by her father, abused by her brothers, beaten by her mother and fondled and raped by a pedophile. After Pecola loses the baby that she has been impregnated with by her father, she loses her mind and ends up thinking that she is now blond and has blue eyes, and that is how the book ends.

Obviously, there is nothing uplifting, of good report or praise-worthy for a child to learn from reading this book. There are images portrayed and language used that will stay in an innocent child's mind and haunt them the rest of their life. As one commentator, Macey France, who has two children in the public schools, writes:

> *The American Academy of Pediatrics studies and develops policies pertaining to youth from birth through age 21, and specifically lists books as part of the mass media environment examined by their institution. The AAP states that exposure to violence in media has a significant risk on the health of children and adolescents and can contribute to aggressive behavior, desensitization to violence, nightmares and fear of being harmed. It is also associated with teen pregnancy and promiscuity. The AAP has also called on schools specifically to do more in the way of preventing young people from being exposed to and negatively impacted by harmful media.*

Ms. France states that in Colorado schools, where the book is being used, the sexually graphic parts cannot be read in the classroom, but have to be read at home. She then asks a profound question:

> *Using just the smallest amount of common sense, we can deduce that if the book cannot be read aloud in the class, could not be viewable if it was a movie and couldn't be played on the stereo if it was a CD, then why is it okay for*

*it to be read and discussed in school of all places? In fact, according to one lawyer, if the incidents in this book were a movie or a picture there would be a very clear cut case for prosecution for **child pornography**.[157]*

Dreaming in Cuba by Cristina Garcia, published in 1992: A title of an article written about the book - "Fifty Shades of the Common Core: **how much porn is too much for high schoolers"** appeared in the *Daily Caller,* September 12, 2013, written by Eric Owens.

Owens described the content of this pornographic book and said it appears on the Common Core recommended reading list (p. 152) between such true classics as Ernest Hemingway's *A Farewell to Arms* and Thornton Wilder's *Our Town.*

Owen's article cites two passages that are absolute pornographic describing two sexual scenes with all the "steamy, erotic" graphic language of a young couple involved in intercourse.

A mother sent an e-mail to *EAGnews* that stated that her son's class was reading the book in the tenth grade of his high school **out loud.** What a book to read out loud! However, to the progressive mind who believes in corrupting young minds (just like Lenin), this book is acclaimed as "Dazzling...remarkable." That is how Michiko Kakutani, a Pulitzer Prize- winning critic described the book in a *New York Times* book review.[158]

Nineteen Minutes by Jodi Picoult – a Father is Arrested at School Board Meeting for Speaking longer than his Two

Minutes: Another book that has a very graphic sex scene (p. 313) between two teenagers was spoken about by parents at a school board meeting May 5, 2014 in New Hampshire. The book was assigned reading for ninth grade students at the Gilford High School.

According to WCVB-TV, the book contains a graphic description of rough sex between two teenagers, which parents were unaware of until the book had already been distributed to their kids.

"I was shocked when I read the passage and not much shocks me anymore. My wife was stunned by the increasingly graphic nature of the sexual content of the scene and the imagery it evoked." Both of them were at the meeting to protest the use of the book that their daughter in the ninth grade had to read.

One of the reasons the school board meeting made national news and that Mr. Baer was on the Glenn Beck show was because Baer was handcuffed and arrested and taken out of the room because he made comments from the audience after he had already had his two minutes worth of speaking out against the book.

"Sir, would you please be respectful of the other people?" a school board member responded to his comments that "This is absurd."

"Like you're respectful of my daughter, right? And my children?" Baer countered. That's when a police officer escorted him out of the room and charged him with disorderly conduct.

His wife, Barbara told a reporter from WCVB, *"I fully understand how he feels. It really is a huge violation. Why should those ideas be put in their minds? They can discuss this some other way. They don't need that kind of imagery."*

In an interview with EAG News, Baer said the following about how the educators and the government think the children belong to them and they get to decide what is best for them:

"Many people in education and government truly believe our children are theirs, that parents are only the custodians who feed them and put a roof over their heads. These school incidents are a byproduct of this 'we know best' philosophy. They believe they have the authority to do this. If people were more complacent, which is hard to imagine, it'd be even worse."[159]

What Can Parents Do? The school was probably using Mr. Baer as an example of what happens when parents become too vocal. Arresting him would frighten other parents into being quiet and not saying anything out of turn or too strong.

In e-mails that were circulating in regards to Mr. Baer's arrest, the following was some good advice given by Ze'ev Wurman, a former senior advisor at the Federal Department of Education and a big critic of Common Core. He mainly recommends making other parents aware as to what is going on. I included one additional suggestion.

On this particular case, the solution is pretty simple due to the easily documented nature of the problem.
1. Make a copy of the 2-3 offending pages of the book under the "fair use" doctrine.
2. Put a cover page explaining what it is, that middle school children were forced or recommended to read it. Don't push on notification/permission issue -- parents don't have the time to read those books anyway so they must trust the system. Just state that the school/district expects/wants/recommends children to read that stuff. DON'T overdo the explanations or your rhetoric -- let the prose speak for itself as much as you can.

3. [My suggestion] On the cover page – include an invitation to the next school board meeting, give the date and time, and recommend that the parents show up and express their outrage, or give the phone numbers, e-mail addresses of the board members and superintendent so they can contact them personally.
4. Make a few hundred copies.
5. Hand them out to MS [middle school] parents at MS events -- weekend ball games, parties, school board meetings, whatever. Expect local administrators to interfere so have more than one parent do it, try to do it on the curb and not on school property as much as possible..[160]

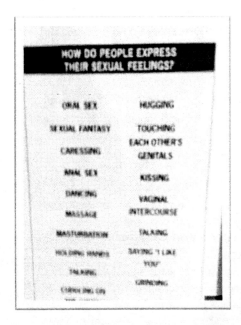

Kansas Middle School Poster Listing Sex Acts as Part of 'Health and Science' Curriculum: In an article by Dr. Susan Berry, Jan. 16, 2014, she tells of Mark Ellis, a father of a 13 year-old girl who was upset by a poster hanging on the classroom door of her middle school that listed sex acts. He was shocked to hear that the poster is part of her school's health and science curriculum. The story was also picked up on a Fox News affiliate in Kansas fox4kc.com.

The poster was, entitled, "How Do People Express Their Sexual Feelings?" and lists such sex acts such as: "Oral Sex, Sexual Fantasy, Caressing, Anal Sex, Dancing, Hugging, Touching Each Other's Genitals, Kissing, Vaginal Intercourse, Grinding, and Masturbation."

Mark Ellis said his daughter, a student at Hocker Grove Middle school in the Shawnee Mission School District, was "shocked" by what she saw on the poster and took a picture of it and showed it to her parents. Her father assumed the poster to be a student prank, until he called the school and discovered it was part of the curriculum. Here is how the conversation went:

"Why would you put it in front of 13 year-old students?" he asked. The principal answered that the poster is "teaching material." That made the father even more concerned about what his daughter is being taught in school.

It upsets me. And again, it goes back to who approved this? You know this had to pass through enough hands that someone should have said, 'Wait a minute, these are 13-year-old kids, we do not need to be this in-depth with this sexual education type of program.'

According to *Fox News*, however, district spokeswoman Leigh Anne Neal said the poster must be viewed in the context of a bigger curriculum, which she identified as abstinence-based for students in middle school.

The poster that you reference is actually part of our middle school health and science materials, and so it is a part of our district approved curriculum. However the item is meant to be part of a lesson, and so certainly as a stand-alone poster without the context of a teacher led discussion, I could see that there might be some cause for concern."

Neal added that the curriculum is similar to those used by other schools around the country and aligns with national standards around those topics, and "It's part of our curriculum in the school district," she said.

In fact, the curriculum, entitled "Making A Difference," is published by selectmedia.org and recommended by the U.S. Department of Health & Human Services (HHS) as a "pregnancy prevention intervention." According to the publisher's website, the goal of the program is:

> *...to empower young adolescents to change their behavior in ways that will reduce their risk of pregnancy and HIV or other STD infection. Specifically, this curriculum emphasizes that young adolescents should postpone sexual activity and that practicing abstinence is the only way to eliminate the risk for pregnancy and STDs, including HIV.*

Module 2 of the program, which is called "Understanding Adolescent Sexuality and Abstinence," offers "an overview of reproductive anatomy, discusses messages about sex, discusses how people express themselves sexually [apparently reinforced by the poster], and the benefits of abstinence."

Nevertheless, Ellis thinks the curriculum should change.

> *This has nothing to do with abstinence or sexual reproduction, actually, a lot of these things. I would like to see that this particular portion of the curriculum is removed from the school.*"

As *Fox News* reported, if the curriculum doesn't change, Ellis will remove his daughter from the sex education classes.[161]

Ellis' Advice for Parents –Be Aware, Stand Up, Take Charge:

A lot of parents view the school as a babysitter. My message is to stand up. Let's take charge of our kids. There are so many out-of-control kids in the nation. It's the parent's job to parent, not the schools. And no matter what the professional educators are saying, that poster had nothing to do with abstinence...

It takes a special kind of stupid to teach children that vaginal sex and anal are examples of an abstinence-based curriculum. I'm afraid many public schools have become perverse sexual indoctrination centers, where teachers provide "how-to" instructions instead of "don't-do."[162]

California Common Core Frameworks Promote Pro-Homosexual, Inappropriate Literature: By February 13, 2014, concerned Californians were supposed to send in comments regarding the "frameworks" [a fancier name for the Common Core Standards] to the State Superintendent and the State School Board trying to make it appear that States still have some control over their own education, and parents' comments would make some kind of a difference. The strategy is that if parents think they have some kind of input, they will be happier supporters of the frameworks. In other words, parents were being "Delphied." (See Delphi technique Chapter I)

Chapter 9 of the frameworks contains language concerning "intolerance and discrimination" in regards to lesbian, gay, bisexual, or transgender students. They quote from GLSEN (Gay, Lesbian, and Straight Education Network) and give recommended books and materials that GLSEN publishes. Chapter 9 states the following:

***Chapter 9 Access and Equity:** (p. 21) Make available and share age-appropriate literature that reflects the diversity of humankind and thoughtfully deals with the complexities and dynamics of intolerance and discrimination. Teach students by example and through discussion how to treat* *diverse others. California students who are not themselves in this population may have parents or guardians who are lesbian, gay, bisexual, or transgender. "All students and their families need to feel safe, respected, and welcomed in school." Gay, Lesbian, and Straight Education Network (GLSEN 2012)*

Only One-sided Views of Homosexuality Allowed in Public Schools: Through the years of successfully using the term of "homophobe" for anyone opposed to their viewpoint, GLSEN has successfully pressured schools to promote homosexuality as normal and censor competing messages. They do not want children to know that there are people who have ever left the lifestyle or that it is possible to do so. A 1999 GLSEN press release states, "ex-gay messages have no place in our nation's public schools."

In more recent years, GLSEN initiated a campaign to send a "Just the Facts" booklet to some 16,000 schools, which warns schools against allowing access to viewpoints that differ from GLSEN's on homosexuality. It claims that faith-based, ex-gay perspectives on homosexuality are harmful. The booklet also states that "experimentation and discovery" are "common" for youth.

Resources for Educators: In GLSEN's 125-page *Tackling LGBT Issues in School* booklet (co-sponsored by Connecticut GLSEN and Planned Parenthood), they promote the following resources:

- A "**Heterosexual Questionnaire**" that asks students, among other questions: "If you've never slept with a person of the same sex, is it possible that all you need is a good gay or lesbian lover?" This resource is promoted as a way to expose "heterosexism" and "make schools safer places."
- A "**Homophobia Scale**" lesson for high-school age students. The scale teaches that "acceptance" and "tolerance" are

"homophobic" attitudes. But "positive levels of attitudes" are "admiration" and "nurturance."

- In short, **GLSEN wants schools to push students beyond tolerance and acceptance into admiration and advocacy for the homosexual activist movement**.

GLSEN's Recommendations for Books that they label as "age-appropriate" and the "highest quality" for elementary school, middle school and high school:

- **Two Moms, The Zark & Me**, (for elementary school) It presents a nightmarish portrayal of a conservative couple basically accosting a child in a park because they learn of his having two mommies. Even a Publishers Weekly review called it "mean-spirited":

  "A boy is taken to the park by his 'two moms,' wanders over to the zoo where he...is picked up by Mr. and Mrs. McFink—ultra conservatives who go ballistic over his family's domestic arrangements....in all, it's a mean-spirited, sniping approach to a topic that deserves thoughtful treatment."

- **Queer 13** (for middle school age) This book is extremely explicit and includes graphic descriptions of a young boy's sexual interactions with an adult man in a restroom—as well as details of how the boy goes on to have more sexual experiences with strangers.
- **The Full Spectrum: A New Generation of Writing About Gay, Lesbian, Bisexual, Transgender Questioning and Other Identities** (for high school and for kids as young as seventh grade) In addition to sexually graphic content, the book openly mocks and gives negative portrayals of several faiths.[163]

Shocking Writing Assignment in English Language Arts – Students Asked to Write that Jews are Evil: In an Albany, New

York, high school, a Common Core writing assignment was so shocking and beyond reason that it made it in the *Times Union* newspaper. The English teacher was attempting to do one of the Four Cs of Common Core – "collaborate" and connect her persuasive writing assignment with history and social studies and give the students something challenging and "sophisticated" to write about.

What did she ask of the students that was so outrageous and got the parents so upset? According to the newspaper article, students were told,

> *You do not have a choice in your position. You must argue that Jews are evil, use solid government propaganda and convince me or your loyalty to the Third Reich. Students were asked to watch and read Nazi propaganda, then pretend their teacher was a Nazi government official who needed to be convinced of their loyalty. In five paragraphs, they were required to prove that Jews were the source of Germany's problems.*

After the article came out in the paper, Albany Superintendent Marguerite Vanden Wyngaard apologized to the families and tried to assure them that there was "no malice or intent to cause any insensitivities to our families of Jewish faith." It was just intended to "challenge students to formulate a persuasive argument." She added that "the exercise reflects the type of writing expected of students under the new Common Core curriculum, the tough new academic standards that require more sophisticated writing."

The Superintendent said she "understood the academic intent of the assignment — to make an argument based only on limited information at hand" [called propaganda]. Still, she acknowledged that "it was worded in a very offensive manner." She did not identify the English teacher or discuss whether the educator faced any discipline. The assignment was given to three classes, but one-third of the students had the courage to say no and refused to do it.

One outraged mother, who sent the story out on e-mail, asks why the assignment was not to write a persuasive article condemning the Nazis for the atrocities they committed killing six million Jews? She is sure there is another agenda.

> *This is purposeful, and it's horrible...there should be nationwide outrage...what they are getting away with is beyond reason! Why didn't they ask these children to write an article condemning the Nazi regime and fascism for the death of millions of Jews and Christians and homosexuals and protestors? Why? Because they have an agenda! And the agenda is promotion of both communism and fascism.[164]*

Scripted, Canned Lessons?   One wonders if this assignment was something scripted for the teacher to do – it was not really the teacher's choice? Maybe she was not allowed to deviate from it as has been stated by other teachers in New York. They are scripted and have to give canned lessons to the students.   They cannot deviate in any way. Maybe such a writing assignment is going on in other schools across the nation.

In Rialto, California, Assignment Given to Argue Whether the Holocaust Ever Happened: May 4, 2014, *ABC Eyewitness News* reporter Amy Powell tells that the Rialto Unified School District came under fire for their "critical thinking" assignment that was given to 8th graders to write "whether or not they believe that the holocaust ever happened."

Parents were outraged as well as the Anti-Defamation League, a Jewish legal organization that defends the rights of Jewish people.

With all the negative publicity the school district was getting, they quickly apologized and dropped the assignment. [165]

Other Ill-Considered Teacher Assignments: The following show two more shocking assignments given out by teachers, this time concerning slavery. Were these their own ideas or suggested to them by the script?

> *In February, 2013, a Manhattan teacher caused an uproar after fourth-graders were given a math problem based on how many daily whippings a slave received.*

> *In January, 2013, Georgia educators attempted to teach division to elementary school students by asking how many beatings per day former slave and abolitionist leader Frederick Douglass received.[166]*

Why would teachers be using such examples? Is this another way to undermine our nation and bring out all the terrible things that have happened so children will not be proud to be Americans? Is it part of the Social Justice agenda that is even permeating math?

A Good Citizen Does not Argue: The following picture is of a poster that was hanging in a 3rd grade class-room in Ohio and a student took a picture of it. It is entitled "What Makes a Good Citizen." All of the descriptions of good citizens sound good until number 6 – "Does not argue." Whoever created this poster wants our children to think a person who argues with his government does not make for a very good citizen. Those behind CC only want nice, compliant Americans who will not argue or make any waves or do very much at all to regain the freedoms we are losing. In fact, if their education is dumbed down enough they won't know enough about their history to know that we ever had those freedoms.

A. What makes a good citizen:

1. Citizens don't liter to keep the environment clean
2. Citizens help schools
3. Citizens fix homes
4. Citizens vote on leaders
5. Citizens pay taxes to the government
6. Does not argue

B. Good things citizens do:

1. Citizens respect each other
2. Volunteer to help each other
3. Obey the laws
4. Don't liter
5. Elect officials

Example of Common Core's False Teachings Concerning our Form of Government: In an English Grammar Assignment the students were to rewrite the sentences giving possessive nouns. There was nothing wrong with the assignment; it was the distorted facts of government that the sentences were about.

Following, you will see the assignment that a mother took a picture of and posted on the internet. The assignment is under a section entitled "Hold the Flag High," which, of course, sounds really good to a patriotic parent. It is not until they read the last three sentences (4, 5, and 6) that red flags go up. [Emphasis added]

Name _____   Hold the Flag High

Possessive Nouns

Directions: Make each sentence less wordy by replacing the underlined words with a possessive phrase. Write the sentence on the line.

1. The job of a president is not easy.
   *The president's job is not easy.*_____

2. The people of a nation do not always agree.
   *The nation's people do not always agree.*_____

3. The choices of the president affect everyone.
   *The president's choices affect everyone.*_____

4. He makes sure the <u>laws of the country</u> are fair.
   He makes sure the country's laws are fair.

5. The <u>commands of government officials</u> must be obeyed by all.
   Government officials' commands must be obeyed by all.

6. The <u>wants of the individual</u> are less important than the <u>well being of the nation.</u>
   The individual's wants are less important than the nation's well being.

Along with being factually incorrect, the last three sentences are teaching a socialist, pro-big government bias. What is wrong with them?

- **The 4th sentence:** The job of the president [executive branch] is to execute the laws, not to decide whether they are fair or not. It is the job of the judicial branch to interpret the laws and determine their fairness.

- **The 5th sentence:** Is it true that government officials commands must be obeyed by all? Maybe in totalitarian countries, but here in the USA, citizens have the right to question those commands. If something is not Constitutional or in violation of their rights, citizens can refuse to obey.

- **The 6th sentence:** Are the individual's wants less important than the nation's wellbeing? That is what a socialist government would want you to think. But, our founding fathers took great efforts to secure the rights of the individual against the encroachment of an all-powerful government. That is why we have the Bill of Rights.

Superficiality, Distorted View of Founding Fathers, Anti-American Bias Found in Common Core Approved Books and Articles: According to Terrance O. Moore, a Professor at Hillsdale

College and author of *The Story Killers, A Common Sense Case Against Common Core,* the writers of the curriculum are only teaching a superficial and biased view of the Founding Fathers, the Declaration of Independence, the Constitution, the Bill of Rights and other historical documents (if they are even mentioned): For example, the only part of the Constitution that is mentioned for 6th graders is the preamble, and the text does not get beyond the words "We the People," before they stop and ask:

> *But, who are "We the People"...Which "We the People?"*
> *The women were not included, neither were white males*
> *who did not own property, American Indians, or African*
> *Americans, slave or free.*[167]

So, by the time the child is finished reading this section, they have been taught that the Founding Fathers were hypocritical, deceptive, racist and disliked women, and the child already has a bias against them.

There is nothing written about the customs of the day, that at the time of the ratification of the Constitution, nowhere on the face of the earth did women have the right to vote yet, or the fact that the Founding Fathers inherited slavery. Most of them wanted to get rid of it as they were writing the Constitution, but they knew the Southern States would never ratify the Constitution if that were the case. They knew that slavery would have to be gotten rid of later. Many of them freed their own slaves themselves in their wills when they died such as our first president, George Washington.

The Northwest Ordinance Abolished Slavery in the New States within its Boundaries: As the Founding Fathers were debating the Constitution, the Northwest Ordinance was being drafted outlawing slavery in all of the States that would be coming in to be part of the

USA. Those States were: Ohio, Indiana, Michigan, Illinois, and Wisconsin.

Other States Abolished Slavery on their Own: In 1777, the year after the Declaration of Independence was signed, Vermont abolished slavery. Over the next few decades other States did the same: Massachusetts, New Hampshire, Pennsylvania, Rhode Island, Connecticut, New York, and New Jersey.

No Praise Given for our Constitution: There is nothing written about how remarkable the preamble was, that this was the first time in history that people had declared themselves sovereign, a free people, no longer under the rule of a king. Instead the students are taught what the founders did not do and to exercise judgment over them.

Only the First Amendment is Taught: The students have no idea that the Bill of Rights have Ten Amendments, nothing about the 2nd one, the right to bear arms; nothing about the 4th Amendment, the protection of privacy; and nothing about the 10th Amendment – that what is not mentioned in the Constitution is left up to the States, such as education. Of course, the writers of the curriculum would not want students to know about this amendment, or they might begin to suspect that top-down, federally controlled Common Core was in violation of it!

Next Generation Science Standards: Guess who is foremost in creating the science standards? The same group that was behind the scenes creating the math and English Language Arts. If you guessed **Achieve Inc.,** you were right. They helped develop the "model tasks for K-12 classrooms to integrate the Next Generations

Science Standards (NGSS) and Common Core State Standards in Mathematics (CCSS-M)."[168]

NGSS"s Green Indoctrination: In an article in *Front Page Mag*, March 4, by Mary Graber, entitled "Common Core's Little Green Soldiers," there is much green, pseudoscience that is being taught to our children especially about man-made global warming now called "climate change." She writes how under Arne Duncan, the Department of Education "has become a propaganda arm used to influence the next generation to accept the idea of catastrophic man-made climate change."

The standards are full of reports coming from the UN, the Environmental Protection Agency, and such groups as the National Wildlife Federation. There is no other viewpoint allowed than those who promote what is deemed "green political correctness." As Mary Graber points out, these children are too young and inexperienced to know that what they are being told is not true.

Green Contests and Activities: In the DOE's *Green Strides* Feb. 28 Newsletter, they announced three contests the DOE is promoting along with various non-profits, government organizations and curriculum companies to promote "fun" contests and activities for students, while promoting Common Core's State Science Standards and further the green indoctrination on climate change.

- **Videos**: The first contest announced is for middle school students to compete with a video challenge called "Climate Change in Focus" promoted by the EPA (Environmental Protection Agency) and the National Environmental Education Foundation. The students are to show "why they care about climate change and what they are doing to reduce emissions or to prepare for its impacts."

  Winning videos will be highlighted on the EPA website. The top three entries will receive "cool prizes like a solar charging backpack." The schools that the winning students attend will receive special recognition and the first 100 entrants will receive a year's subscription to *National Geographic Kids Magazine.*

- **Young Reporters:** A second contest is for ages 13 – 21, sponsored by the National Wildlife Federation's Young Reporters for the Environment. It invites students to report on an environmental issue in their community in an article, photo or photo essay, or short video." Entries should "reflect firsthand investigation of topics related to the environment and sustainability in the students' own communities, draw connections between local and global perspectives, and propose solutions."

- **"Champions of the Earth" Nominations:** Students are encouraged to make nominations for a special award for those who go the extra green mile called "Champions of the Earth," a "UN-sponsored award for the environment, Green Economy, and sustainability." Among the 2013 laureates is Martha Isabel Ruiz Corzo, who orchestrated a public-private biosphere reserve status for a region in Mexico, and Brian McLendon, of Google Earth.

More Green Propaganda: Students are exposed to more green indoctrination through taxpayer funded textbooks and videos and online materials supported by Public Broadcasting. Many students, of course, have had to sit through Al Gore's documentary, "An Inconvenient Truth," which should really be labeled "Inconvenient Lies" for its total distortion and exaggerations of any true science.

The Next Generation Science Standards, like the standards for math and ELA, are intended to be "transformative" and reflect a new vision for American science education." They also pretend that they were created by State educators as is also claimed with the math and English standards, but they were all produced by Achieve who then invited others to join with them to give the appearance that they were "State-created and led."

"Transformative," No More Memorization: Transformative means the standards call for "new performance expectations" that "focus on understanding and applications as opposed to memorization of facts devoid of context."

"Short Shrift to Knowledge:" Science professors Lawrence S. Lemer and Paul Gross object to the fact that memorization is no longer required. They call it "short shrift to knowledge." They also object that the standards bypass essential math skills in favor of "process," which they stated in the fall of 2013 on the Thomas B. Fordham Foundation blog. [169]

"Lots of Fluff:" Lerner and Gross believe the Common Core standards, in all disciplines, are written with "a lot of fluff to conceal their emptiness." Is that why we are constantly hearing the words "rigorous, rigor, higher order thinking skills, etc.," when their proponents talk about them? They have to disguise the truth.

Lerner and Gross Criticize the following about NGSS:
- **"Inconsistencies** between strong NGSS assertions and what was actually found by the mathematicians of the reviewing group."
- **Confusion** – because of the focus on "process" rather than the correct answer.
- The **"slighting of mathematics,"** (postponing Algebra to the 9th grade, teaching less and less real, traditional math) which does "increasing mischief as grade level rises, especially in the physical sciences." Physics is "effectively absent" at the high school level.
- **Shirking of the necessary foundations in math and science knowledge.** The best science education seems to be one based on integrating rigorous content with the practices that scientists and engineers routinely use in their work—including application of mathematics.
- The **"practice strategy"** – Common Core teaches that "students learn science effectively when they actively engage in

the practices of science." Lerner and Gross say "cognitive science contradicts that claim." Beginners don't and can't 'practice' as do experts. They don't have the prior experience, knowledge, extensive build-up in long-term memory of scaffolding: facts, procedures, technical know-how, solutions, or vocabularies.

- **"Inquiry learning"** – Lerner and Gross say the "practice strategy" is an extension of one of the fads of the early 1990s called "inquiry learning" which had "no notable effect on the (mediocre) performance of American students in national and international science assessments."

- **Ideological lessons which only teach one biased viewpoint to very young children and are thus indoctrination** – such as: Kindergartners are being taught "Human impacts on Earth systems." "Things people do can affect the environment, but they can make choices to reduce their impact."

Lerner and Gross believe that human impacts on Earth systems are huge topics, when approached legitimately. They present quandaries to scientists at the top levels far beyond the understanding of kindergartners. Yet NGSS impose them on kindergartners. **The objective, of course, is not teaching legitimate science, but indoctrination.**

Ten States have already voluntarily adopted the Standards. Mary Graber ends her article with, "Such efforts, coordinated by the Department of Education, threaten the future of science itself."[170]

Science will also be affected by the Lowering of Math Skills: Since the teaching of algebra is being postponed from the 8th grade to the 9th, there is no room for calculus the senior year of college. Sandra Stotsky states how this will affect the sciences:

The main problem with NGSS is that it eliminates high school chemistry and, in effect, physics (since the math for it isn't there). It is science for dummies.[171]

Wyoming Rejects the NGSS because of the Teaching of Man Made Global Warming or Climate Change as an Exact Science: In an article published May 2, 2014, by *Fox News*, it was revealed that an environmental group is trying to get enough signatures on a petition to overturn a ruling made by the State legislators in Wyoming that they refused to adopt the NGSS for their State.

The group called "Climate Parents" is accusing Wyoming legislators of putting "Coal over Kids," since Wyoming is the largest coal producing State in the nation, and those who support the idea of manmade global warming believe the burning of coal is one of the causes of too much greenhouse gases in the atmosphere. Climate Parents would like to see Wyoming close their coal mines.

A rebuttal to Climate Parents was given by Amy Edmonds, police analyst for the Wyoming Liberty Group. She told the newspaper, *the Laramie Boomerang* that a Conservative think tank had given the NGSS only a "C" rating. She said the following in support of the decision of the State legislators:

The Next Generation Science Standards are just inferior standards for the state of Wyoming. Anyone who reads the standards will understand that there is not a fair and balanced view of climate change. The idea that climate change is settled science is open to debate.[172]

UN Children's Book Using Green Fear Tactics: One of the many books that is teaching green indoctrination is called *Rescue Mission Planet Earth, a Children's Edition of Agenda 21.* It was published on Earth Day, 1994 by King Fisher Books.

The book is pretending that various children of the world submitted writings and drew pictures showing their deep concerns for what is happening to poor mother earth. However, many readers believe the pages are a little too well written and the illustrations too well done to be coming from children

Population Control: *Rescue Mission Planet Earth*, has several pages devoted to population control: One shows hiundreds of storks flying in the sky delivering babies. In the middle is a depiction of God frowning, not looking very happy at all. Then one reads the words, *"The earth groans each time a baby is born."*

Indoctrination Promoting Sustainable Development: The book begins with an introduction by the Secretary General of the UN, who back in 1994, was Boutros Boutros-Ghali. He states that the large (40 chapter) UN book on Agenda 21 contains a special chapter devoted to children and youth in **sustainable development**, which stresses the need for their "active involvement in matters related to environment and development."

The book is to show that the children of the world are very concerned and actively involved and giving advice and "lessons" to other children. Mark Affleck, a blogger and writer, states the following about the book:

It is really an "indoctrination manual" designed to spread fear, exaggerate concerns, and rob the innocence of our children. There is a smog poem on page 11 written [supposedly] by a poor indoctrinated child from Poland that is utterly heart-breaking. There are warnings about a hole in the ozone-layer, vanishing mountains, expanding deserts, destroyed rain forests, polluted seas and rivers, etc.[173]

There are pictures in the book attached to headlines about environmental abuses, but no clear indication that the photo is a result of the issue discussed, but to a child this would all be very convincing. Affleck adds:

The purpose of the book is to push a specific agenda. The pushers of Agenda 21 have no sense of decency. There is no science in this book; it is all theory, hype and emotion. It is also quite revealing as to who these propagandists really are.

First Grade Text Book and Workbook That Teaches Social Justice Advocacy: In Utah, parents discovered a little book that is being used for "language arts and writing." It is beautifully illustrated and looks innocuous enough, but what it is really trying to do is turn the little first graders into social advocates for social, liberal causes. They are to learn how to use their "emotional, feeling" voices to plead for causes before their city council, etc. because "emotional words" cause people to act. They are to look at what is wrong in the world and how to organize their community for a "call to action." This is for first graders – six year olds!

There is a workbook that goes along with the textbook that teaches them more about emotional words. This same book *Voices* is to follow them through each grade of elementary school, all with the same purpose – to train them to be advocates for social changes.

In the third grade book *Voices,* the teacher is told she is "to measure attitudes, beliefs and dispositions and promote growth and changes in attitudes and behaviors."

Informational Texts Promoting Liberal Philosophies: There are many little booklets to go along with the other prescribed ELA books and all seem to have a liberal bent to them. There are several promoting the UN and the UN Declaration on Human Rights. Students don't get to learn hardly anything about the U.S. Bill of Rights, but they do get to read every one of the 30 plus rights in the UN document. Of course, the UN books are supporting global warming and all the other pseudo-science beliefs that go along with it. There is always a call to action at the end of each book. What children can do about this problem and that problem.

There are also booklets about the lives of famous liberals, such as Sonia Sotomayor, Supreme Court Justice, appointed by Obama, who has quite a controversial past. There is a book promoting the Highlander Center in Tennessee and the causes it believes in such as: such as the ACLU, hate crimes legislation, gay and lesbian issues. The one thing the Highlander Center book leaves out is the fact that it was closed down on several occasions by the FBI because it was proven to be a communist-training center. [174]

Common Core's Strange New Math: Complaints are coming from across the nation from parents, students, and honest teachers of how weird the Common Core math is and how they do not like it. Students who were once great mathematicians are getting poor grades. They now hate math. Just as the picture of this little boy shows, children are confused, frustrated, and just space out, because it does not make any sense.

They come to school, having done the math in the traditional manner and have all the answers correct, but they are marked down and get a C or a D. The teacher tells them she does not necessarily want the correct answer. She wants the correct process.

My son, who is a very good CPA and really enjoys his job, when shown the new CC math that his wife is supposed to teach in the 3rd grade, said, if he would have had such math, he would have hated it and would have never ended up as a CPA.

Why are educators having to switch to such a system that is so confusing and obviously not better? What if the electricity was not working or for some reason calculators could not be used, a good mathematician could still figure out some one's income taxes and do it quickly. If my son tried to use CC math, it would take ten times longer. His clients would not care "if the correct process was being used." No, all they want is the correct bottom line figures. Parents hear the mantra that the prior math was too extensive, "a mile wide and an inch deep." Students were expected to do too much, so they didn't learn it well enough. Now, with Common Core math, they will be learning concepts "a mile deep and in inch wide." So students spend an entire class period on one question? They are also saying that "drill kills." Now children won't have to spend the time memorizing math facts.

"Common Core Conundrum": In an article by Eric Erickson, in *Townhall,* April 18, 2014, he states that all the problems of Common Core pale in comparison to **its biggest problem - math**. He says how the "education elite" have done it again "rejected the tried-and-true way of teaching traditional mathematics in favor of the trendy and novel." But this time, the methodology is so different and so confusing, the majority of parents cannot help their children. And some proponents of Common Core say that is a good thing:

Common Core supporters have gone so far as to release studies showing that children whose parents do not help them will outperform, over the long term, children whose parents are engaged.

According to Erickson," *The justifications to maintain the madness keep growing."*

Children have to Write Essays to Explain their Math Steps: No longer is it correct to just add 2 plus 2 to get 4. Now a child must explain why that is so. If a child decides that the answer is 5 instead of 4 but provides a logical reason for the answer, teachers are encouraged to give the child points. If the child has the correct answer but does not write his little essay, he could get a D on the assignment. After a while, even for the best students, the essays are getting really old and trite, and they are tired of writing them.

Building Familiarity Before Competence: Erickson writes that his own son, a second-grader, attends a private Christian school that is using Common Core. In one year, his son has been exposed to "time, money, addition, subtraction, measuring, multiplication, division and fractions and is now headed into math involving parentheses." "Before one concept is grasped, new concepts are approached." Common Core seeks to "build familiarity before competence." [So much for the Common Core mantra of going "a mile deep and an inch wide." It looks like their math is just the opposite - spread out all over the place, at least a mile wide and not even an inch deep at all.]

How Does this Affect Teachers? They are frustrated, too. They see students who once liked math now shying away from it, and they have to deal with frustrated parents, too. Many teachers also wonder why we have to "reinvent the wheel" when the wheel was working really well.

As Erickson writes, *"It is not a bad idea to have some uniformity of education in a mobile society. But reinventing several-thousand-year-old basic concepts goes too far."*

Erickson Believes the Ballot Box is going to be a Crucial Way to Fight Common Core: If a politician is in favor of it, voters will reject him. *"This sleeper issue could impact local elections nationwide."*[175]

Examples of the Strange Common Core Math Strategies: The Truth in American Education website shows examples of the strange new ways of working problems under Common Core math sent to them by attorney Jane Robbins, who has done a series of excellent introductory videos that can be seen on various websites including CUACC.org. The math problems are coming from a workbook used in Atlanta, Georgia. The strategies for doing simple addition and subtraction are called: "number lines; 100 block; place value strategy; part-to-whole; comparing, and removing." The examples shown even have a "parents' cheat sheet" for them to try to understand what their child is to do to work the problem. [176]

Common Core Math Baffles not only Students but also their PhD Parents: According to a report from the *Daily Caller,* one North Carolina father was thoroughly stumped with the following Common Core math sheet his five-year old son brought home to him where the child was to make up his own problems – "telling three subtraction stories."

"I have a Ph.D., and I have no idea what is supposed to be done with this homework assignment," said the man, who wished to remain anonymous. When the doctor spotted the "K.OA.1." towards the top of the worksheet, he recognized the assignment as part of the Common Core curriculum for k -math in Oklahoma. [177]

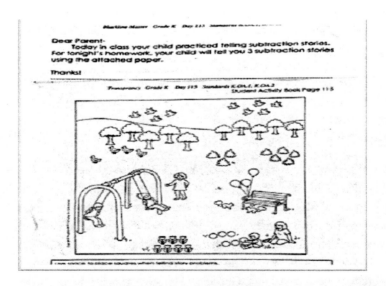

Electronic Engineer Father with Higher Math Training Could not Figure out his 2nd Graders Math Assignment: A homework assignment posted on the Facebook page for "Parents and Educators Against Common Core Standards" shows just how frustrating the progressive Common Core initiative has become to people with even the most prestigious of degrees such as electrical engineering.

The worksheet presents the student with the following problem: "Jack used the number line below to solve 427-316. Find his error. Then write a letter to Jack telling him what he did right, and what he should do to fix his mistake."

Confused by what was being asked, one second-grade boy left the sheet completing blank, prompting the teacher to respond with a green question mark at the top of the page. The boy's father, who has a Bachelor of Science Degree in Electronics Engineering, wrote the response shown on the next page back to the teacher:[178]

The father's name is Jeff Stevert. Somehow, Glenn Beck heard about this incident and saw the letter that Jeff had written. He contacted Jeff and was able to interview him on his show. He said that the teacher's response back to him was that she totally agreed with him. Jeff believes the majority of teachers also agree that this kind of math is ridiculous. Why waste so much time and complicate math, when you can come up with the answer very quickly and simply and save hours of time?[179]

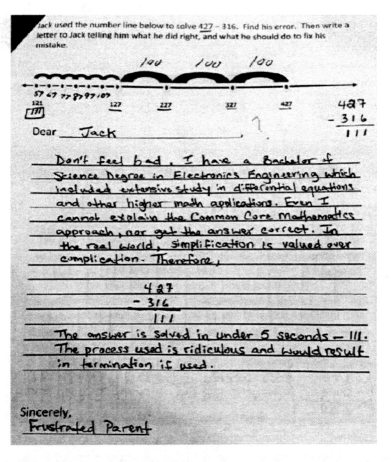

Jack used the number line below to solve 427 – 316. Find his error. Then write a letter to Jack telling him what he did right, and what he should do to fix his mistake.

Dear _Jack_____,

Don't feel bad. I have a Bachelor of Science Degree in Electronics Engineering which included extensive study in differential equations and other higher math applications. Even I cannot explain the Common Core Mathematics approach, nor get the answer correct. In the real world, simplification is valued over complication. Therefore,

$$427 - 316 = 111$$

The answer is solved in under 5 seconds — 111. The process used is ridiculous and would result in termination if used.

Sincerely,
Frustrated Parent

Estimating: The next problem shows how Common Core even has a new method of estimating. Notice that instead of rounding up to a higher number as we have always been taught when a number is over 50, they round down. What is meant by "front end" estimation? Is there a "back end"?

Find the sum. Use front-end estimation to check that each answer is reasonable.

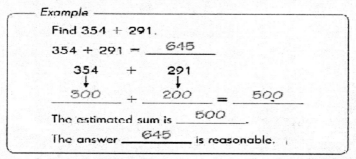

Example

Find 354 + 291.

354 + 291 = _____645_____

354 + 291

↓ ↓

_____300_____ + _____200_____ = _____500_____

The estimated sum is _____500_____.

The answer _____645_____ is reasonable.

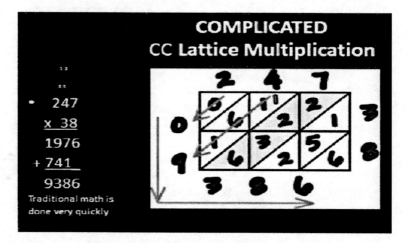

Lattice Method of Multiplication

Instead of being able to actually line the numbers up 247 x 38 and do traditional multiplication, as is shown above on the left, the students have to put the number into a strange lattice format and work the problem multiplying across inside the squares. It takes so much longer to set up the lattice, put the numbers where they go and to multiply across, and it is much more difficult and hard to understand.

College Students Also Baffled: In a recent piece by *Campus Reform*, students at George Mason University were thrown for a loop by a Common Core subtraction problem that is indicative of math lessons taught in elementary school classrooms. They were shown the following problem and asked to react to it. All of their reactions were essentially the same. "Why complicate something so easy? It doesn't make sense." **From *the Daily Caller*, Common Core math problem[180]**

Old Fashioned Way	New Common Core Way			
32	32 – 12 =___	12+	3=	15
-12		15+	5=	20
20		20+	10=	30
		30+	2=	32
Common Core	Add the middle Column			20 = answer

Again, such a simple subtraction process that takes just a few seconds to get the correct answer - is made to be so hard and complicated, and the child ends up adding rather than subtracting to get the answer. How confusing is that? Why put a child through such a process?

No wonder children, parents, and teachers are beginning to hate math with the Common Core methods. Is that what this is all about – dumbing down the math, frustrating the children who otherwise would love math and would have been motivated to go on and become great mathematicians?

Comedy Central Host, Stephen Culbert, Exposes the Sham of Common Core Math: Popular comedian and satirist Stephen Culbert, who will replace David Letterman as the host of the

Tonight Show, made fun of Common Core on his show, April 8, 2014. Here are some of the statements he made:

I have long opposed Obama's Common Core education curriculum that sets uniform standards across all the States. Different States have different values. I don't want my kids ending up on Colorado's drug education course that classifies weed as a condiment.

As much as I didn't expect it, I may be coming around to the common core, as it turns out Common core testing prepares our youth for what they will face as adults, constant stress and confusion...and passive, aggression note taking.

He then plays several brief news clips from different television stations with peoples comments: "Critics say these tests are hurting not helping students." Parents say, "Kids are anxious and uptight;" "it's stressful," "It's ridiculous." "I wouldn't allow my children to take the test today. They are stressing over it and getting upset."

He then gives the humorous example of the note writing of one second grader who was supposed to write and explain how he got his math answer. He wrote: *"I got the answer by talking in my brain and I agreed with the answer that my brain got."*[181]

The Math Standards are Promoting Social Justice: Phil Darro, one of the five writers of Common Core, who worked with Jason Zimba to produce the math standards, proudly states in a meeting before a group of teachers, *"The reason we have standards is because of the social justice agenda- to assure that all kids get enough math to have a decent opportunity."*

On the power point presentation that he gave with his speech is shown the following words: "Social Justice – the main motive for standards." Oak Norton, who is the webmaster for Utahns Against Common Core, where the video clip can be found, makes the following comment about social justice:

> Common Core set minimum standards for all students which means minimal learning for those who could accelerate. Thus social justice is achieved by holding down the achievers to the level of the lowest common denominator and by forcing them to learn what you want them to learn instead of letting them become individualized and accelerating their education as they can.[182]

If the Standards are Really so Great why did the CCSSO and NGA add an Escape Clause? Mercedes Schneider reminds us of the *disclaimer* attached to the standards. This is a good question to ask our school board and other elected officials that if the standards are so great, why did their creators not stand by them and give a guarantee for how well they would work? Instead they give a disclaimer that they will not be held liable if they do not work.

> THE COMMON CORE STATE STANDARDS ARE PROVIDED AS-IS AND WITH ALL FAULTS, AND NGA CENTER/CCSSO MAKE NO REPRESENTATIONS OR WARRANTIES OF ANY KIND, EXPRESS, IMPLIED, STATUTORY OR OTHERWISE, INCLUDING, WITHOUT LIMITATION, WARRANTIES OF TITLE, MERCHANTIBILITY, FITNESS FOR A PARTICULAR PURPOSE, NONINFRINGEMENT, ACCURACY, OR THE PRESENCE OR ABSENCE OF ERRORS, WHETHER OR NOT DISCOVERABLE. [Emphasis added.][183]

Chapter VI

Computers and Collection of Data – Intrusive Snooping, Longitudinal, from Cradle to Grave, Health Risks of Wi-Fi Radiation in Every Classroom

Futuristic Story of Education Now Coming True: The following was written by a friend Al Duncan in a novel that he wrote that was first published in 1999 called *the Master Plan*. It is a story about the future, when our nation and the world has been taken over by the United Nations and their goals for a one-world government have finally been achieved. This is a glimpse into what education can become like when computers are the teachers and humans are just facilitators.

Fred Moore is seven years old and a student in Public Education Center 419. Fred's classes consist of him alone. Pupils frequently gather in groups, for seminar-like discussion. However, most of Fred's time is spent at the learning console, which consists of a computer.

Fred's computers like all the other Concenter computers around the world—are connected to the main terminal in the educational Resource Center. There, a team of psychologists, programmers, expert teachers of everything from arithmetic to zoology, remedial specialists and guidance counselors comb Fred's record, and his progress is tabulated by the computers. No one knows Fred's grade level and it doesn't matter. He works his own pace. No one can come between Fred and the curriculum we have laid out for him.

...The global educative process is clear and easily understood. Education is tied directly to jobs—the job is our critical point in the State. We intend to start our education process at birth, linking instruction with productive labor. Our teaching is a continuous, lifelong education. That is why we are raising children in communal nurseries; any form of theology and history is suppressed.

Our education process gives incentives...to the one who cooperates most effectively with others. Our education process molds Fred's cognitive structure including all of his facts, concepts, beliefs, and expectations. We modify his valences and his values. We prepare him for the realization of his best self in the higher loyalty of serving the State. World citizenship, a global principle is the standard education of every child. [184]

What a scary story could be the future of our children and our nation! As you will see in this chapter, we are not too far away from that point where computers will be the teacher and plan the career for every child using the enormous data collection that is now made possible through those computers.

With Modern Technology and the NSA, Data is Stored on all Adults: As we are finding out more and more of the secrets of the NSA (National Security Agency) from the whistleblower Edward Snowden, we have come to realize that with the use of computers, cell phones, smart phones, iPads, GPS tracking system, smart meters on our homes, and all sorts of modern technology, data is being collected on all of us adults constantly. It is being stored in gigantic NSA facilities such as what was finished in the fall of 2013 at a National Guard base in Bluffdale, Utah. The building cost over

$1.2 billion, is 1.5 million square feet; with powerful NSA computers filling 100,000 square feet. [185]

"a person has no legitimate expectation of privacy..."

As the message on this picture shows, we, adults, have more or less gotten used to the idea that data is being collected on all of us. What is being done with that data, no one seems to know? But we think if we are law abiding citizens, maybe we will be okay and that data will not be used against us.

However, most parents did not think this same data would be collected on children at our public schools. For some reason we thought schools were safe havens that could be trusted to watch over our children and protect their privacy. Sorry, that is not the case.

"Common Core's Data Collection is not New, No Different than Before?" Administrators and teachers have a standard answer when asked about the data collection – "It's nothing to worry about. We've been doing it for years. Common Core is no different." Well, either they are not informed or they are not telling the truth.

Data Collection is the Driving Force Behind Common Core: The data collection is much bigger than ever before, with over 400 points of data, much more intrusive, and it is really the driving force behind Common Core. It is the tool needed to achieve the ultimate goal - to prepare our children to be part of a global workforce, with their careers already chosen for them, their schooling selected for them to fit that career. And with the data collected to know what is remiss in the students' attitudes and belief systems, the computers can do the programming/reprogramming to make sure that students graduate and move onto college and career with the proper attitudes, belief systems and behaviors to be better cogs in the global workforce and proper global citizens.

As you will discover, there is also much money involved, as with all of Common Core. Your child's data is worth a pretty penny to someone who is willing to pay for it.

The Family Educational Rights and Privacy Act (FERPA), which used to be in place to protect children's and families' private lives, was amended Dec., 2011, by the Obama administration by executive order to exceed the agency's statutory authority and thus allow invasive data to be collected on students and teachers. It is now "open season" on our children's private lives.

"Correct Dispositions" is one of the things listed as being tested as the students take their various tests and assessments with their computers. All the data that is being collected on students and teachers includes this term – "correct disposition" – just another term for the right liberal mindset or political correctness.

Many education schools discourage, even disqualify, prospective teachers who lack the correct "disposition," meaning those who do not embrace today's "progressive" political catechism. Karen Siegfried had a 3.75 grade-point average at the University of Alaska Fairbanks, but after voicing conservative views, she was told by her education professors that she lacked the "professional disposition" teachers need. She then began studying to be an aviation technician instead."[186]

Cradle to Grave or Womb to Tomb: The collection of data will begin at birth and continue on until a person dies. With Obama Care and all the data collected from health records, it can really begin when the fetus is developing in the mother's womb.

History: It is true that data collection is not a new idea. Dictators have been doing it for centuries. With modern technology, however, it is now so much easier, and so much more data can be collected and stored.

Data Collection in the USA: Remember the infamous "Dear Hillary Letter" that Marc Tucker, President of the NCEE (National Center for Education and the Economy) wrote to congratulate Hillary Clinton after the election of her husband to the presidency in 1992? It somehow was leaked out to the conservative media and people became aware of its shocking contents. In the letter, Tucker essentially said that everything that he and Hillary had been dreaming of with modern technology, socialist education, central planning and data collection could now be made possible with her powerful position in the White House. He wrote of a computer database, a.k.a. "a labor market information system," into which school personnel would scan all information about every schoolchild and his family, identified by the child's social security number.

The data would include: academic, medical, mental, psychological, behavioral, and interrogations by counselors. The computerized data would be available to the school, the government, and future employers. Guess what? That is exactly what the Common Core now makes possible.

State Longitudinal Data System: Longitudinal means it crosses State lines and can go to colleges, to federal agencies in the education profession but also third parties – the private sector. The data can be sold to the highest bidder. Advertisers pay heavily to find out private information about children, parents and teachers.

The Assessment Tests will be the Biggest Gatherers of Data: The USDOE (U.S. Department of Education) has agreements with PARCC and SBAC (in charge of the assessment tests) **requiring them to provide the USDOE complete access to all student data.**

This includes biometrics (finger prints, retina scans, DNA); health records, diet, food diaries; how much exercise they have; personal data, such as religion, political persuasion, household income, etc.; **"behavior, disposition and habits of mind,"** and **stress levels taking tests.**

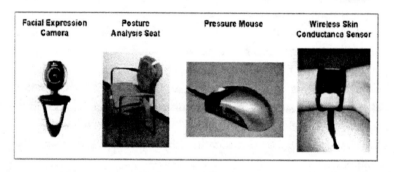

Promoting Grit, Tenacity, and Perseverance: Critical Factors for Success in the 21st Century is the name of a publication that was printed February, 2013 by the U.S. Department of Education Office of Educational Technology. On page 45 appears the above startling picture of the tools that will be used to access and record stress levels and other traits as a child is taking the assessment tests.

Data mining techniques that measures blood volume, pulse, stress levels, and facial expression – to show and record "frustration, motivation/flow, confidence, boredom and fatigue."

As the child is taking his test, a camera will be recording his facial expressions; the chair he is seated in will record his posture; the mouse he is using will record his stress level – how tightly he is clutching the mouse or how hard he pushes on it, etc.; and the wrist band will record his blood volume, pulse, and perspiration levels.

Why are they doing this? These tools will supposedly help show and record a student's "frustration, motivation, flow, confidence, boredom and fatigue." What if the child is not having a good day, or is all stressed out with the black band on his wrist and knowing all this information is being recorded on him. It would make most people a little bit nervous! Could they really show their true selves under such circumstances?

Assessment Tests More Concerned About Data Collection than Test Scores? Is this why California had to go ahead and issue the assessment test in the spring of 2014 to ever 3 million students, even though schools were not ready for it with not enough computers, or iPads, etc., and even though parents and teacher were told it was not going to be scored? It was just a test of the test. If that were really the case, could not just a few school districts be chosen to issue the test and try it out? Why did the entire State have to give it? Obviously, the scores are not the most important part. It is the data that is being collected on the children that is most important.

What will this data be used for and where will it end up? Could it be sold to the highest bidder? Could it determine if the child can go on to college or will he be sent to a trade school? Will it determine what kind of career your child will be allowed to have?

How is the Data Collected? Teachers are told that they will be the primary ones most responsible for collecting and taking the data. Lap top computers or i-Pads issued by the schools will gather data as the children take their tests and as they do assignments at home with their families.

InBloom was one of the systems where the vast amount of data was going to be be warehoused and managed. It was the non-profit corporation briefly mentioned in Chapter III that was developed and funded by, you guessed it, the benevolent Gates Foundation to the tune of $100 million. They describe themselves as "a nonprofit provider of technology services aimed at connecting data, applications and people that work together to create better opportunities for students and educators." It promised to streamline how teachers and administrators accessed student records. The system was supposed to extract student data from disparate school grading and attendance databases, store it in the cloud and funnel it to dashboards where teachers might more effectively track the progress of individual students.

Originally nine states, representing more than 11 million students, were participating in the development and pilot testing of the inBloom technology services to ensure they meet the needs of states, districts, teachers and students. They were Colorado, Delaware, Georgia, Illinois, Kentucky, Louisiana, Massachusetts, New York and North Carolina.

Five states have already selected districts to be part of the pilot testing: Jefferson County Public Schools, Colorado; McLean County Unit District No. 5 (Normal) and Bloomington Public Schools District 87 (Bloomington), Illinois; Everett Public Schools, Massachusetts; New York City Department of Education, New York; and Guilford County Schools, North Carolina.[187]

The InBloom/ Ruport Murdoch Connection: There is one other important detail that not too many are aware of. The operating system for inBloom was developed by the Amplify division (formerly Wireless Generation) of Rupert Murdoch's News Corp, the owner of *FOX News*. InBloom itself seemed to downplay their involvement with *News Corp*/Wireless Generation, even though it was a key partner in the Shared Learning Collaborative, which gave rise to inBloom.

Back in 2011, the Wireless Generation was also poised to win a no-bid $27 million contract to build an ARIS-like portal for New York State as part of the requirements for the state's Race-to-the-Top bid. ARIS stands for "Achievement Reporting and Innovation System" and was a data-collecting portal for the New York City Department of Education, but was widely seen as a failure. Joel Klein had just left his post as New York Schools Chancellor to become CEO of Wireless Generation. However, following the hacking scandal at *News of the World*, a *News Corp*-owned British tabloid, New York State declined to approve the Wireless Generation contract.

Estimated Profits of a "Non Profit": While inBloom itself was a non-profit, one of its expressed aims, as the *New York Times* points out, was to "bolster the market for educational products." The K-12 education software market alone is estimated at **$8 billion** according to the Software and Information Industry Association. Rupert Murdoch had pegged the education-technology market, which also includes hardware and networking technology, as worth **$500 billion.**

Costs to Schools: Even though the information gleaned from individual students was supposed to provide the vital information needed to develop and hone the products, schools would still have to pay dearly not only for the products that are made possible by inBloom but for using the data-collecting portal itself. Starting in 2015, inBloom was to charge States and districts between **$2 and**

$5 *per student* each year for storing data on the site.[188] That is a huge expense for a State as large as California with over 6 million children in the public schools.

Unique Student Private Identification Number (USPI): Parents are told to not worry about the data being stored – that the data is "aggregate." That means it is done on a wide range of children and cannot be used to identify one certain student. That is not true. From information coming from Utah, we find out that every student has a "unique student private identification number" which must be used when a student logs in on his computer to do research, read assigned e-books, write essays, do other assignments and take tests including the big assessment tests.

This means that third parties could already have the USPI for every student, making it really easy for them to reattach the identity to any "de-identified" data they might get under the "research" provisions. Also, anyone helping in the computer labs, with online communications with the parents about logging in to these services etc., would have both the identity and student ID number in very unsecure situations and transmissions.[189]

InBloom Suddenly Announced on April 21, 2014, that they were Closing their Doors: They were involved in an $8 billion industry collecting data from prekindergarten to 12th grade. They had received "seed" money from Gates for $100 million. What could possibly have caused them to call the whole thing off?

According to BITS, a blog for the *New York Times,* the venture ran into roadblocks in a number of districts and States "over privacy and security issues."

The inBloom database included more than 400 different data fields about students that school administrators could

*fill in. But some of the details seemed so intimate —
including family relationships ("foster parent" or
"father's significant other") and reasons for enrollment
changes ("withdrawn due to illness" or "leaving school
as a victim of a serious violent incident") — that parents
objected, saying that they did not want that kind of
information about their children transferred to a third-
party vendor. That led some schools to recoil from the
venture.*

When parents in Louisiana discovered that InBloom had their
children's social security numbers, they made such a fuss that
Louisiana withdrew from InBloom. The school board of Jefferson
County Colorado followed. In April, 2014, after New York State
legislators passed legislation prohibiting the state department of
education from giving student information to data aggregators like
inBloom, education officials also reversed their plans to use the
service.

After losing the services of New York, Iwan Streichenberger, the
chief executive officer of inBloom, announced they would be
closing, that "*personalized learning was still an emerging concept,*"
and was "*the subject of mischaracterizations and a lightning rod for
misdirected criticism.*" He added: "*We have realized that this
concept is still new, and building public acceptance for the solution
will require more time and resources than anyone could have
anticipated.*"[190]

However, even though one data-collecting company has closed,
there are still many different systems to take its place, and there are
grants in place to entice the States to go along with the collection.
Take for example what is happening in Nevada.

SAIN in Nevada: Christina Marie, who is fighting Common Core
in Nevada, wrote that their grant application for the SLDS (State

Longitudinal Data System) in their State is called SAIN – "System of Accountability Information in Nevada." She writes, "Isn't that a hoot considering how insane all of this is?

How the USPI System Works: Christina Marie has done research on how the State system works. The USPI (Unique State Personal Identifier) will be attached to all the PII (Personal Identification Information) from each student and teacher.

Christine was told that the USPI matching system will receive only an individual's personal information necessary to generate an accurate match. Once the record is matched and a USPI is assigned, the other systems are cross referenced in a table that will allow for the query of data using the USPI, "and no personal identifiable information will be passed."

> *Strong encryption methods will be used to pass the initial request from the originating agency to the USPI system. No permanent student level data will reside on the USPI system. Personal information will be used only to make the initial match and then purged from the system.*

Is Purging or Destroying the PII Data Truly Doable? Is that really true? Christina spoke to an IT expert in Nevada who believes that to destroy data would be a pretty big claim considering the amount of data. Additionally, he said the cost would be so immense that the state might claim to have purged the information when in reality they would not spend the time and/or money all the while crossing their fingers that nothing comes back to haunt them.[191]

Price for Nevada Dad to See the Data on his Children - $10,194! According to a *FOX News* report on May 16, 2014, for John Eppolito to even lay eyes on the data the schools have collected about his four children will cost him $10,194! Why would the price tag be so expensive? According to what the Wyoming State Department of Education told him, "the system is not set up to extract the data." Here is what they issued to the Fox News:

Upon continued insistence from the parent, [Nevada Department of Education] staff assessed how much programming time would be required to write new queries and develop a data table to create readable reports for the parent Staff determined that it would take at least 3 weeks (120 hours) of dedicated programming time to fulfill the parent's request. At the applicable wage rate of $84.95/hour, the requested work resulted in a $10,194 price tag.

Eppolito was told, he could only see the data, however. He could not get rid of it. Of course, with such an expensive price tag, there will not be many parents who will go through the process.

The Fox News reporter, Perry Chiaramonte, stated that Nevada has spent an estimated $10 million in its seven-year-old System of Accountability Information in Nevada, known as SAIN. Each night data from county school systems is uploaded to the State database and potentially shared with other counties and states, businesses, etc.

In an interview with Martha MacCallum of "America's Newsroom" *FOX News* that was shown the morning of May 16, Eppolito stated that it is the SBAC and the PAARC consortia that are demanding that the States collect the data and pass it on to them. There are over 400 points of data collection, everything from test scores, to discipline, to mental health. Who knows all that is collected and where it will end up.

Eppolito is a real estate agent in the Lake Tahoe area and a former math teacher. He is leading the group, Stop Common Core Nevada. Eppolito wonders why the State is collecting data that parents can't even view. "This data is for everyone except the parents," he stated. "It's wrong."[192]

Student Achievement Backpack (SABP) in Utah: From a You Tube clip made by a concerned mother in Utah, Pamela Smith, we learn about a new Utah law (SB82) that was passed in 2013 called "Student Achievement Backpack," that essentially mandates that all personally identifiable data collected on students, from various forms, assessments and computer adaptive programs must be sent to the State, which then sends it on to the federal government and other public and private organizations. The data collection is also mandated on teachers and staff.

Utah received $96 million from the federal "Stimulus money" in 2009 to maintain their SLDS data collection. As Pamela Smith states, "The federal dollars built it; State taxes are required to maintain it. This takes needed money out of the classrooms and redirects it to "control the classroom."

Student Interoperability Framework (SIF): Utah is now plugged into a new system, where student data is provided to all 50 States, federal agencies and third parties. On their website one can read: "One wire, with one plug, open, global standard, seamless, real time data transfer." Here students', staff's, and teachers' information is being stored in separate, individual backpacks and kept indefinitely for research and analysis.

The National Data Collection Model (NDCM) was provided as the ideal model for States to follow. All States are working towards compliance to this model. The NDCM is requiring 100s of data points such as: voting status, nickname, bus stop arrival time, health information, behavioral assessments, ability grouping and biometrics. Ms. Smith takes a closer look at the behavioral assessments and the biometrics.

Another Utah bill, H15, mandates that data must be collected and sent in on behavior from preschool and beyond. It goes into the child's virtual "backpack," the name for the file where it is stored, and where information is collected the rest of the child's life.

What are biometrics? They are personal, visual, body traits to identify a child such as: fingerprints, eye retina scans, facial characteristics, voice prints, DNA, handwriting samples, etc. Pamela Smith adds, "Even law enforcement agencies can't gather most of this information even on suspected criminals." But look what they are gathering on our innocent children!

Teachers Play an Important Role in the Data Collection: As with everything that is a little nefarious, one must paint a rosy picture of it to make it appear innocent and actually good for the children. Such is the case with data collection, as can be seen on the chart on the next page: **"Ms. Bullen's Data-Rich Year."** Notice the words right after the heading– **"When teachers are empowered with data, students do better."** The chart is produced by Data Quality Campaign and a larger version can be seen at dataqualitycampaign.org.

The chart has, obviously, been created to try to convince the teachers that their role in collecting data will help the children improve. As one can see from the pictures on the chart, a teacher has to go through 18 steps in keeping the data throughout the year on just one student. How much harder will that be on a classroom full of students? There are also other teachers, the principal and a new entity called "data coaches" that the teacher has to work with.

Questions to Ask? How can this data be safely stored? What kind of government does this to their own people? Should a government be allowed to collect such data on their own people? Where will the data end up and what will it be used for?

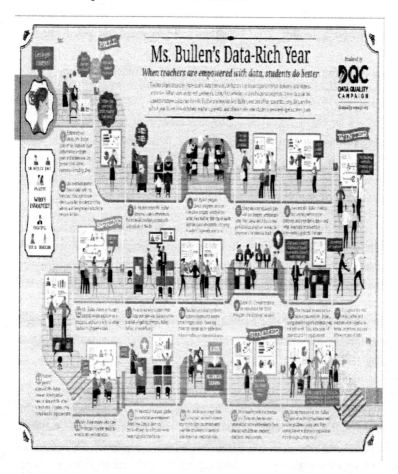

CCSSO is asking for Such Data on not just Students, but Teachers and Staff: The Council of Chief State School Officers, which mainly consists of State superintendents of schools from across the nation (but not all of them), is joint owner of the Common Core standards along with the NGA (National Governor's Association). It is their goal to have timely, actionable, and assessable data. This goal was accomplished when the SLDS was built in every State.[193]

Personal Stories - Report on Sneaky Data Collection on Students: Written by a Missouri resident, Beth Myers, a former teacher, a policy researcher and advocate, who holds a PhD in education: - "FYI potential homeschool parents." Her story was sent out over the internet as a warning to parents of what to do before pulling their children out of the public school and home schooling them. The data on your children goes on and will be shared outside the district even though promises are made to the contrary. Missouri has a workforce database that collects personally identifiable student information from pre-K to the workforce [which I am sorry to say is what just about all States have.]

Myers first tells how she was chosen to have an internship with the FDOE when she was working on her doctorate in education. It was just a few months after Arne Duncan had been appointed secretary. It was then that she heard discussions that they would be revising the FERPA ([Family Education Rights Privacy Act] regulations that had protected personally identifiable student information/data (PII). In December, 2011, that is exactly what happened, the USDOE revised FERPA, essentially gutting the law.

In September, 2013, Myers spoke to the State school board about her concerns with student data privacy and the sharing of personally identifiable student information with the state's workforce database.

The following month she spoke to her own local school board about the same issues.

The superintendent and school board assured me and the public that the district took data privacy seriously and that the only data shared outside the district was that which was sent to the state department of education.

A month later, in November, 2013, Myers and her husband decided to withdraw their son from public school because of their concerns over Common Core and began homeschooling him. They completed all the required withdrawal paperwork for both the State and the local school district and brought it back to the school. They documented that their son was moving into a homeschool program.

Graduation Alliance had the Son's Data: On December 9th, Myers received a phone call from a local chapter of "Graduation Alliance," which is part of a national organization started by Colin Powel called "America's Promise." The young man on the phone said that:

*...he had RECEIVED INFORMATION that my son had withdrawn from the district, that there was no record of his having enrolled in another district or education program, and that there was no record of his having graduated. His organization wanted to offer me online courses so my son could complete his coursework and graduate. When I asked him how his organization had access to my son's information, he stated that it was **PROVIDED to them by MY DISTRICT** (which had only two months prior assured me that data was not shared beyond the state DOE!!).*

Greatly disturbed, Myers contacted her local superintendent by e-mail who answered back that that the district had indeed shared her son's information, that the district had a contract with this organization, and that it was "a good program."

At no time in his response did he apologize for having shared my child's information or for misidentifying him as a dropout rather than a homeschooler. I now do not know who has my son's information, if he is misidentified as a dropout in some workforce data system somewhere, or how that misidentification may affect him in the future.

Advice for Parents Removing their Children from a Public School to Home school. Beth Myers gives us these words of council from her own experience:

I would recommend that you make sure that when you fill out the appropriate paperwork, you clearly mark the reason for dropping as enrolling in homeschool... NEXT, I would recommend that you contact the district directly (a formal letter to the district superintendent) and advise them that you have elected to homeschool and have formally withdrawn your child from the district.

I would inform them that because you have terminated your relationship with the district, any further activity related to your child's personal information, beyond reporting to the state that your child has withdrawn from the district, should cease.

I would request that your child's DIRECTORY information... be removed and emphasize that your child's information should not be shared with ANY outside agency (e.g., non-governmental, non-profit, for-profit, non-educational governmental agency) WITHOUT YOUR EXPLICIT CONSENT.

Most States do not have a State-Level Privacy Law: Myers advises us:

Because the federal student privacy law has been gutted

*and most states do not have a state-level privacy law, I
have had no recourse regarding the sharing of my son's
information. I am very active now with parents and
legislators to formulate legislation at the state level to
protect student data and parent rights.*[194]

Intrusive Questionnaires: As an example of just how intrusive the
data is, the following comes from *The Blaze,* Glenn Beck's
television show. Mike Opelka was able to get a copy of a
questionnaire that was given to Sophomore students at Poolesville
High School in Maryland in the Montgomery County School
District, (which is Common Core compliant).

The Questions were Asking such Privacy Issues as: What's your
religion? Your sexual orientation? Were you born in the United
States? Your parents' political affiliation? Your parents' income?
What race do you identify with? Should "assault rifles" be banned?
Who's to blame for the government shutdown? How do you feel
about Obama Care? Do you live with one parent or two? How
many siblings do you have? What part of Montgomery County do
you live in? What middle school did you attend?

This was a survey that no one was allowed to opt out of. Parents
were outraged when they found out about it, and some of them
contacted Glenn Beck who reported about it on his show. When his
investigators contacted the Montgomery County School District,
their officials denied that the survey existed. When told that it was
actually posted on the school's website, within an hour it had "been
scrubbed" from the internet.

When questions persisted, Dana Tofig, the school district's
public information officer, finally acknowledged the survey's
existence and confirmed that it had been removed. He insisted,
however, that it was voluntary and was part of a class project put

together by students, and that no one would know who was answering the questions.

Parents say otherwise, that it was put together by teachers who were trying to assess how politically correct the students were, and that the students had to log on to their computers to their *Edline* accounts to take the questionnaire. *Edline.net* is an online education support system for parents, students and teachers, that parents say could be easily traced. Those giving the survey could easily figure out who the student was from the answers given to the intrusive questions being asked.

According to parents, students were instructed to take out their cellphones, log in to *Edline* and take the survey. There was no opt-out offered, and in one instance, a student who did not wish to take the survey was coerced by an "authoritarian" teacher. The official response from the school administration was:

> *The results of the survey were only going to be analyzed by the AP Government classes, and not provided to anyone else. All responses, regardless of where they were submitted, were done anonymously, and neither the students nor the teachers would have had access to the demographic data on a student-by-student basis.*

The Blaze was curious about the truth about the anonymity of the students and their answers, so they contacted *Edline* and spoke to a woman named Tina, who identified herself as a "system operator." When she was asked about anonymity, Tina responded, "I can't imagine how they (students) could retain anonymity if they logged in using their user name and password." [195]

States and Districts who Get Core Waivers to get out of NCLB will have even more Data Collection: As you will see from the following article, eight districts in California decided to apply and received waivers (August 8, 2013) to get out of the requirement of NCLB, something that the State School Board of California had turned down. The waivers are for only one year and are affecting schools attended by one million students.

The Eight Districts are: Los Angeles, San Francisco, Long Beach, Fresno, Oakland, Sacramento, Santa Ana and Sanger.

Hoops to Jump Through: For any waiver, just as for any grant received, there is a price to pay and rigid requirements to be met. To receive the waivers, the eight districts had to be willing to do the following:

1) Implement their own system of college-and-career-ready standards separate from the rest of the state.
2) Largely "monitor their own progress," which is a nice sounding term for **"collect more data" not only on students but also on teachers.**
3) Agree to fully implement the more rigorous Common Core State Standards in the coming school year.
4) Implement assessments aligned to those standards by the 2014-15 school year. **[The assessment is how the most data will be collected.]**
5) Redesign their teacher evaluation and accountability system, which usually means tying the teachers' salary to the test and **more data collected on teachers.**

School Quality Improvement Index: This is the new name for the accountability system that the 8 districts will be held to. It is based 60 percent on academic factors such as student performance and graduation rates, 20 percent on a "social-emotional domain" that focuses on absentee, suspension and expulsion rates, and 20 percent on the "culture-climate domain," which focuses on how students, staff and parents evaluate school performance.

Dean Vogel, president of the California Teachers Association, was not very happy with the eight districts applying and receiving their own waivers. He called it:

> *...absurd, counterproductive and divisive and sets up a new bureaucracy to oversee the districts. The CORE waiver distracts from the good work already in progress by local educators across the state. This will create confusion for educators, students and parents.* [196]

The Federal Department of Education began issuing waivers for No Child Left Behind in 2011, after education professionals for years criticized the 2001 law for unintentionally "incentivizing States to set lower academic standards to meet its requirements."

Since 2011, 42 States, the District of Columbia, and for the first time **eight California school districts** have been approved for the waiver. Of those states, 34 and the District of Columbia have waivers that will expire at the end of this school year - 2014. Those states must now present plans showing the conditions for the original waivers were being met now, as well as for the 2015-16 school year. [197]

Study Done by Fordham Law School about Data Collection and Privacy Issues through Cloud Computing in Public Schools:
[Fordham Center on Law and Information Policy (CLIP), Fordham Law School (12/13/13)] Following is a summary of their findings:
- Data-driven decision making is at the center of education policy debates.
- School districts are turning to evolving technologies and cloud computing to satisfy education objectives and save costs.
- Public schools are rapidly adopting cloud-computing services and transferring increasing quantities of student info to third party providers.
- Privacy issues are becoming more salient and contentious.

- Protection of student privacy in the cloud computing is generally unknown both to the public and to policy makers.
- Recommendations to the schools based on their findings to improve the protection of student privacy in the context of cloud computing.
- Their study was of a national sample of school districts, large, medium and small school systems from every geographic region of the country. They used the open public record laws, and requested all of the district's cloud service agreements, notices to parents, and computer use policies for teachers. All of the materials were then coded against a checklist of legal obligations and privacy norms. The purpose for this coding was to enable a general assessment and was not designed to provide a compliance audit of any school district nor of any particular vendor.

The key findings from the analysis are:
- 95% of districts rely on cloud services for data mining related to: student performance, support for classroom activities, student guidance, data hosting, as well as special services such as cafeteria payments and transportation planning.
- Cloud services are poorly understood, non-transparent, and weakly governed: only 25% of districts inform parents of their use of cloud services, 20% of districts fail to have policies governing the use of online services, and a sizeable plurality of districts have rampant gaps in their contract documentation, including missing privacy policies.
- Districts frequently surrender control of student information when using cloud services: fewer than 25% of the agreements specify the purpose for disclosures of student information, fewer than 7% of the contracts restrict the sale or marketing of student information by vendors, and many agreements allow vendors to change the terms without notice.
- FERPA generally requires districts to have direct control of student information when disclosed to third-party service providers.

- The majority of cloud service contracts do not address parental notice, consent, or access to student information. Some services even require parents to activate accounts and, in the process, consent to privacy policies that may contradict those in the district's agreement with the vendor.
- However FERPA, PPRA (Protection of Pupil's Rights Amendment), and COPPA (Children's Online Privacy Protection) contain requirements related to parental notice, consent, and access to student information.
- School district cloud service agreements generally do not provide for data security and even allow vendors to retain student information in perpetuity with alarming frequency. Yet, basic norms of information privacy require data security.

Suggestions: In response to these findings, Fordham CLIP proposes a set of specific, constructive recommendations for school districts and vendors to be able to address the deficiencies in privacy protection. The recommendations address transparency, data governance, contract practices, contract terms and a national research center and clearinghouse. [198]

Bill Gates Recommends Common Core and Robust Data Collection for Teachers and Students: The following is from a speech Gates gave in 2009 to the National Council of State Legislators: [Emphasis added]

*If your State doesn't join the common standards, your kids will be left behind; and if too many states opt out—**the country will be left behind.** Remember—this is not a debate that China, Korea, and Japan are having. **Either our schools will get better—or our economic position will get worse.***

Common standards define what the students need to learn; robust data systems tell us whether they're learning it—and they tell us a whole lot more than that. The stimulus package contains funding for longitudinal data systems; I hope you will use this funding to support *systems that **track student performance from early childhood education through high school and college and into the workplace.***

Student performance should be linked to the teacher and the curriculum and the instructional tools. It should let us know what the best schools and teachers are doing differently and what kind of teacher training promotes student achievement. It should help us improve college completion rates, and determine what curriculum leads to career success.

Gates states that 47 states have adopted portions of a strong data system, but "we still have a long way to go." He does warn, however, ***"If you do build this system and get this data, you may have to deal with people who don't want you to use it."***

Gates and his Children are Exempt from Common Core: Bill and Melinda Gates are similar to President Obama and Michelle, who send their children to private schools where there is no Common Core and no data collection on them. As Mercedes Schneider writes in her commentary about Gates speech:

*For years, Gates has been pushing his version of so-called education reform for **Other People's Children**. His kids attend Seattle's elite Lakeside School, a place where there is no corporate reform "pushback" because there are no corporate-driven reforms.[199]*

A School District Sells their Student's Data: In case you thought it could not get any worse, well it just did! The Sweetwater School District in Chula Vista, California, needed close to $22,000 to buy a new stage, new flags and banners and to get the Castle Rock Middle School all spruced up with a coat of paint and new fans in the cafeteria in anticipation for the arrival of Secretary of Education, Arne Duncan, in September, 2013.

Since they could not think of any other way of raising the money, the superintendent and principal decided to sell their students' data to the highest bidder. And who was the highest and only bidder? A branch of the federal Department of Education, called "Promise Neighborhood/South Bay Community Services."

According to an article that came out in the *San Diego Reader*, December 3, 2013, Castle Park Middle School is a Chula Vista Promise Neighborhood school.

> *Promise Neighborhoods are funded by the Department of Education and claim to offer "cradle to career" services. South Bay Community Services is the organization that oversees and distributes the $60 million government investment in Chula Vista.*

The investigative journalist writer of the article, Susan Luzzaro, was very persistent and was finally able to obtain copies of the e-mails that went back and forth between the principal and superintendent. Here is the one that reveals the selling of the data:

> *On August 2 Principal Bleisch wrote to Alt: 'By the way, FYI-SBCS [Promise Neighborhood/South Bay Community Services] is prepared to give my school a good chunk of change (over $100K of PN money allocated last year for staff that was not used.) The catch is that they are kinda using the **data-sharing agreement as leverage**.) They promised to expedite this money transfer as soon as we deliver on the data agreement'* [200]

One wonders how many other elected school district trustees, whom we are supposed to be able to trust, who tell us how much they value our children, are capable of trading in their data for a "mess of pottage" or for "thirty pieces of silver"? If you are familiar with *the Bible*, you know that the mess of pottage is a symbol of someone who is willing to sell his birthright or his soul for immediate rewards.

The "thirty pieces of silver" is a symbol of treachery and betrayal, what Judas, one of Christ's disciples, received from the Jewish high priests for betraying Christ. Are teachers, administrators, school board trustees and superintendents, etc. willing to sell our children's data for their own gain?

How to Fight the Data Collection in State Legislature: This is advice coming from the Missouri Education Watch Dog, which has been fighting Common Core for many years. It is written by their leader and editor Gretchen Logue.   She warns us that much of the data legislation that is going through some States such as Louisiana and Missouri is just window dressing and does not really protect the privacy of children or their parents. She writes:

> *These are bogus privacy bills introduced by senators or representatives on behalf of the state educational agencies allegedly offering data protection with the personally identifiable information; it is allowing third parties and various agencies to access **without your consent.***

Gretchen tells of a mom who testifies in Louisiana about how their bill was actually granting the state agency even more authority to gather data information and provide access on students. There is a video of her testimony which echoes what other parents are saying throughout the United States. These are some of the main points from the video:

- Kids are becoming a data index.
- Statist and elitist mentality pervades.
- Parents have been villainized (portrayed as villains) in every way possible.
- Parents are omitted in everything…"we matter nothing."

- This is my children's information.
- There are unintended consequences.
- There is a freedom and right to privacy and this bill does nothing to protect this right.
- I am the sole legal authority over my child.
- You must fully restore the right over data privacy, collection and collection storage for my child and not give it to a governmental agency.
- We are afforded due process and protection for effective due process and right to privacy.
- There is a denial of these rights.
- There is no due process in this bill for parents.
- FERPA is meaningless.
- Parents don't count because we are not required to consent, and SEA [State Education Agency] can determine just about anyone as an authorized representative [to receive data].
- Louisiana can go further than FERPA.
- SSNs [Social Security Numbers] have been uploaded to third party vendors.
- The buck has to stop with our children.
- Parents are denied the divine right to protect their student's data and this bill totally negates my right as a parent and gives it to government.
- We are adopting a village mentality rather than have parents have the right to protect their children.
- Pass a bill that places students/parents first and foremost in traditionally free America.
- NGOs are supplanting us in so many ways. How do you counter NGOs and governmental agencies? In a traditionally free America you keep these agencies (state and private) in check with one word: Consent. **You need consent from the person to whom that information belongs. My information belongs to me, not the government.**

- The countries that streamlined the data tracking initially were Russia and China. [We are becoming more like them each day.]
- **What have we gotten in America with increased data tracking? We've gotten less freedom and more government.**

Who is the Real Author of so-called "Data Privacy Bills" that do nothing to stop the informational gathering? Since the data bills that are appearing in other States are all similar, Heather believes they have one main author and are probably coming from the controversial group called ALEC, American Legislative Exchange Council, which has a template for all State law makers for the year 2014. "Legislative-Advocacy Group's Model Bill Tackles Privacy of Student Data": Here is what is written about it:

> *The template being provided to state lawmakers by the controversial American Legislative Exchange Council, known as ALEC, would require state school boards to appoint a "chief privacy officer," create a data-security plan, publish an inventory of all student-level data being collected by the state, make sure that contracts with some vendors include privacy and security provisions, and ensure compliance with federal privacy laws.*
>
> *The group's model legislation mirrors a recently enacted bill in Oklahoma that is widely regarded as the first attempt in the country to comprehensively address growing concern over the collection, electronic storage, and sharing of oceans of student-specific information. Such data cover matters from academic performance to family background to disciplinary and health records.*

Although the mother on the video did not mention ALEC by name, ALEC is one of the NGOs heavily invested in education reform. Is it any wonder why politicians are not receptive to parents and the taxpayers when they are compelled to support the system that is increasingly being taken over by private organizations?[201]

What Can Parents Do to Fight the Intrusive Data Collection? Thanks to the Pacific Justice Institute, a wonderful law firm that represents especially Christians when their religious rights are being infringed upon, **an opt-out form has been created for parents to opt their children out of the Assessment Tests. It is following the State of California Department of Education Codes:**

33308.5. (a) Program guidelines issued by the State Department of Education shall be designed to serve as a model or example, and shall not be prescriptive. Program guidelines issued by the department shall include written notification that the guidelines are merely exemplary, and that compliance with the guidelines is not mandatory.

60615 Notwithstanding any other provision of law, a parent's or guardian's written request to school officials to excuse his or her child from any or all part of the assessments administered pursuant to this chapter shall be granted." State tests are mandatory for districts to administer but optional for students to take (with parent opt out).[202]

Concerns about Radiation from Computers and Wi-Fi: Before leaving this chapter, there is something else that parents and teachers need to be aware of. As all children in schools across the nation are going to be taught with computers, more Wi-Fi will be connected in the schools. Wi-Fi is a source of pulsed radiation that scientists are becoming concerned about. Children's skulls and bones are not yet developed enough to combat the constant radiation that comes from Wi-Fi and constant exposure to computers.

Just google "Wi-Fi Dangers to Children's Health," and an amazing amount of information comes up. There were 46,900,000 hits of people who share this same concern.[203]

On the website safeinSchool.org, you read the following:

"We are parents who fully support the use of computers and the incorporation of technology in education, and we believe that it must be implemented in a SAFE manner."

Doctors and Scientists around the world have warned against unnecessary exposure of children to RF/microwave from wireless technology and recommend safer WIRED internet connection instead, both in school and at home.

SafeinScnools.org website lists the following Major Concern:
• "Scientists urge halt of wireless rollout and call for new safety standards: warning issued on risks to children and pregnant women.
• Scientists who study radiofrequency radiation from wireless technologies have issued a scientific statement warning that exposures may be harming the development of children at levels now commonly found in the environment.
• Pregnant women are cautioned to avoid using wireless devices themselves and distance themselves from other users...
• Current U.S., Canada and ICNIRP standards for radio-frequency and microwave radiation from wireless technologies are entirely inadequate. They never were intended to address the kind of exposures from wireless devices that now affect over 4 billion people.
• The combined effect of cell phones, cordless phones, cell towers, Wi-Fi and wireless internet place billions of people around the world at risk for cancer, neurological disease and reproductive and developmental impairments.
• We are already seeing increases in health problems such as cancer and neurobehavioural impairments, even though these wireless technologies are fairly new in the last decades or so for the

general public. This finding suggests that the exposures are already too high to protect people from health harm.

• Safety standards also ignore the developing fetus, and young children who are more affected.

• The Scientific Panel urges a halt to the rollout of new wireless technologies, especially those that cause exposures for pregnant women and for children."[204]

Encourage your school to use wired connection for internet, and lessen their exposure and use of cell phones as schools are doing in New Zealand, Australia and other countries in Europe.

Rate of Autism Skyrocketing: As of February, 2013, the rate of autism in the USA has risen to 1 in 50 children.[205] What could possibly cause such a rise? Many doctors and scientists believe it is the bombardment of RF and EMF waves with the huge rise in use of wireless technology and the effect that has had on the baby in the womb and in new borns. Two studies show that EMF radiation could be a contributing factor, if not the actual cause of autism:

1. In 2007, Tamara Mariea and George Carlo conducted a study to assess the role of EMFs from wireless devices in the etiology and treatment of Autism.

   Researchers found that EMFs (specifically from wireless devices) trap heavy metals in cells, causing heavy metal toxicity. This accelerates the onset of autistic symptoms and also impedes therapeutic clearance of the metals. The findings also suggest that EMFs probably work in conjunction with other environmental factors (such as vaccines) and genetic factors to cause Autism.

2. The second study was conducted by Dietrich Klinghardt, Director of the Klinghardt Academy of Neurobiology in Seattle.

   The researchers measured the mothers' body voltage and microwave exposure in their sleeping environment, and also those of their autistic children. The study strongly suggests that electromagnetic radiation in the sleeping area of the mother during pregnancy, as well as that in the sleeping environment of the children, may be contributing, if not causal, factors in Autism.[206]

Again, do your own research to verify the accuracy of the above reports. One also has to realize that there is much money invested in computers, Wi-Fi, smart phones, cell phones, smart meters, etc. Could that be the reason that we are not hearing very much about the harmful side effects to our health of this technology?

Chapter VII

Common Core Assessments

Two Different Consortia Tests – PARC and SBAC; Field Testing; Data Collection; Testing for "Attitudes, Behaviors, Beliefs, Values, and Dispositions; the Scoring of the Tests and what is Done with the Results, Opposition Mounting, Opt Outs Possible?

Picture of 7th graders practicing for the PARCC Assessment test at the Marshall Simonds Middle School in Burlington, Mass.[207]

Two Different Consortia that Created the Tests: The two Consortia are Smarter Balance Assessment Consortium (SBAC), that 22 States belong to including California, and the Partnership for Assessment of Readiness for College and Careers (PARCC) that the rest of the States belong to – except for some that have dropped out and are trying to find a different form of assessment like Utah,

Kansas and Alaska. In total 39 States belong to one of the two Consortia.

SBAC members are: California, Nevada, Oregon, Washington, Idaho, Montana, Wyoming, North Dakota, South Dakota, Iowa, Missouri, Wisconsin, Michigan, West Virgina, North Carolina, Delaware, Connecticut, Vermont, New Hampshire, Maine, Hawaii, U.S. Virgin Islands

PARCC members are: Arizona, Arkansas, Colorado, District of Columbia, Illinois, Indiana, Louisiana, Maryland, Massachusetts, Mississippi, New Jersey, New Mexico, New York, Ohio, Pennsylvania, Rhode Island, and Tennessee

Funding Came from the DOE: The federal Department of Education gave $230 million to pay for the development of the tests that the two groups have shared. Would you not say that is one more example of how the federal government is a little too much involved in what is supposed to be something that is to originate with the States?

What about States Input? Did the individual states have very much input into how the Assessment turned out? According to Attorney Emmett McGourty, the input was the same as in writing the standards; it was "suggestion box" recommendations. And those who gave input have no idea if their suggestions were taken or not. For any local teacher or administrator to think they actually were involved in the writing of the assessments, they were probably "Delphied" into thinking so, just as with the writing of the standards. (Look in Chapter I for the definition of Delphi.)

What States Belong to Each Consortium: Smarter Balanced Assessment Consortium (SBAC) had originally 31 member States They are listed alphabetically:

California, Connecticut, Delaware, Hawaii, Idaho, Iowa, Kansas, Maine, Michigan, Missouri, Montana, Nevada, New Hampshire, North Carolina, North Dakota, Oregon, Pennsylvania, South Carolina, South Dakota, US Virgin Islands, Vermont, Washington, West Virginia, Wisconsin, and Wyoming

Partnership for Assessment of Readiness for College and Careers or PARCC is a 22-state consortium, including these states: Arizona, Arkansas, Colorado, D.C.,   Florida,   Georgia, Illinois, Indiana, Kentucky, Louisiana, Maryland, Massachusetts, New Jersey, Mississippi, New York,   North Dakota, Ohio, Oklahoma, Pennsylvania, Rhode Island, and Tennessee.

The Behind the Scenes Leader of the SBAC Assessment is Linda Darling Hammond, (LDH) who is a very progressive, left-leaning Stanford education professor, who has written several books on her education philosophy. She is recommended by her good friend and associate, Communist Bill Ayers, as "his favorite education expert."[208] So, obviously, they must share the same radical education philosophies.

Because of her far-left reputation that precedes her, she has tried to keep her name hidden, so that no one would know that she has been directing the writing of the SBAC assessment. However, a book that was published by the California Office of Education in January, 2013, *Recommendations for Transitioning California to a Future Assessment System*, reveals and thanks her for her leadership. On page ix in the introduction, we read, "*A special note of gratitude is extended to Linda Darling Hammond, Ph.D.,*

Professor at Stanford University, for her continued guidance throughout this project."

LDH also helped with the writing of C-SCOPE, the controversial, left-leaning digital learning system that has been in the State of Texas since 2007 and is written about in Chapter II.

Linda Darling Hammond was originally being considered by Obama for his Secretary of Education, but she was so far left, not even the Democrats would support her, so Obama picked a more moderate Arne Duncan instead.

PARCC – Partnership for the Assessment of Readiness for College and Careers. PARCC is the second consortium that some States belong to that is supposed to be submitting questions for the Assessment of Common Core. And who are the leaders for it? One would think that maybe the creators of the Common Core Assessment would make even a small attempt to have the test be somewhat fair and balanced between liberal and conservative ideology, by choosing a conservative to lead the second consortium, but no, that is not the case at all. We have a radical liberal leading the SBAC consortium, so we need at least one of the same mindset leading the PARCC consortium. Guess who that might be?

Enter left-leaning Sir Michael Barber, whom you have already become acquainted with earlier in Chapter II, who started the U.S. Education Deliverology Institute that is partnered with Achieve and is the Chief Education Officer for the Pearson Foundation that is publishing the e-books and the tests. Again we ask the question, why is a British subject chosen to head up an American consortium for education reform? Does there not seem to be a little "conflict of interest" that he is so involved in promoting every aspect of Common Core, something he and Pearson are benefitting financially from?

The selection of Barber illustrates that Common Core is a global plan. It is not just for American students; it is for students worldwide. And one of the strong beliefs of Sir Barber is that every child is a "citizen of the world," and there should be no borders between nations.

Sir Barber's Formula for Earth Oneness: In a talk that Sir Barber gave for the Council on Foreign Relations, that can be seen on the You Tube link following this paragraph, he showed the following formula: $E(K+T+L)$ and he explained that K is knowledge, T is thinking, L is learning and E = ethics, but not the kind of ethics that have anything to do with Biblical morality or right or wrong. No, since Sir Barber is an atheist, his ethics are centered on earth worship. To him, ethics stands for "shared understanding of earth and sustainability that every child in every school around the world will learn." And what do you get when you work this formula of E multiplied by $K+T+L$? According to Sir Barber, the answer is - "citizens of the world," the answer to all the world's problems. [209]

"Whole System Revolution": Another formula that Sir Barber gives is under the title of "whole system reform": He shows that standards + human capital + structure and accountability + systemic innovation = Whole System Revolution. He expects this to be a worldwide revolution with no turning back to the old traditional education ways. [210]

The Delivery Chain: If you would like to know more of Sir Barber's views, check out the power point presentation that he has created and is up on the PARCC website. His "delivery chain" for Common Core is full of one graph and chart after another. It refers to our children as human capital throughout. It truly sounds like a formula for a factory to deliver its product. And what will that product be? One thoroughly indoctrinated, cookie-cutter molded **"global citizen of the world."**

Regional Centers: What is especially interesting is Slide No. 20 and 22, where the delivery chain is shown going from State to Region/County to district, to school to classroom. So, they are already planning for regional centers and regional government to be in place and have included it in the delivery chain? This supports the statement made by Sandra Stotsky earlier about the plans to end local and State school boards and replace them with large, regional unelected boards.[211]

Implementing Common Core State Standards and Assessments, the workbook that Achieve and Sir Barber's U.S. Education Delivery Institute have published together to train State and district leaders in Common Core is also full of one chart and graph after another reviewing, analyzing, organizing, implementing and evaluating the delivery of the "systems." Those poor teachers and administrators using it would have to record their every action, every move and every thought.

Concern for Liberal Content in Common Core Instruction in Preparation for the Assessment: Now that we know the backgrounds and left-leaning ideology of the leaders of the two consortium creating the Assessment, Linda Darling Hammond and Sir Michael Barber, should we not be just a little concerned about the liberal slant that will probably be found in the Assessment because of their being at the helm in its writing? And will that liberal slant not be taught throughout the year in the classroom in preparation for the test? As is written in the book about California's Assessment System, "what gets tested is what gets taught." [212]

Strange Results of the Assessments: Two States have already tried the PARCC Assessment - Kentucky and New York - to test for how well the students are learning the Common Core curriculum. There were some very strange results for both States. They both dropped 30% in proficiency as had been predicted.

Following is an excerpt from an article about the results from the State of New York that questioned their accuracy and what could be achieved by manipulating the scores to the predicted outcome. [The entire article can be seen at www.CUACC/org]

Many Questions to be asked about Common Core Assessment Results for English and Math from the State of New York y Orlean Koehle, August 9, 2013

Could these Results be Fraudulent – Deliberately Lowered to Achieve an Agenda? Many people are starting to question the accuracy of the results including superintendents and principals. Following this article is a link to a PDF letter written by Joseph V. Rella, the Superintendent of the Comsewogue School District in Port Jefferson Station NY to State Senator Kenneth La Valle, in which he questions what really is going on and pleads for the senator's help.

He quotes from Principal Carol Barris, the award-winning Principal of South Side High in Long Island, New York, whose article about the assessment results appeared in the Washington Post, August 7. Both of them raise suspicions of what is really going on. Mr. Rella states, "If it sounds too good to be true, it is," and conversely, "if it sounds too bad to be true, it's not!" Were the student test results deliberately lowered to fit the predicted outcome of only "30 - 37 percent proficiency?

Why? What Benefit would it be to Have Low Test Results? *Mr. Rella quotes Principal Carol Barris:*

To make much money: *"...test makers, book publishers, data management corporations – all making tremendous profits from chaotic change." "When the tests scores drop, they prosper. When the tests change, they prosper. When schools scramble to buy materials to raise scores, they prosper." "There are curriculum developers earning millions to create scripted lessons to turn teachers into delivers of modules in alignment with the Common Core (or to replace teachers with computer software carefully designed for such alignment)."*

To create the appearance that Common Core is as wonderful as it has been lauded to be. *By making the test scores look bad this year, by next year when the assessment is given again, the scores will be much higher proving that Common Core is working, and all the fuss and bother and chaotic changes and enormous costs are worth it.*

To "dismantle the public schools:" *Mr. Rella states, "Clearly the agenda is to shake confidence in our public schools [so] that other alternatives (charter schools, vouchers, etc.) look more attractive. It is nothing less than the programattic dismantling of the public schools!"*

Why dismantle public schools and encourage charter schools? *Mr. Rella does not answer that question. But as has already been stated, some believe the number one reason to make charter schools look better is to destroy local control and representative government over our schools – what every good socialist country* has done. *In the majority of States, when a public school becomes a charter school, it no longer comes under the jurisdiction of an elected school board. It is now under the direction of a private group, a business, or a corporation that has taken over, but it still receives tax paying dollars to help run it. If parents have complaints, who do they go to? If there is no longer an elected official over the school, there is no accountability to the parents. We now have education without representation.*

To promote public/private partnerships*: When you have a corporation now running the school but still receiving tax paying dollars, you have a partnership of a private entity with the public (government), which is really fascism, exactly what was going on under Mussolini in Italy and under Hitler in Nazi Germany. Why is that so bad? In America, along with the three branches of government that were so designed to keep a check and balance on each other's power, business has traditionally served as a fourth check on the power and corruption of big government in our nation. When you have both big business combined with big government then there is no check and balance. Together they become bigger, more powerful and more corrupt.*

The Sad Effect such Faulty Test Results will have on the Aspirations of Young children: *The children in New York spent a long time preparing for the test, and in April, they spent two grueling days, four hours a day taking the assessment. Mr. Rella stated, "Today we crossed a major line. The majority of our young children will receive the clear message that since these tests are predictors of college success -- they are not college material in the 3rd, 4th, and 5th grades???!!! That message is unconscionable. It is hurtful to our children. I pray it is not lasting."*

At the end of the letter that Superintendent Rella sent to Senator La Valle, he stated the following sincere plea: "If you believe that any of this is valid, then please help us. We are being systematically deprived of our rights as Americans to appeal. No one is listening."

The passionate Superintendent then pleads, "If not, then I request on behalf of our residents, your constituents, you initiate proceedings to have me be removed as Superintendent. If this assessment system is truly valid, then during my tenure as Superintendent, our students went from 90% proficient to about 30% proficient. At best this is gross negligence, at worst this is willful malpractice."[213]

New York Rally Against Common Core and the Unfair Assessment: The letter by Dr. Rella caused a ground swell of opposition to rise in New York, and Dr. Rella and others added more to that ground swell by hosting a rally at the football stadium at one of the high schools in his district on August 14. Dr. Rella spoke and said the following: "Common Core hurts children!" "Let's Stop it, Fix it or Scrap it!"

He also started a new mantra – instead of "Race to the Top," he is calling it, **"Lace to the Top."** Everyone who joins him in this battle is to wear neon green shoe laces. So every time you look at your shoes, you are reminded of the battle to stop Common Core.

Dr. Rella also reminded people of the statement made by the Commissioner of Education for New York, John B. King Jr. (who, in spite of his statement, is still was a supporter of Common Core). His statement was later repeated by the head of the Chicago teacher union, Karen Lewis, who is very opposed to Common Core and has helped influence her union to adopt a resolution against it. Both King and Lewis said:

Common Core is like flying an airplane still under construction. It has never been field tested. We are flying the plane as we build it.

Dr. Rella said at the rally, ***"We are turning in our ticket. We are no longer on the airplane Field Testing for Common Core"***

The Field Test for SBAC: Students in the 3rd through 8th grades in the 22 States that signed on to be part of the Smarter Balance Assessment Consortium participated in "field testing" in the spring of 2014. Supposedly, there are no scores for the children taking the test, "no repercussions and no consequences." But this trial run or field test is to help determine "minimum passing scores and whether the questions meet the standards:

Test results won't be used to judge students or schools. They'll be used to set the bar next year, correct errors and make *changes to questions. More than 3 million students — picked from third through 11th grade classrooms — were chosen for the trial run.*

Could that not have already been determined by those preparing the test? Teachers across the nation used to prepare their own tests before national standards came into existence. We would know if the questions met what had been covered in our classes, because we had taught the material in those classes. We didn't need a costly trial run for the whole State. This just shows how far removed Common Core assessments are from local classrooms and local and State control.

Opting Out of the Tests: Every State, by some provision in their State Ed codes allows parents the freedom to opt their children out of a test. The administrators are just not informing the parents that they have that right.

As in the example of Nevada, only parents who asked for a way out of having their children be tested were given an exemption, other parents were left in the dark that such a thing was even possible.

How Many Opt Outs in California? "We haven't heard of many, officially or anecdotally," said Pam Slater, spokeswoman for the California Education Department, which is testing 3.2 million students in the target grades.[214] Of course, not too many parents who opt their children out make the front page of the newspapers. However, one did, as you see in the following. She is a reporter.

LA Times Journalist Opted Her Teenage Daughter out of the Test: Karen Klein wrote an article "Why My Family is Opting out of the Common Core Testing" that was published April 8, 2014.

Why did they make that decision? It was mainly testing burnout. When her daughter found out that she could opt out from the test, that is exactly what the family did. The mother wrote:

> *Her test results could, in an immeasurably small way, have helped the state draw up better exams in the future. Right now, I think the small, joyous rebellion of saying no, during the last year we have the chance, is more important for both of us. Take that, world of Scantron![215]*

Mother in Sacramento Suspended from the School because her son was passing out Opt Out Forms to fellow Students: Katherine Duran, co-founder of Concerned Parents of Elk Grove, an advocacy group to inform parents about CCSS, and a mother of a 12-year old who attends Mark Twain Elementary School in the Sacramento City Unified School District in California, had allowed her son to bring opt-out forms to school to give to his friends to get out of the assessment tests, as he had already done.

The opt-out forms were created by the Pacific Justice Institute, under the direction of founder and president attorney Brad Dacus. They let the school administration know that "pursuant to California Education Code §§ 51513, 60614, 60615, and 20 U.S.C. § 1231(h)," the child is to be exempted and excused from the following activities:

1) Taking any and all statewide performance assessments, including but not by way of limitation to, academic, achievement and annual tests, and Common Core interim and formative assessments, administered pursuant to sections 60600, et, seq. (Calif. Educ. § 60615);
2) The administration of any test, questionnaire, survey, examination or evaluation, containing any questions or items relative to my child, or my personal beliefs or practices or practices in sex, family life, morality, or religion (Calif. Educ. § 51513);

3) The administration of any test, examination or assessment as part of a statewide pupil assessment program relative to my child, or my personal beliefs or practices in sex, family life, morality or religion, or any question designed to evaluate personal behavioral characteristics, including, but not limited to, honesty, integrity, sociability or self-esteem (Calif. Educ. § 60614);

4) The administration of any survey, analysis or evaluation that reveals: (1) political affiliations or beliefs of my child or me, my family, neighbors or friends; (2) mental or psychological problems of my child or his or her family; (3) sexual behavior or attitudes; (4) illegal, anti-social, self-incriminating, or demeaning behavior; (5) critical appraisals of other individuals with whom respondents have close family relationships; (6) legally recognized privileged or analogous relationships such as those of lawyers, physicians and ministers; (7) religious practices, affiliations or beliefs of my child or me, or (8) income (other than that required by law to determine eligibility for participation in a program or for receiving financial assistance under such program). (20 U.S.C. § 1232 (h)).

The notice then states that the school is to "keep this signed, written notice on file in my child's cumulative folder. This form supersedes all prior Opt-Out forms." There is a place for the child's name, grade, date, school, parents signature, and a place for the principal to sign, showing that he has received it.

Following is a picture of the cover letter that Katherine Duran created that went along with the official opt out form explaining to the parents a brief background of CCSS, the Smarter Balance Assessment test, data collection and why parents should opt out.

Christopher Duran had the cover letter, the opt out forms in nice envelopes to pass out to his friends so no teacher or administrator would have to see them. The cover letter was very respectful. It acknowledged the group's support of the school, its teachers and administration. It stated:

This is NOT a war on our schools. We love our teachers and principals. Opting out now will ultimately protect teachers and prevent them from being subjected to the unfair evaluations and accountability mandated by the federal government. Teachers, principals and administrators across the United States have expressed their disapproval of every aspect of the Common Core initiative.

Duran said that her son told her at the end of the day, March 20, when she went to pick him up what happened. Somehow, one of the teachers must have seen the envelope, confiscated it and took it to the principal. Later in the day, the school principal, Rosario Guillen, made an announcement over the loudspeaker that the forms were inappropriate and were to be collected.

After hearing her son' story, Mrs. Duran went into the office to speak with the principal. She said Guillen admonished her saying, *"I'm very concerned you put your son in this position; it is inappropriate....what you did was inappropriate."*

Duran was very polite in her reply. She told the principal that it was her son's idea. *"My son is also very concerned about the inappropriateness of Common Core and the tests and wanted to share that. I believe he has a right to share with his friends, the same as it would be for party invitations, Valentines."*

Principal Guillen replied, *"I'm very uncomfortable with this, and I'm ending our meeting, and now I'll have to run all of this past the district, they're not going to like it."*

Duran reached for the 8 envelopes to take them with her. The principal slapped her hand down on Duran's and said, "No, they are not yours anymore." Duran, who has arthritis in that hand and was responding to the sharp pain of that slap, kept her composure and stated, "Respectfully, I will leave one for you but I'm taking the rest with me. Good afternoon." She grabbed them all except for the one and left.

The next Monday, Duran said police arrived at her door and delivered a letter from the school principal. Duran was told in the letter that she was suspended from setting foot on the campus for 14 days *"unless the purpose relates to the legitimate educational needs of your children who attend Mark Twain. In such case, you must obtain my permission in advance."*

Gestopo Tactics Used on Duran's Son: Her gutsy son continued to hand out opt out forms for the next few weeks, up until the time of the assessment test being given. The school administration was furious. They tried in every way to find the letters, searched his backpack and lunch box. They interrogated him, kept him out of class for 90 minutes, but the next day he would show up with more opt out forms.

Katherine Duran and Assemblyman Tim Donnelly Appeared on the Glenn Beck Show, April 9, 2014: Glenn Beck got wind of the story and had Katherine and California Assemblyman Tim

Donnelly, a candidate for governor, as guests on his show. Donnelly is running on a strong anti-Common Core platform.

When Beck asked Katherine how she found out about Common Core, she said it was from watching his show. It was all his fault. He helped her to realize how bad this was for her children and how we are losing our freedoms if we allow this takeover of education.

Donnelly told how he is being asked to speak all across the State at various anti-Common Core forums where large numbers are assembled. People tell him that when they have handed out flyers to alert parents of the forums by standing on the sidewalk of the school, principals tell them, "This is inappropriate, and you are disrupting the flow of traffic. You don't have a Constitutional right to be here." Parents have to stand firm and say, "We are on a public sidewalk and we have every right to be here."

Beck asked if there are some teachers who confide in him and Katherine that they do not like Common Core either. Donnelly answered: "Yes," he has had conversations with teachers who tell him that "they are being forced to teach a curriculum that they know is bad for kids, but they are afraid to speak out. If they speak out they are penalized, threatened, or intimidated."

Beck asked what is it going to take to turn this around? Donnelly answered that it is going to have to start with parents like Katherine taking a strong stand and uniting with other parents.

Katherine, however, said that most parents still do not know what Common Core even is. They don't have any idea that the test taken is any different than any other test their children have taken. The kids are tested throughout the year, so it is no big surprise that parents hear that another big test is coming up the end of the year.[216]

Big Push Back in the State of New York – large numbers opting out of the Assessment Tests: In Brooklyn New School, 240 parents out of 300 students at the elementary school were opted out of the English Language Arts testing. Even a greater number is expected for the math.

Signs that Parents are Holding in front of the School:

Opponents of the testing say the tests are just too long: kids spend up to 90 minutes a day on the exam for three straight days. Common core testing is expensive. Estimates suggest states spend anywhere from $800 *million to $10 billion on the program each year. So rather than teaching a well-rounded curriculum, opponents of common core say educators are forced to teach to the test.*[217]

Over 30,000 Opt Out of New York's Schools: On April 3, 2014, some 30,458 students had opted out. Here is a link to the spreadsheet compiled by the 31 courageous and dedicated parents who are tracking the number of NY opt-outs so far. Later it was estimated that 5% of parents had opted their children out – that would be closer to 60,000 students.[218]

A Substitute Teacher's Evaluation of the Test – "Testing What Isn't Worth Learning." A teacher in Sonoma, California, writes the following letter to the editor for the Sonoma Index-Tribune:

As a substitute teacher, I observed fifth graders taking the pilot test for Common Core (which doesn't count this year). As a retired elementary teacher who also taught high school math in summer school, I'm familiar with the many difficulties students have in this subject.

The absent teacher (who's gone for two weeks) asked me to fill out progress reports, and I was glad to see that many kids are at grade level. In fact, during class it's clear that more than half the class understands this week's topic (multiplying fractions and mixed numbers).

But this Common Core math test was sneaky and complicated. When students asked my help to understand a question on their computer screen (it's not a paper booklet), I would read the question to myself in case there was something I could clarify. But, no, it was just a convoluted "gotcha" question that they had to decipher.

Like Sonoma Valley's students, many of my current students are English Language Learners. Didn't it occur to anyone that word problems make it difficult to tell whether they get the wrong answer due to the English used to pose a question, or because of poor math comprehension?

Dr. Arthur Costa, a leading education professor at Sacramento State (now retired), said it well: "What was educationally significant and hard to measure has been replaced by what is educationally insignificant and easy to measure. So now we measure how well we've taught what isn't worth learning."

Lauren Ayers, Sonoma

Chapter VIII

Citizens of the World

United Nations

As you will read in this chapter , the intent is for Common Core to be a global education program. It is not just for the USA. It is the plan for every nation, being promoted through the UN.

"Citizens of the World": This is one of the mantras that is being blatantly used to promote Common Core. One would think those behind Common Core would want to be a little discreet or clandestine in using these words, but no, they proudly state them as if this is something all Americans should want their children to become. The goal is to have Common Core taught in every country and village around the world and to have all of our children believe that they are global citizens, to no longer think of themselves as citizens of any one sovereign nation.

An attractive, colorful pro-Common Core insert in the Santa Rosa (California) Press Democrat newspaper, August 26, coming from the Sonoma County Office of Education, stated the following on the back page under the large heading of **"Global Citizenship"**:

> *Our interconnected world requires diverse individuals to interact on a local and global scale...As students are engaged in thinking about the world and the larger community, they are acquiring skills that enhance their role as responsible global citizens.[219]*

245

Before we can be United Global Citizens, we must first be All States United in Common Core: Notice the above picture that comes from the main website promoting Common Core, www.corestandards.org. The picture no longer has five States missing. All are now united in their adoption of Common Core. This is the ultimate goal. In a totalitarian nation, no wiggle room is allowed for any State to opt out. All must be united and involved.

It is also interesting to see that the original bright, golden color of the States that had signed on is now changed to the brown color of those States that had refused. Is this to portray the dumbing down effect that Common Core will now have on the entire nation? It is also interesting to see the shock wave pattern spreading behind the map of the USA. Is this to signify that Common Core is meant to spread around the world and bring all children to the same mindset?

Common Core is already Global: If you google "Common Core, Sustainable Development," Africa pops up with the exact same words as in being taught here in the USA. Google Common Core UK, and the same thing happens – just with more emphasis on preparing children for the workforce – to be the cogs in the global economy.

A lady who moved to Brussels wrote back to a friend who sent her e-mail message on to others. She wrote:

> *Common core has made its way to the math curriculum at the International School of Brussels - the school that the state department employees and the new ambassadors send their kids to. We are very upset at the moment because they are requiring Justin to repeat Algebra I even after he finished last year with an "A." Lots of change here, difficult with the kids at the moment.*

Success in the Global Economy: David B. Cohen, a California teacher writes in his blog of March 2011, entitled "Common Core Confusion," how he cannot seem to get straight answers concerning the national, top-down aspects of Common Core and what its real purpose is all about. He quotes Alfie Kohn, a writer of an article in *Education Week*, who wrote that is seems to be all about "success in the global economy":

> *If you read the FAQs page on the common-core-standards Web site, don't bother looking for words like "exploration," "intrinsic motivation," "developmentally appropriate," or "democracy." Instead, the very first sentence contains the phrase "**success in the global economy**," followed immediately by "America's competitive edge."*[220]

Main Emphasis - Prepare Students for a Global Economy: Dr. Terry Metzger, Assistant Superintendent of the Rincon Valley Unified School District in Santa Rosa, CA, spoke for a women's breakfast of the Sonoma County Forum on May 15, 2014, about Common Core and told them that the main emphasis in her school district is "Students must be prepared for a global economy." (See the article written about her entire talk very revealing talk on CUACC.org)

The Hidden Cs of Common Core

Organizations that Are Promoting Common Core worldwide:
To help all students everywhere around the globe be prepared for a global economy, along with the Bill and Melinda Gates foundation, the Pearson Foundation and other previously mentioned American millionaire corporations there is one from India that is promoting Common Core worldwide.

CORE Education and Technologies Limited: CORE's headquarters are in Mumbai, India, where it was begun in 2003. It now has offices on four continents: American, Asia, Europe, and Africa.

The company is headed by Sanjeev Mansotra, Chairman and Global CEO (CORE Group). Their international headquarters are located in Atlanta, Georgia and in London. CORE has diversified into an integrated education company and provides solutions to 7 States in India, 3 Caribbean nations, 20 States in the US, 40 Institutions in UK and 8 African countries. They have approximately 3,125 employees worldwide.[221] It is the listed as the fastest growing IT company in the State of Maharashta, India. It provides vocational and technology education K-12 and higher education worldwide. [222]

Harvard Promotes Wide World Common Core Standards "Teaching for Understanding Framework: It is amazing to read what is up on the Harvard website – almost the exact "newspeak" language that one hears everywhere from the supporters of Common Core: [All of the familiar mantras supporting CC are put in bold.]

As an example of how WIDE World supports educators as they align their curriculum with Common Core standards we are pleased to share a unit of study developed during our Teaching for Understanding course.

The WIDE World online professional development program is specifically tailored to generate significant improvement in student learning and engagement by:

- *Helping educators build their students' **deep understanding** and **strong content** knowledge as they prepare them for **college and career readiness***
- *Emphasizing **rigorous content** and high-order cognitive skills*
- *Integrating ongoing assessment practices into lesson planning*
- *Enabling **collaborative** local and **global communication** among educators as they share effective models of instruction*

*Here are a few of our courses that prepare and support educators as they work to cultivate the **high order thinking skills** necessary to meet the Common Core Standards:*

- *Teaching for Understanding: Focus on Student Understanding*
- *Making Thinking Visible: Building Understanding Through **Creative** Thinking*
- *Teaching to Standards with Technology*
- ***Differentiated Instruction**: Strategies for Effective Classroom Practice[223]*

Letter from a teacher in Bosnia/Herzegovina – Common Core is in their country as well: Thanks to Charlotte Iserbyt, the author of *Deliberately Dumbing Down of America*, for the following letter:

My name is Bojan Kerezovic, and I am a primary school teacher. We are now having almost all of the things - reforms, innovations and restructuring that you have warned us about... The government now shifted into the higher gear in this process of restructuring our once fine education system into workforce training... They don't even hide it from us! It is almost exactly as you have been telling us for years.

Most of teachers, parents and administrators are unaware, ignorant or simply don't care. I need all the knowledge and documentation I can get so I can protect what is left of our education system and warn other teachers, parents and administrators and, perhaps, even to write a book about that myself. It would be great if you can give me some advice about writing a book on this (where to look for proofs, documents, who to speak to, what to look for, etc).

I have downloaded the book from your pages a few years ago, marked it all up and read it a few times - it is all the same here! Since we have been under socialism a long period of time (and still we are), average citizen thinks that this is the way it should be... People here have no idea about all of this...

Common Core and UN Agenda 21 -- Mass Producing Green Global Serfs: Highlights from an article by Alex Newman from the *New American* website:

Global, Green Citizens Require a New Form of Education: Newman writes that one of the key agendas behind the deeply controversial Common Core standards is not openly spoken about. But official UN documents and statements by top world leaders reveal the clandestine plan to transform American children, and students around the globe, into what globalists refer to as "global citizens" ready for the coming "green" and "sustainable" new world order.

Of course, these plans of a "top-down, planned, and regimented society" would be completely at odds with "the U.S. Constitution, national sovereignty, individual liberty, God-given rights, Judeo-Christian values, and Western traditions."

A major component of the scheme is so-called "sustainability" and a radical UN program known as Agenda 21, encompassing virtually every facet of life "how man interacts with the environment." To prepare humanity for this green vision, however, will require a new form of "education."

UNESCO calls it "Education for Sustainable Development." On its website, UNESCO, "United Nations Education, Science and Culture Organization, "the self-styled global education agency, actually boasts of its plans. *"The UN Decade of Education for Sustainable Development (2005-2014) seeks to mobilize the educational resources of the world to help create a more sustainable future."* "There are many paths to sustainability" and they are all mentioned in the 40 chapters of Agenda 21, the official document of the 1992 Earth Summit. Education is one of these paths. *"Education alone cannot achieve a more sustainable future; however, without education and learning for sustainable development, we will not be able to reach that goal."*

Where does the Name Common Core Come From? UNESCO and Muller

1984 UNESCO published a document Developing a Common Core

UNESCO's Earth-worshipping "Earth Charter" was the central theme of Outcome Based Education and now Common Core.

The goal is to bring all educational standards under one common roof of compliance and global academic philosophical and religious sameness.

Robert Muller – wrote the "World Core Curriculum"

Former UN Assistant Sec. General, a social Marxist, who wrote *The New Genesis* with the UN as the savior of the world.

* Muller made this statement, *"In the middle of my life I discovered that the only true, objective education I had received was from the United Nations..."*

Before the term "sustainability" was in vogue, the late UN Deputy Secretary General Robert Muller, the architect of UNESCO's "World Core Curriculum," offered some insight into the purpose of UN-led, globalized pseudo-education. The goals were:

1) Group Think – Part of the Greater Whole, Collectivism: "Assist the child in becoming an integrated individual who can deal with personal experience while seeing himself as a part of the greater whole, as part of a group consciousness." Children are to no longer think of themselves as individuals, with "limited, self-centered objectives." In other words…smash individualism and notions of individual rights and replace them with collectivism.

2) Traditional education out - reading, writing, critical thinking, math, real history, actual science, and more are no longer to be taught.

3) In its place, impose "The World Core Curriculum" on humanity, a standardized Common Core education on all nations.

4) Teach a "Green World Order." What will it consist of?

Arne Duncan laid out the plan in a speech given at a "Sustainability Summit" in 2010:

- Teach the UN Sustainability Agenda through Common Core.
- Teach green citizens and prepare them to contribute to the workforce through green jobs.
- Centrally planned, UN-directed "green" economy and the "green" world order will determine what jobs citizens will have, and central planners will train them accordingly. [This was tried by Obama's green czar, Van Jones, but after his own words exposed him as a communist, his plans did not go anywhere.]
- Duncan states that other U.S. agencies and departments "have made important contributions" linking education and sustainability.
- Much of the green sustainability indoctrination will be funded with "stimulus money."
- At the global level, the World Bank, multiple UN agencies, Big Labor, Big Business, tax-funded NGOs (non-governmental organizations), and more are all involved in harmonizing and globalizing education as well.

Change the World: As Duncan made clear in a 2010 speech to UNESCO, the Obama administration's goal is to work closely with UNESCO to change the world through education:

> *Our goal for the coming year will be to work closely with global partners, including UNESCO, to promote qualitative improvements and system-strengthening and 'education is the most powerful weapon which you can use to change the world.' [a quote by Nelson Mandela]*

UNESCO Mission Statement:

...The world is looking for new ways to build peace and sustainable development...and sustain the hope of a new humanism.

UNESCO exists to bring this creative intelligence to life .... and the conditions for sustainable development must be built.

Globalization will Intensify: Arne Duncan apologized that the U.S. had not done enough in the sustainability movement but promised that efforts will be intensified.

> *Today, I promise you that we will be a committed partner in the national effort to build a more environmentally literate and responsible society.*
>
> *We at the Education Department are energized about joining these [UNESCO] leaders in their commitment to preparing today's students to participate in the green*

economy, and to be well-educated about the science of sustainability.

Restructure Human Civilization: What does Duncan, UNESCO, Common Core and Obama really mean when they talk of educating our children about "sustainability" and the "green economy"? In essence, according to UN documents and reports, the idea is to **restructure human civilization into a "centrally planned global society under the control of international institutions such as the UN"** — all under the guise of saving the planet and "sustainable development."   They say this even though they know central planning does not work and has always and everywhere produced environmental devastation in addition to human misery. But maybe **human misery** is what the global elite want for all the rest of mankind, while they can live a care free life of wealth, and live off the hard labor of the lowly minions.

Human Existence Must Dramatically Change: UN documents explain that under the "green economy" banner, literally everything about human existence must dramatically change: Lifestyles, opinions, education, health, consumption, production, agriculture, diet, law, taxation, industry, governance, and much more.

> *Transitioning to a green economy requires a fundamental shift in the way we think and act,' explains a 2012 UN report entitled "Working towards a Balanced and Inclusive Green Economy.' A more recent UN report, developed with help from Obama policy architect John Podesta, noted that the 'worldview and behavior' of every person on Earth must be 'dramatically altered.'*

What about American Traditions, Self-Government and Christianity?   Newman writes: According to UN documents, "national sovereignty, individual liberty, free markets, unalienable rights, traditional values, self-government, **Biblical Christianity**, and more **must all be pushed aside."** Wow, that certainly explains why our history text books have been so altered, with very little in them to support the idea that America is an exceptional nation, one to be proud of and that we were built on a Judeo-Christian foundation.

Preparation for Green Careers and Green Citizens: Arne Duncan stated that he would *"build the science of sustainability into the curriculum, starting in kindergarten and extending until the students graduate from high school."*

The Same Sustainability Education is Happening Across the Globe: At the 2012 UN "Conference on Sustainable Development" in Rio, chaired by an anti-American Chinese Communist, every national government represented committed to do what Duncan described. They made the following pledge called "The Future We Want":

> *We therefore resolve to improve the capacity of our education systems to prepare people to pursue sustainable development, including through enhanced teacher training, the development of curricula around sustainability, the development of training programs that prepare students for careers in fields related to sustainability.* [Of course, "we" in this pledge does not represent the people, but the "legions of bureaucrats, dictators, presidents, and mass-murderers at the UN sustainability summit — not the public."]

The Higher the Education, the Greater the Threat to Sustainability: UNESCO's website makes it abundantly clear why we see such a dumbing down of standards through Common Core, the global education plan for the world. Traditional and classical notions of education have no place in the sustainable "green" world order. In a stunning admission in the UN toolkit for global sustainable education, they explain:

> *Generally, more highly educated people, who have higher incomes, consume more resources than poorly educated people, who tend to have lower incomes. In this case, more education increases the threat to sustainability.*

Read that sentence again! **The more education people have -- threatens the elitists' vision of "sustainability."** Let there be no doubt about the real purpose of Common Core and its deliberate dumbing down of the minds of our nation's children! This is the broader globalist vision for `education, and it has been burrowing its way into U.S. schools for decades.

Do we Choose Continued Globalization, a Green Economy, and the Dumbing Down of Education or a Well-Educated Citizenry and Liberty? As Alex Newman states at the end of his article:

> *With the ongoing globalization of education under UN and Obama administration guidance, Americans are at a crossroads. One alternative is putting a stop to it all now, withdrawing from Common Core, rejecting unconstitutional federal bribes and mandates, and restoring proper education to promote a well-educated citizenry capable of critical thinking and maintaining liberty. The other option, as globalist voices have made clear, is a "green" economy — and everything that radical vision entails. **We must choose wisely.***

Chapter IX

Comments and Testimonials of Teachers, Administrators, Professors, Parents and Students against Common Core

There are so many testimonials now coming from teachers. At first it was only parents, but teachers are becoming more courageous as they see the detrimental changes happening to their students, as well as to the teaching profession, which they used to love and enjoy.

Much of Common Core Math is Developmentally Impossible for First Graders: This is coming from Marni Pehrson, who has her own blog and shares the following compelling story from a teacher who wishes to remain anonymous. The teacher she has named Mrs. Jones. It is entitled:

"Breaking the Spirits of the Best and Brightest"

"Six-year-old Latisha studied problem number two on her math test. She closed her eyes, scratched her head and then re-read the problem. Her face grew distraught, and Mrs. Jones could see tears forming in the child's eyes.

"Don't worry about that one, Latisha, just bubble it and move on," the teacher encouraged. But Latisha wouldn't continue. She stuck her thumb in her mouth and concentrated harder. "We haven't learned this yet, sweetie, move on to number three. I know you can get number three," Mrs. Jones encouraged.

The teacher knew the question was impossible for Latisha, and it wasn't because the class hadn't learned it yet. Developmentally, problem two was impossible for her entire first grade class. Mrs. Jones' mind went back thirty years to her university days where she first learned Jean Piaget's theory on cognitive development. Children's brains develop in stages and her class hadn't reached the stage where they could answer these questions.

Which number line does **not** represent 53 + 8 = ☐

Sample 1st grade question. This was answered incorrectly.

Trying to teach her 6-year-olds how to answer a fourth of the problems on this test would be a cognitive impossibility. It would be like reasoning with a newborn that a ball you showed her still exists now that you've put it behind your back. For the newborn, it no longer exists. Her brain hasn't wrapped around the concept of object permanence.

Mrs. Jones walked around the room, noticing some children haphazardly coloring in bubbles, not worrying about which answers they got right or wrong. But her brightest students were reduced to thumb-sucking and emotional upset, stuck on questions that their little minds wouldn't be able to answer for several more years.

The teacher's heart ached for her children. She wanted to help explain the cryptic questions, but there was an observer in the room, insuring she could do no such thing. The Common Core tests had to be administered without assistance.

Mrs. Jones encouraged Latisha one more time to continue to the next question and wondered how much longer she would remain a teacher in the school system. Between the endless regulations and documentation, militant demands by school authorities and now Common Core testing that was breaking the spirit of her students, she didn't know if she could take it much longer.

Many have addressed concerns over Common Core, but as I sat over my Thanksgiving dinner listening to this school teacher relate her first-hand account, I nearly broke down in tears. Why?

Because I felt sorry for little Latisha and the other children having an upsetting moment? Yes. Because I felt for the teacher being forced to work under conditions that broke her spirit? Yes. Because as a child I would have been like little Latisha, and I know what it would have done to me? Yes!

More importantly, I know the damage experiences like this inflict on people long-term. I spend my days helping the best and brightest break through fears, overwhelming, self-doubts and old programming from their past – most of it caused by small traumatic moments in childhood — like little Latisha and her thumb-sucking classmates just experienced.

In moments like this, the child's mind grasps to make sense of reality. She's trying to make sense of the world, how it works and who she is in it. Most likely, Latisha and her friends are forming opinions that act like core beliefs, driving their subconscious minds for decades unless they find some way to remove or counteract them.

Inside Latisha's mind, she's probably thinking and feeling with great emotion: 'I'm dumb, math is hard, I can't learn, Tests are impossible, I'm a failure. There's no use in trying.' One-time traumatic events coupled with strong emotion can seed beliefs like this into a child's mind until they become the person's mode of operations. Her entire life filters through those beliefs and impacts her choices and outcomes.

With Common Core, the rising generation will be repeatedly exposed to this kind of abuse throughout their school years. Whether created in ignorance of basic child development or as a malicious attack on teachers and students, the results of Common Core on children are the same – the best and brightest are being demoralized and programmed for failure at a core level."[224]

Common Core is Developmentally Bad for K-3: An article that was published in the Washington Post written by two experienced childhood teachers Edward Miller and Nancy Carlsson-Paige also state how developmentally poor the standards are for K-3 children.

They quote recent critiques of the Common Core Standards by Marion Brady and John T. Spencer who state that the process for creating the new K-12 standards involved too little research, public dialogue, or input from educators.

> *We reviewed the makeup of the committees that wrote and reviewed the Common Core Standards. In all, there were 135 people on those panels. Not a single one of them was a K-3 classroom teacher or early childhood professional. It appears that early childhood teachers and child development experts were excluded from the K-3 standards-writing process.*

When the standards were first revealed in March 2010, many early childhood educators and researchers were shocked. *"The people who wrote these standards do not appear to have any background in child development or early childhood education,"* wrote Stephanie Feeney of the University of Hawaii, chair of the Advocacy Committee of the National Association of Early Childhood Teacher Educators.

How is this affecting teachers? Dr. Carla Horwitz of the Yale Child Study Center notes that many of our most experienced and gifted teachers of young children are giving up in despair.

> *They are leaving the profession, because they can no longer do what they know will ensure learning and growth in the broadest, deepest way. The Core Standards will cause suffering, not learning, for many, many young children.*[225]

Child Psychologist Dr. Megan Koschnick States, "Common Core Standards are Developmentally Inappropriate and Cause

"Enormous Stress": At a large conference on Common Core held September 18, 2013, at Notre Dame University, Dr. Koschnick made the following remarks:

> *Why do we care if [Common Core standards] are age inappropriate? Well, you can answer that with one word – stress. Instead of thinking about what's developmentally appropriate for kindergarteners, they are thinking [college] is where we want this kindergartener to end up, so let's back track down to kindergarten and have kindergarteners work on these skills from an early age. This can cause major stress for the child because they are not prepared for this level of education.*[226]

Teachers complain Common Core-linked lessons are little more than scripts to read: According to Perry Chiaramonte, Fox News, December 8 2013:

> *A growing number of teachers say the national standards, ...have combined with pressure to "teach to the test" to take all individuality out of their craft. Some teachers told FoxNews.com the new education approach is turning their lessons into little more than **data-dispensing sessions,** and they fear their jobs are being marginalized.* [Emphasis added]

Now teachers aren't as unique. It means anyone can do it. It's like taking something done by humans and having it done by a machine." - Michael Warren, New Jersey public school history teacher

In a Washington Post blog post, a Delaware public school educator penned an anonymous letter complaining that **Common Core was taking the joy out of a profession she loved.**

> *Teaching used to be a fun job that I was deeply passionate about. I used my own creativity, mixed with a healthy dose*

of perseverance, dedication and cheerleading to encourage my students, most labeled 'special needs,' to believe in their own abilities and self-worth.

I was given a curriculum and told by my administration to teach it 'word-for-word. In a meeting with my administration, I was reprimanded with 'Don't forget, standards drive our instruction.'

Another New Jersey public school teacher who asked not to be named, said the **rigid new instructions for teaching have left her and her colleagues feeling like "robots."**

I'm unable to do projects anymore because we have so much other stuff to do that is based on the Common Core. All the teachers at my school, all we talk about is how we don't teach anymore and we feel like robots just doing what we are told to teach and can't have any creativity for the students to enjoy themselves.[227]

Principal Karl Krawitz Speaks Out Against Common Core: He is the principal at Shawnee Mission East High School, just outside of Kansas City, Kansas.

I think Common Core [is] going to set education back even further because you're dictating curriculum...what people are supposed to regurgitate on some kind of an assessment that's supposed to gauge how well kids have learned the material and how well teachers have taught the material. The reality is tests don't do either one of those things.

Krawitz, who still teaches chemistry at his school, says "Common Core proponents also assume that there's a consensus about what should be taught." But there is no consensus. Krawitz worries that Common Core will impose more testing. *"And there's a big thing people need to understand: Testing in this country is big business,"* He says the testing industry stands to make tons of money. *"To me, the real question is not who makes money. The question is, is it worth it? I would do everything I can to keep Common Core out of this school,"* he says. [228]

Carol Burris, a high school principal on Long Island, NY, She was chosen as "The Empire State's 2013 Principal of the Year," even though she has been speaking out against Common Core for two years and has written extensively about what she calls a "flawed Core implementation."

She writes that when the CC curriculum was first introduced and promoted in 2009, its creators said "unequivocally that principles of equity would be at the center of its eventual implementation. She was impressed by this and had at first supported Common Core believing that educational standards would be raised "through a rich curriculum and equitable teaching practices (that) states could voluntarily adopt."

But five years later, Burris is strongly opposed to Common Core and writes of the "growing discontent by students, parents, unions and legislators" who are complaining about a myriad of issues -- including the lack of equality and the fact that academic standards are *not* being raised.

Assessment Tests: After two years of testing, Burris has seen scores from Common Core testing in New York "drop like a stone – and achievement gaps dramatically widen."

Among Black Students and those with Disabilities it is Worse:

The percentage of black students who scored 'Below Standard' in third-grade English increased 'from 15.5 percent to a shocking 50 percent post-Common Core implementation. In seventh-grade math, black students labeled 'Below Standard' jumped 'from 16.5 percent to a staggering 70 percent.' Evidence also showed that 75 to 84 percent of students battling disabilities fell into the 'Below Standard' range too.

"College Ready" Scores Plummeting: Burris points out that if Common Core tests scores were used in New York State's "college-ready" scores that students need for graduation, the State's "four-year graduation rate would have plummeted to 35 %. It is even worse for students with disabilities (5 %); blacks (12 %), Latino (16 %) and English-language learners (7 %)." [229]

In a Letter to Dianne Ravitch, Burris Writes about the Math – "It is Disjointed, out of Sync, Wrongheaded and Destructive"

I have looked closely at the 8th grade math test sampler for NYS. The questions on topics are more difficult than the questions on the same topics on the Algebra Regents given in high school for the graduation standard. Last year only 73% of NY's students passed that Regents.

*This disjointed, out-of-sync testing program that is based on the ideals of David Coleman and others, rather than on the reality of developmental learning for a diverse body of NY students is **wrongheaded and destructive.***

Burris Writes of the Enormous Salary David Coleman is Earning and the Money he is Making off from Common Core:

Mr. Coleman earned considerable fees for his consultation to the New York State Education Department (over 60K in a few months). Last year, he went to the College Board for a starting package of 750K. The College Board is now selling CCSS prep curriculum through Springboard, and former employees are Regents Fellows developing the tests. Clearly the Common Core has been quite profitable for Mr. Coleman and others.

*However, **that profit is being made at the expense of our students.***

Three Teachers From Missouri Speaking out Against Common Core on the Glenn Beck Show with Guest Hosts Stu Burguiere and Pat Gray, 4/9/14: Susan Kimball, Tonya Pobst, and Heather Drury are all educators in the state of Missouri who have taken a stand against Common Core, a controversial new set of academic standards that critics say will "dumb down" America's children and open the door for data mining activities on students.

Pobst Believes Teachers have a Duty to Students and Parents to Speak out, but Teachers Have Lost their Freedoms:

When my students walk into my classroom, I have a responsibility not only to those students — I have a responsibility to those parents. These parents are entrusting me with their children ... and I feel it's my duty, morally and ethically, to let them know that this is how your child has to be taught now. I don't have any freedom.

Susan Kimball said Teachers are Given Scripts to Read:

The new standards are so controlled that — rather than just being given the material to teach — teachers are given "scripts" to read. If a student responds to a lesson with a certain question, teachers are told to read a corresponding line from the script. Educators have no power to alter the curriculum to cater to the needs of students who learn differently.

Heather Drury said Parents are Unable to Help their Children or Examine What they Are Learning:

Because of the radically different way subjects like math are being taught — parents will be unable to help their children, leaving America's youth completely dependent on the state for their education. It's trying to keep parents kind of out of the loop of what's going on in our schools. That's very concerning to me.

Kimball added: *"They say they're not, but they're changing our history and I've seen some examples of that. And that scares me to death, to be honest."*

All three teachers are worried that their jobs are at risk because they are speaking out, but they hope their stand will encourage other teachers to voice their concerns, as well.

Georgia Teacher Quits but Posts a Letter to her Students Explaining Why She Left - Because of Common Core: The following letter was posted on Dianne Ravitch's blog on November 14, 2013. It is from Meg Norris, a certified seventh-grade teacher in Georgia and a doctoral candidate. After 18 months of trying out Common Core in her classroom, she could no longer believe in or go along with "what she was mandated to do." She saw her once happy students become frustrated and upset struggling with the Common Core standards that were not written by teachers and written in ways "far beyond the students' understanding."

She finally felt compelled to walk away from her dream job of teaching to fight against the implementation of Common Core and its high stakes, standardized testing. She is now banned from her former school because of her stance. This is the letter that Meg Norris wrote to her students and which she posted online for all to read and share [Emphasis added].

"To My Students:
I did not return to the classroom this year and I want to apologize. I am truly sorry for having left you. It was the hardest decisions I have ever made. I want you to understand why I left. It had nothing to do with you. I still love you and believe in you. You are still amazing and you can do anything you want to do. I did not give up on you. I left to fight for you.

I saw you struggling with Common Core skills. Even with the new curriculum from the district, no matter how I broke it down for you I could see you didn't understand. I saw the frustration on your faces. And when time ran out and we had to take the county's test (on the county's schedule), **I saw the tears roll from your eyes. You failed. I saw you missing school more days than normal. I saw you with long sleeves covering up the cutting scars on your arms. I saw how the sparkle in your eyes dimmed. I saw the small bald spot on your head where you had pulled out your hair.** *And it wasn't just in my class.* **You hated going to math. You came early every day for homework help, but it didn't make any difference. You still could not understand.**

I want you to know none of this is your fault. It is not you. I know the school, the county and the state call it "rigor." That is a horrible word. Look it up in the dictionary for me. **Rigor is for dead people. You are not failing because it is too hard. You are not failing because you are not working hard enough. You are not failing because of your teachers. You are failing because Common Core was not written by teachers. Common Core was not written to help you.** *Let me explain why this hurts you so much.*

Your brain, as it develops, can only learn certain things at certain times. **Common Core is trying to force you to learn things your brain is not ready to learn.** *Researchers for decades have* *found that the things Common Core requires you to do are impossible until you reach high school, at the earliest. No matter what your teachers do to get you to learn it, you aren't going to be able to. There is nothing wrong with you. Your brain was designed perfectly. Common Core standards were not.*

Common Core was written by businessmen trying to make money off of you. You and your learning are a grand experiment in corporate profits. *If you fail at school, if your teachers fail to teach you, these corporations can sell more books, workbooks, tests, software and technology to schools and even to your parents to try at home. None of it will work. These same businessmen want to convince states to let them and their companies take over your schools. Your parent's tax dollars would then go to these companies.* **Over $600 billion is spent on education every year in this country. This money should go to your education, not to private companies.** *It is very similar to what was done to prisons several years ago.*

Common Core is the first time in the history of this country that a privately written and copyrighted plan has become public policy. There is no research to back it and it has never been tested. *Politicians are pushing it because these corporations are giving them money to push it.*

When I left I met with members of your Board of Education and told them what was happening. They ignored me. I went to the local newspaper and they ignored me too. When I spoke to the state Senate education committee they dismissed me as a political nut job. When I came back to chaperone your fall dance I was told I was "no longer one of you" and I could not come in because of my position on Common Core. Ghandi once said, "First they ignore you, then they ridicule you, then they fight you, and then you win." **We will win. We will win for you and every student after you. This is not political. This is for the future leaders of our country. These corporations don't want to teach you how to think.**

It is time for you to talk to your parents. Help them understand that **opting you out of state testing will protect your personal information as well as stop the data that is being used to unfairly judge you and your teachers.** *Schools where more than 80% of kids* *have been opted out are cancelling these stressful tests that measure nothing. There is a new test coming to replace the CRCT, which is why politicians like Governor Deal and Superintendent Barge want to keep Common Core.* **Have your parents demand a portfolio of your work be kept and that your hard work be used to decide if you should go on to the next grade, not a random test.** *Any test not written by and graded by your teachers should never be allowed in the classroom.*

Please do not worry about me. I am strong and people have called me worse names and banned me from much better places. **Standing up for what is right is not always the easy thing. I knew that when I left my classroom. I have 32,000 other teachers from all over the country who are standing with me. I have education experts and child psychologists standing with me. I have politicians standing with me. I have famous authors standing with me. And the group is growing.**

Just this week I got an email from Judy Blume, author of famous children's classics like Tales of a Fourth Grade Nothing, Blubber, Are You There God, It's Me Margaret, Forever, and Tiger Eyes. She shared with me that she was a horrible test-taker. She is very grateful that she is not in school taking the kinds of tests you are taking. Can you imagine how horrible it would be if our favorite authors gave up because they could not do well on standardized tests that meant nothing? I don't want to find out.

Talk to your parents and let them know what is happening in your classrooms. Every time you take a test or a survey, tell your parents. Be brave and keep making me proud. You can be anything you want to be. I am always here for you."
Mrs. Meg Norris, Ed.S. 7th Grade (former) teacher Georgia[230]

Statement by a Teacher in Rhode Island Who Resigned on You Tube: Stephen Round was not allowed to speak at a school board meeting where he wanted to resign publicly, so he decided to do it on You Tube. Here are some of the statements he made and the reasons for his resignation:

Rather than creating lifelong learners, our new goal is to create good test-takers. Rather than being the recipients of a rewarding and enjoyable educational experience, our students are now...experiencing a confining and demeaning education...on the misguided notions of 'educrats.'

He quit his secure $70,000-per-year plus benefits teaching job and stated he would rather tutor kids *"than be part of a system that is diametrically opposed to everything I believe education should be." He then announced, "I've had it. I quit!"*

Stephen Round, 13-year elementary school teacher at Providence School District, Rhode Island, (spoken on a You Tube video)[231]

Wyoming Teacher Received a Gag Order from her School that She could not Speak about Common Core: by Shane Vander Hart, April 24, 2013 [Name withheld to protect privacy and career]

I am currently a teacher in a smaller district in Wyoming. I attended a Wyoming Department of Education (WDE) training for the ELA Common Core Standards in July, prior to starting the 2012/2013 school year. I came to this training knowing only that Wyoming, along with 45 others states were choosing to adopt the standards fully by 2015.

The WDE presenters were suggesting we use some of the methods I had been trained to use in Utah, and had previously used when I taught there. Since our state and district benchmarks would not be fully aligned with textbooks, curriculum, and testing until 2015, I wanted to get a head start.

I looked into what my former colleagues were doing in Utah. This is when I discovered the movement that Three Moms Against Common Core had started that Christel Swasey has been a HUGE part of. I was FLOORED! I had no idea that there was a different train of thought, let alone a movement against the implementation of Common Core.

This piqued my curiosity and caused me to do some researching. I quickly realized how ignorant I really was about our country's education system and how the Department of Education affects what happens in our schools. It was truly ignorance on my part, as I only saw how things happened on a local level and never really thought about the effects of national legislation affecting a small town in Wyoming.

The more I researched the more I become aware of how much I didn't know! I also began forming my own opinions about how this could potentially limit local voices from parents, teachers, and administrators. I chose to share my research and opinions with my administrator and a few close colleagues privately. I emailed links to the research I'd done, along with my views on what is happening and how it could potentially affect us as parents, and teachers.

After the email was sent I met one-on-one with my administrator, where we discussed common core and the research I had done and continue to do. Basically, I left that meeting knowing that he disagreed with what my opinion is. However, I left with the feeling that we would agree to disagree. He also pointed out the fact that our state and district would be moving forward with common core and I would need to be on board with it.

The next day I was approached by a fellow teacher whom I'd shared my concerns with. They asked if I would be comfortable sharing those same concerns during a grade level meeting, as others were curious. I agreed to do so. During the meeting I spoke of several movements in various states that are pushing to repeal the adoption of common core, or at least give more time to consider it. I spoke of being shocked that I was ignorant of any controversy surrounding the Common Core. I shared my feelings, concerns and opinions. I suggested they become aware that there are two sides to this and to be prepared to have an opinion. I pointed out that questions could come from concerned parents or others in the community. I also shared that my main concern was with the changes to data privacy and losing local control.

When I was finishing my administrator said that there would be no more emailing, or talking about the common core amongst the staff. There was a finality to his tone and the meeting was quickly over at that point.

I then received an email from my administrator reminding me of our district policy of not using school resources to push political concerns or agendas. He also stated that there was to be no more discussion about common core unless it was on an "educational" basis between staff members.

Ironically, I had several teachers contact me outside of school that same day, to say they were shocked at my administrator's tone. They feel I was being genuine in sharing information that was previously unknown and could potentially affect educators. Several staff member have also approached me saying that they are grateful for this information and are now researching it on their own.

The question being asked in my school now is...Why can't educators do what they do best? Research, question, inform?? Isn't it better to question and discuss things, even if we don't agree on them as to find what is best for the children we have been entrusted with? Should we turn a blind eye, and be lead like sheep off the cliff?

What is wrong with forming an opinion, discussing it, whether we agree with each other or not? Why stifle this? I don't think he realized that he just gave fuel to what was once a single voice!

At this point my union representatives are looking into this as a form of suppressing free speech. I also have an appointment set up to meet with our district's superintendent so that I may better understand the position our district is going to take on this. At this point the staff at my school believe they will be reprimanded if they speak with parents concerning common core for something other than its educational use.[232]

In the summer of 2013, this courageous teacher resigned from her teaching position so she could speak out. She is now leading a group to fight Common Core in Wyoming. Her name is Christy Hooley. The group she has organized is **Wyoming Against Common Core.** She has her own blog to keep people alerted as to what is going on.[233]

Parents Speaking Out Against Common Core: There are thousands of anti-Common Core comments by parents that one can read on face book posts across the nation. I recommend "Parents and Teachers Against Common Core Standards," started by Angela Weinsinger, who at the time she started the site was serving as the President of her school board, Travis Unified School District, located on the Travis Air Force Base in California. She now has over 18,000 people who have joined her site.

Parents are Dropping out and Homeschooling Because of Common Core: WICHITA, Kan. -- Just mention the Common Core and you'll get a reaction from parents Justin and Jennifer Dahlmann. "We both get a little tight in the chest," Justin said.

The Dahlmanns pulled their older girls out of their private school because of Common Core. The girls were beginning to struggle in school was no longer enjoyable for them. The parents didn't know why and began to do their own research on the new curriculum and found out how "overbearing it was." They also did not like that parents had been kept in the dark as to what was happening.

"The standards are making education more confusing rather than helping students to think more critically, as supporters claim." The Dahlmanns told the school administrators "As soon as you drop the standards, we'll put our kids right back in there'"

The Dahlmanns say from their research they believe that the standards have essentially come from the federal government, that in order to get Race to the Top money or No Child Left Behind waivers, States had to implement a new set of standards in each State that signed on. "The only standards they [the federal government] would accept are Common Core standards."

For the Dahlmanns, homeschooling their children is, in essence, a form of protest of the "overbearing" standards they believe are coming from "the top down."

They say what concerns them the most is that most parents have been told little, if anything, about the standards. They hope no matter the conclusion parents reach, they at least will take a closer look and ask questions about what their children are being taught.

"If this does nothing more than wake people up to becoming more involved with their children, that's great," Justin said. Absolutely, parents need to become more involved in this!"[234]

Common Core is expecting WWII historical interpretation from young people who know so little about it:

Bunch of nonsense!!! My daughter read a small book on Japanese interment and she was asked to write why this happened. The answer her teacher gave as an example was way different from one I would give.

You can't compare the standards of the 1940's to today's standards. It is all about interpretation. How can you grade an interpretation in middle school about WWII when you have only read a 4-page paper? In part, history is taught so we won't make the same mistakes as in the past.

Math is taught in such a difficult way, that I have to re-teach her so that she understands. End results the same, but far less steps. Hopefully parents will get involved in their children's homework, so they can make intelligent decisions regarding Common Core. [posted by guest]

Common Core is like a brightly tied up box with sinister lies inside and so much more!

*You know what? The more I looked into it, like all things that are **sinister**, it's packed in a nice, little box with a pretty little bow on top, but once you untie the bow, and start unpacking these so-called federal educational standards, you realize it's **all a pack of a lies**.*

It's like a magician: In the right hand, he's holding these sparkling uniform standards that will purportedly level the playing field. But in his left hand and behind his back, he's holding the other components of this total education initiative.

If it were simply standards, it would just be unconstitutional, but not horrible. But it's so much more, and it's the so much more that is truly horrible.

The government will tell you there is no central database that is part-and-parcel of Common Core, but that's an outright lie. They're tracking over 400 data points, from parents' political and religious affiliations to how much money they make, what the child eats, behaviors and attitudes toward sex...everything.

Of course it's all tied to this administration giving out money if you implement it. Bribery in its truest form, and another way to collect data on its citizens. [Posted by Ben]

Common Core Math is a Failed Costly System – Home School Using Saxon Math:

Unfortunately, this failed system will cost the taxpayers of Oklahoma (and all other Common Core states) more than they'll need to pay to generate early grade mathematics results!

... all one has to do is compare homeschool mathematics grades to those of public schools. Though status quo educators will tell you it's because homeschool students get much more attention than those in a regular public school classroom, I disagree.

Most homeschools use SAXON mathematics programs. These programs have decades of proven results in the classrooms in which they are used. Why do we not use these in public schools today - opting instead for perennially FAILED programs like Everyday Math? Parents and taxpayers need an answer to this question TODAY!

A Post From another Math Teacher Who Loathes Common Core- May 12, 2014

I will be straight up and say I loathe Common Core. I teach high school math and Common Core is horrible. We didn't need to revamp how we teach math. I keep hearing that we need to have more word problems and that that is what CC will do. Will it didn't work.

I have never had such a miserable group of Freshman. Miserable, nervous, anxious and terrified about failing. Kids come in to retest, retest, and retest some more. They are learning how to retest, but not learning the actual math.

When CC was implemented, we lost one-quarter of our basic Algebra. One-quarter of a basic beginning language was removed. We were given one day to "review" basic beginning operations that usually take a full 2 weeks as most students coming in to high school are clueless about beginning basics.

This is not teaching. Everything is data driven, and not student centered.

Teachers are leaving the profession in droves. That is not discussed in the media at all. Common Core is ridiculous and criminal in its course content. Students are less informed and are uneducated to even the previous standards before Common Core.

I urge teachers and parents to work to remove Common Core in their state and bring education under the control of parents and school boards.

Signed lbgage

Expert Mathematician and Engineer Ze'ev Wurman Believes Common Core Marks the Cessation of Education Improvement in the USA: Wurman is a prominent software architect, electrical engineer and longtime math advisory expert in California and Washington, D.C. He believes Common Core delays math proficiency: with addition and subtraction until 4th grade; with basic multiplication until 5th grade, and skimps on logarithms, math induction, parametric equations and trigonometry at the high school level. He states:

> *I believe the Common Core marks the cessation of educational standards improvement in the United States. No state has any reason left to aspire for first-rate standards, as all states will be judged by the same mediocre national benchmark enforced by the federal government.*
>
> *Moreover, there are organizations that have reasons to work for lower and less-demanding standards, specifically teachers unions and professional teacher organizations. While they may not admit it, they have a vested interest in lowering the accountability bar for their members...This will be done in the name of 'critical thinking' and '21st-century' skills, and in faraway Washington, D.C., well beyond the reach of parents and most states and employers.*[235]

Specifics Exposing Common Core – Mercedes Schneider, a High School English teacher and outspoken critic of Common Core, who has her own blog writes to NEA President to tell him all that is wrong with Common Core "Let's Help NEA's Dennis Van Roekel Forsake His Common Core "Guessing," January 18, 2014.

Mercedes is responding to an interview with Dennis Van Roekel, the President of the NEA, National Education Association, in the Jan. 14 *Education Week* , where Van Roekel says that he has yet to hear anyone offer specific disagreements or a better alternative to Common Core; so Mercedes takes on that challenge and writes an excellent letter to him. She cites the following as a specific standard that needs changing:

> *By the end of grade 10, read and comprehend literary nonfiction at the high end of the grades 9-10 text complexity band independently and proficiently.*

Mercedes writes that this standard is bad for the following reasons: It "completely ignores how students develop the prior knowledge necessary in order to critically approach texts." It sounds good that a teacher should be able to hand a "high end" text over to her students and have them "comprehend…independently and proficiently." But in reality, the students need assistance. Why? Because they are 15, and the teacher is much older and experienced. "They learn by interacting with me as I broaden their exposure to the world via my own."

> *In short, this standard ignores the fact that students learn via active and dynamic relationship with their teachers. The building of a student's knowledge base involves continuous exchange between teacher and student. It also requires a teacher's expert opinion to determine when and to what degree a student is able to handle a text on his or her own.*

> ***Moreover, the standard advocates that "one size fits all,"** that all of my students are automatons who will be on grade level with reading when they arrive in my classroom and that I should be able to move them forward at the same rate, a rate "equaling" one year of reading comprehension. **This standard assumes sameness.***

Mercedes also tells Mr. Van Roekel, that what she has written is not her "best guess." It is from two decades of classroom experience, with 13 of those years spent teaching high school English.

What else is missing from the Standards? **The entire democratic process** – "CCSS is as "top-down" as it gets, and with a dash of "facilitated democracy" to offer pseudo-legitimacy." Teachers had very little input and were never asked if "CCSS should happen in the first place.

She then gives him a copy of an anti-CCSS resolution that her school St. Tammy Parish in Louisiana, drafted in October 2013. It says the following:

*WHEREAS, our belief is that **Common Core State Standards do not justify the disruption to instruction, accountability, professional development and teacher preparation that follows adoption of these standards and PARCC** assessments in our system; and **we further believe that the Guaranteed Curriculum, state approved, adopted and implemented in the St. Tammany Parish Public School System meets the needs of every child, every day in St. Tammany Parish.** [Emphasis added.]*

Mercedes gives other good arguments against the standards and then states why Van Roekel and the NEA are supporting them: *"The union wanted to create these lessons"... after it received $3.8 million from Gates in July 2013– the same month that NEA formally endorsed CCSS."*

She challenges her fellow teachers also to respond to Van Roekel and express all the "specifics" of what they do not like about Common Core. "Van Roekel needs us, American teachers. What he will choose to do with our words is anyone's "guess."[236]

Rethinking Schools, Volume 28 No.2 - Winter 2013/14
The Problems with the Common Core
by English Professor Emerita Dr. Sandra Stotsky

This is a revised version of a talk on the Common Core State Standards (CCSS) delivered in Portland, Oregon, Sept. 20, 2013. The CCSS have been adopted by 46 states and are currently being implemented in school districts throughout the United States. These changes include:

- *A 10-year experiment in the use of federally mandated standards and tests called No Child Left Behind (NCLB) that has been almost universally acknowledged as a failure.*
- *The adoption of **test-based teacher evaluation frameworks** in dozens of states, largely as a result of federal mandates.*

- *Multiple rounds of budget cuts and layoffs that have left 34 of the 50 states providing less funding for education than they did five years ago, and **the elimination of more than 300,000 teaching positions.***
- *A **wave of privatization** that has increased the number of publicly funded but privately run charter schools **by 50 percent,** while nearly **4,000 public schools have been closed** in the same period.*
- *An appalling **increase in the inequality and child poverty** surrounding our schools, categories in which the United States leads the world and that tell us far more about the source of our educational problems than the uneven quality of state curriculum standards.*
- ***A dramatic increase in the cost and debt burden of college access.***
- ***A massively well-financed campaign of billionaires and politically powerful advocacy organizations that seeks to replace our current system of public education**—which, for all its many flaws, is probably the most democratic institution we have and one that has done far more to address inequality, offer hope, and provide opportunity than the country's financial, economic, political, and media institutions—with a **market-based, non-unionized, privately managed system.**[237]*

Catholic Professors Sign a Letter to U.S. Catholic Bishops Denouncing the Common Core State Standards: The letter was sent to more than 100 dioceses and state that Common Core is doing "a grave disservice to Catholic education" and they urge the bishops to ignore the standards or to give them up.

The letter was written by Law Professor Gerard V. Bradley at the University of Notre Dame, with 132 professors from various disciplines and institutions signing on.

The letter states that the standards are "contrary to tradition and academic studies on reading and human formation," and it accuses Core proponents of seeking to "transform 'literacy' into a 'critical' skill set, at the expense of sustained and heartfelt encounters with great works of literature. It calls Common Core "a recipe for standardized workforce preparation" and cites criticism of the standards by James Milgram, professor emeritus of mathematics at Stanford University, and Sandra Stotsky, professor emerita of education at the University of Arkansas – "saying the standards aren't strong enough to prepare students for even minimal college work. The full text of the letter can be found posted on the *Washington Post* blog, Nov. 2, 2013.[238]

Foreign Exchange Student from Denmark Speaks out Against Common Core from What She has Seen in Her High School in Idaho: Mathilde Vold-by-ravn, age 17 from Aarhus, Denmark, attended school for the year 2013-14 in a small farming community in Idaho. The town's name has been withheld at request of her host family. A fellow Eagle Forum member who lives close by had heard how unhappy Mathilde was with her American education experience and asked her if I could interview her for my book. She was happy to share her experience with me. In a phone interview, in February, 2014, she reported the following about her year in America, comparing her education here to what she had back in Denmark, and specifically speaking out against Common Core:

Mathilde was told before she came to America to expect that the American schools would be behind Denmark in education. So she expected it to be easy, "but not this easy!" she said. In Denmark she was used to having 3-4 hours of homework a night; here in America, she hardly has any.

Her parents are teachers in Denmark. She says that she calls them almost every night to report on the strange education she is experiencing in her high school in America.

She said that the majority of the boys in the high school are just there to be able to play sports. That seems to be all that they care about. The girls are not too different. No one seems to be too interested in college.

Mathilde said that for English Literature, the Common Core standards are supposed to cover 15 in the junior year, but as of February, they had only covered three of the standards. She said the standards are written in crazy sounding language with words that the teachers do not even understand.

The students had to take a test at the beginning of the school year and one at the end of the semester to show how much they had improved. The students knew nothing about the subject for the beginning test. She thought it was a complete waste of time, effort and energy. Of course, there would be some improvement made if you knew nothing about the subject to begin with. The students were told that there was 80-90% improvement, but no one ever received a test back to verify that. She thinks it is very deceptive!

She was taking Algebra II but dropped out of it, because she had already had it in Denmark, and how it is taught under CC is so confusing that most kids now hate math. Common Core is making the kids so frustrated. They can't wait to get out of school.

She said that some kids do absolutely nothing, hardly ever turn in an assignment and yet still pass the class. Why is that allowed? The teachers are afraid to give the kids a bad grade because that makes them [the teachers] look bad, and it is a bad reflection on the school and also their standing in the community, so they let the students slide by with very little work done.

For the English Literature book reports that the kids are supposed to give every month, the kids just pick a short story. If they don't come to class prepared to report on it, then they can just stand up and read the book cover and get a grade for their book report.

The kids all got free iPads from the school supposedly to do their homework on and to use to take the tests. The kids just took them home and put lots of games and videos on them. They use them in class and play their games or watch videos on them when they are supposed to be doing assignments.

It is also very easy to cheat on the tests given on iPads. The teacher just sits at her desk and does not see what is going on. If the student does not do well on a test, he can retake it and retake it until he gets a good grade. One student retook a history test 5 times.

Mathilde said the American history text book that the school is using is not accurate and history has been watered down. There is nothing in it about the Founding Fathers, the Constitution, or the Bill of Rights. One of the assignments was to write about three names or events from World War II. It was very hard for most of the students. One student wrote about Stalin, Hitler and couldn't think of another person, so he included Picasso.

She had amazing teachers back in Denmark, and school was very challenging and exciting. But that was not her experience here. The family she has been staying with she really likes, and she has met lots of nice people in the little town she was in, but as far as education has gone, it has not been her best experience.

Fortunately, she already had graduated from high school last year at age 16, so she will not have to play catchup, but she will have to work extra hard this summer to be ready to start college in the fall.

What she has heard of Common Core is that it will be the plan for the whole world, being pushed through UNESCO and the United Nations. She is afraid she will find it back in Denmark as well, and if she does she will speak out against it as well there. She wears a "NO to Common Core" button to school.

One would like to think that her high school is an isolated case, but as has been written about in Chapter II under "cheating," the NCLB system, now coupled with Common Core entices teachers and administrators to dumb down assignments and tests and to fudge on grades to save their jobs and the school's future. It is happening in many schools across our nation.

What a sad state of affairs the education in America is now in – as the next chapter portrays – it is a sinking ship!

The Hidden Cs of Common Core

Chapter X

Chronological History of Education Leading to Common Core

The History of Progressive Education in America

How we Got to Where We are – from a Ship of Liberty to our Sinking Ship of Education

There is a story of a U.S. naval ship in the early days of our nation that was lost at sea in a terrible stormy night. The captain and admiral on board saw a distant light and heard a faint voice over the roar of the waves saying, "Turn your ship ten degrees starboard."

The admiral said to the captain, "The nerve of the captain of that ship telling us to turn ours. Who does he think he is? You get on the megaphone and tell him to turn his ship."

So the captain did. "You turn your ship ten degrees starboard." There was silence. Then again they heard the voice a little louder this time again saying, "Turn your ship ten degrees starboard."

This time the admiral got on the megaphone and said, "This is the admiral of the United States Navy. Who do you think you are telling us to turn our ship?"

They heard the voice answer back. "This is seaman, Jim Jones. My ship is the light house. You turn your ship at once or you will be crashed on the rocks of the shore."

Now the admiral and captain swallowed their pride, heeded the warning, and quickly turned their ship in the nick of time and escaped from being crashed.

The moral to this story is that it does not really matter if you hold a lofty title like an admiral, or captain or have a PhD or master's degree. If we see and understand the dangers that we are in, then we need to become a voice of warning, like the young man in the lighthouse, become aware, informed, and active to try to turn our ship of education around before it is too late.

There are many hardworking, dedicated, diligent teachers and administrators who also share this same concern about the state of education today. The purpose of this chapter is to not to criticize educators but to expose the system under which they now have to teach and where all the changes in education are coming from.

What are the danger signs:

• The top one percent of U.S. students (all advanced placement) continue to place last or next to last in international testing in science and math with other leading industrial nations, **yet U.S. students rate themselves the highest in self-esteem.** (*The Conspiracy of Ignorance,* Martin L. Gross, 1999.)

• **In 1993, 59%** of California high school graduates entering California State Universities had to take remedial English and math. Twenty-one years later – **2014, it is now 90%** who require remedial math and 75% who require remedial English.[239] We have yet to see what the statistics will be because of Common Core. But, of course, the entire college courses of math and English are to be aligned to Common Core (or dumbed down), if David Coleman, President of the College Board, has his way, so no one will be able to tell just how bad things are.

• **"American college students feel good about themselves, but they can't read or write - and they're rude and apathetic."** Linda K. Ross, English teacher at Santa Rosa Junior College as reported in the *Press Democrat. Nov. 3, 1996* A similar statement was made by Henry H. Bauer, a university chemistry professor that college students seem to care less about studying or getting good grades and feel an entitlement that the professors must pass them anyway.[240]

• **In 2010, it was reported "The illiteracy rate for prison-inmates is 75%; 85 % of all juveniles** who come into contact with the juvenile court system are functionally illiterate."[241]

• **"The high school dropout rate of Hispanics (30%)** is the highest of any ethnic group, four times that of whites, three times that of Blacks, and it has not budged since bilingual education began." (*U.S. News and World Report*, Sept. 25,1996)

• **1999 figures show the numbers have not improved among Hispanics**. Only 55% of Hispanics graduate from high school, blacks - 73%, and whites -82% (Forbes.Com, "Diploma Missing," by Peter Brinelow, May 28, 2001)

• **By 2011, dropout rate of blacks in California had risen also to 30%** "...the dropout rates also illustrate that African American students (30.1 percent) and English learners (31.1 percent) are more likely to drop out than their peers."[242]

• **"The high school diploma has been made nearly worthless, since it no longer guarantees any particular level of educational achievement. The college degree is losing its value**. A year after graduation, 44 percent of graduates are in jobs that don't require a four-year degree. That should be no surprise: Many have a college degree without having a college education." Joanne Jacobs, "College degree lite," *Press Democrat*, Feb. 23, 1995

How has our education ship gotten so off course? In the early 1900s, our nation was praised around the world for our well-educated citizens. Literacy rates were in the nineties. We had brilliant scientists and inventions and great advances in our standard of living.

What has caused such a big difference? **Did this happen by chance or was it planned?** To answer this question, this chapter will write of five things: I) A glimpse into the educational philosophy back when our founding fathers established our nation and wrote the Constitution and what our early schools were like. II) What has caused this philosophy to slowly change? III) The people involved in that change. IV) The new terminology and methods that are running our schools and what effect they have had. V) What the legislation was that has caused tremendous changes in our schools.

I. What the ship of education used to be like when our nation was first founded and what the education philosophy was governing our schools:
• **There were simple schools that were mostly religious academies, or no schools at all.** Our Founding Fathers were home-schooled or had private tutors. Later small simple schools were begun with religious instruction. The Bible was the first grade primer. The *New England Primer* was published in 1690 and used until the early 1900s. It was based on *the Bible*. For example, in teaching the alphabet, the words were: "A is for the apple that Adam and Eve ate in the Garden of Eden."

As an example of the part religion was intended to play in our nation, read what the Northwest Ordinance of 1787 stated, Article 3:

> *"Religion, morality, and knowledge being necessary to good government and the happiness of mankind, schools and the means of education shall forever be encouraged to teach them."* [243]

• **Traditional Definition of Education**: The following was what education was all about and what its objectives were: *"The imparting to the next generation time-honored truths, facts,* *knowledge, culture, traditions and morality based on Judeo-Christian principles that will help children live happy, useful, productive lives."* [Notice there is no mention of children being trained for one certain career.]

• **Liberal Arts Education:** The curriculum was a wide, broad, strong foundation that prepared students to be ready and able to choose whatever career they would like. They were proficient in English, science, math, history, geography, several foreign languages (including Latin and Greek), arts, music, and sports.

• **Governing the ship was the Tenth Amendment to the U.S. Constitution, which states that anything not mentioned in the Constitution was to be left to the States.** Education was one of those items. It was not to be touched by any federal agency or under federal control. Education was left under state or local control, because education was a family decision, left under parental rights.

• **The United States Flag of liberty** was flying on the mast. Children were taught the U.S. Constitution, Bill of Rights, and patriotism. They were proud to be Americans. Our founding fathers recognized that it is only through being well educated in truths, correct principles, knowing their own history and form of government that the people of our nation could maintain their freedoms and be self-governing.

• **True academic basics** were taught with the "Three R's- Reading, Writing, and 'Rithmctic," plus a wide range of the classics, art, Latin, French, and other foreign languages. Students were taught by phonics and were so literate, they were capable of reading the Bible in the first grade.

• **Very high literacy rates**: The United States became known for its high literacy rates that continued until 1910. For ages 10 –14, only 1 in 1,000 could not read in 10 States. In the worst States it was 22 out of 1,000. (U.S. Bureau of Education, 1910.)

Result: Education worked. America had the highest literacy rate of any nation. The goal of education was achieved. We did have happy, useful, productive, moral and free Americans, who did live by the Golden Rule and by the Ten Commandments.

II. What Caused the Original Education Philosophy to Change?

How do you change a free, independent nation into a place where children now belong to the community, to the State, to the supreme leader or to the collective? You slowly gain control of the minds of the young preschoolers, the elementary school children, the high school children and the university students - the next generations. What caused these changes?

• **1789-1799 The French Revolution had taken place - a socialist revolution.** It was not fought for the same reasons as the American Revolution. Its purpose was to destroy religion and to spread socialism. They succeeded. The socialist philosophy spread through France, Germany, and the rest of Europe. It greatly affected the education system. In Germany, it was mostly found in Prussia and the Frankfurt School.

• **The Prussian Definition of Education: "*Parens Patria*"** which is Latin for "The father land is the parents, children belong to the state." Schools were all centralized under a powerful State government. The purpose of the State schooling was not intellectual training but the conditioning of children to "obedience, subordination, and collective life." Whole ideas were broken into fragmented "subjects," and school days were divided into fixed periods "so that self-motivation to learn would be muted by ceaseless interruptions." The goal was to produce students who would be: 1) obedient soldiers for the army 2) obedient workers for mines, factories, and farms 3) well-subordinated civil servants, trained in their functions 4) well-subordinated clerks for industry 5) citizens who thought alike on mass issues 6) national uniformity in thought, word, and deed."

• **What kind of teachers does such a system require?** "Where the whole tendency of education is to create obedience, **all teachers must be pliant tools of government."** John Taylor Gatto [244]

• **What kind of government works best with such a system of education? A dictatorship**. People are already used to being told everything they should think and do. Under such an all-powerful state-run, state-controlled system of education, it was very easy for a dictator such as Hitler to gain total control over education and impose his Nazi propaganda, as was stated by him in the following:

When an opponent declares, 'I will not come over to your side, 'I calmly say, "Your child belongs to us already. What are you? You will pass on. Your descendants, however, now stand in the new camp. In a short time they will know nothing else but this new community.(Given in a speech in 1933) [245]

III. The People and Dates involved in Transforming American Education into Progressive / Socialist Ed:

• **1796-1859 – Horace Mann – Influenced by the Prussian System and Spread it to America**: Horace Mann, known as the Father of Public Education, was also one of the early fathers of the "progressive, or socialist" education. He visited Prussia in the summer of 1843 and came back to report in glowing writings about how wonderful the Prussian system was.[246] Mann served in the State legislature of Massachusetts and became the secretary for the Massachusetts Board of Education in 1837. He started the first public school and the first state-controlled and financed teacher college (Normal School) in Lexington, Massachusetts, to prepare teachers with the proper world socialist view. [247]

• **1844-1924 Stanley Hall**, a student of Horace Mann. He also traveled to Germany (in 1879) and studied in Berlin and Leipzig (Prussia) and came back a convinced atheist and evolutionist. He was the most popular speaker at NEA conventions and helped create the NEA Child Study department, the beginning of experimental psychology labs on children. In 1883, he began the first formal psychological labs on children at John Hopkins University. "Hall objected vehemently to the emphasis on teaching traditional subjects, e.g., Latin, mathematics, science and history, in high school, arguing instead that high school should focus more on the education of adolescents than on preparing students for college."[248]

• **1874-1949 Edward L. Thorndike** taught psychology at Columbia's Teachers College for 37 years. He carried the experimental work on animal behavior and child behavior much further. He developed and formulated "behavioral psychology" – the psychological basis for progressive education. He wrote:

> *The best way with children may often be, in the pompous words of an animal trainer, 'to arrange everything in connection with the trick so that the animal will be compelled by the laws of his own nature to perform it.'*

He had very little regard for man as anything other than an animal. *"Human nature is simply a mass of original tendencies that can be exploited for good or bad, depending on what learning takes place."* [249]

• **Evolution** had a big influence on these early American socialists and on education. As Samuel Blumenfeld wrote:

> *Evolution is at the very basis of modern public education where the child is taught that he is an animal linked by evolution to monkeys. His school materials have been designed to teach him as an animal with stimuli-response techniques which are now universally used throughout American education. So we ought not to be surprised when students act like animals and call their school 'The Zoo.'* [250]

• **1894-1930 John Dewey,** a student of Stanley Hall, formulated the social aims of progressive education, of which he is called its "Father." He was part of the faculty at Columbia Teacher College in New York City from 1904 to 1930. Prior to that he had been the head of the philosophy, psychology, and education department at the University of Chicago, 1894-1904, where he created his famous "Obligatory School," where he tested certain philosophical and psychological ideas on real live children. His purpose was to show how education could be reformed *"to create little socialists instead of little capitalists"* who, would eventually change America's economic system. He also was an atheist and helped write the Humanist Manifesto that taught atheism.

- **1891-1937 Antonio Gramsci,** Italian Communist, who was imprisoned in Italy under Mussolini, had great influence also on promoting socialist/communist ideals in American public schools. Through letters that he wrote from prison, his followers began implementing what he called "the long march through culture." He suggested that cultural Marxism could be sold by "capturing the schools, the churches, the culture and media."
- **Education Mafia:** Columbia University and its Teacher College became the undisputed training center for "progressive education." Its graduates were then placed in strategic prominent positions as the heads of teacher colleges, universities, superintendents of schools across the nation where they made sure only the "progressive," socialist philosophy of education was being taught.

IV. The New Socialist Teaching Methods and Terminology and Their Effect on America: Is there any question that our American schools have changed compared with what we used to have and with what the typical socialist schools are like today? The list below describes how this has happened:

- **Transforming the classroom for more, social contact.** Instead of rows of desks for individual work, children sit in circles for group work.
- **Creating a new religion - Secular Humanism** - where man is venerated rather than God. Dewey wrote the Humanist Manifesto, and under his guidance Secular Humanism became the official religion of the public school supported by government funding.
- **Some of the humanist beliefs now in our public schools and quotes supporting them**:
- No belief in God - "no deity will save us; we must save ourselves;"
- Only evolution is taught, creationism is not allowed;
- No absolute truth, no strict moral standards, no ethics that have a theological or ideological sanction,
- Only situational ethics taught - "Ethics or truth that fits the situation and stems from human need and interest." To deny this distorts the whole basis of life. We strive for the good life, here and now." This is why drug prevention classes do not work because the

children are being taught situational ethics along with them. "Here are all the facts about every form of drugs, now you decide what you are going to do with this information - what is right for you."

• Free sex - "individuals should be permitted to express their sexual proclivities and pursue their life-styles as they desire."

• **Any Christian who does not agree is labeled "intolerant**."

Intolerant attitudes, often cultivated by orthodox religious and puritanical cultures, unduly repress sexual conduct...Such repressive attitudes prevent children from attaining their full potential as sexual beings.

• **Self-reliance, self-esteem** - "maximum individual autonomy (autonomous means "without outside control.") - to no longer have to depend on one's family or others for excessive guidance and decision-making help." This has fostered the wedge between child and parent, child and authority, child and values.

• **Values Clarification** - "We are not clear about our own values... Young people brought up by moralizing adults are not prepared to make their own responsible choices. How can a young person arrive at his own values...where does he learn whether he wants to stick to the old moral and ethical standards or try new ones?" [251]

• **Hegelian Dialectic** - create a crisis - thesis, put the blame on someone else -antithesis, resolve the crisis by including the antithesis in the solution - synthesis. The solution always requires more big government and government spending, which helps to cause a new crisis, and the process starts over again.

• **Delphi technique** - manipulating people towards a pre-conceived agenda, making them think they were part of the process and helped create the goals, so they are willing to support them.

• **Consensus building** - through the techniques of a skilled facilitator, everyone is brought to consensus about an issue that they never intended to agree to.

• **Fear tactics such as loss of job or funding** - teachers and principals are threatened with a loss of their job if they don't go along with the agenda. School districts are threatened with a loss of funding if they don't accept all the strings that are attached.

• **Fear Tactics are also used in teaching pseudo-science** such as global warming, hole in the ozone layer, oceans are rising, loss of natural resources, etc., so the poor student is so paranoid about hurting Mother Earth, they will believe and support the draconian laws, costly regulations, and restrictions on their freedoms and use of resources, even their own use of their own property.

• **Attacking literacy – reducing the ability to read.** Dewey and his colleagues decided that the reason why Americans were so independent is that they were too literate. According to Dewey, high literacy makes people too individualistic, "selfish," less dependent on government, and "detrimental to building a socialist society:"

> *The greatest enemy to socialism was the private consciousness that seeks knowledge in order to exercise its own individual judgment and authority.* **High literacy gave the individual the means to seek knowledge independently.**

> *...the time has come for a thoroughgoing examination of the emphasis put upon linguistic work in elementary instruction... The plea for the predominance of learning to read in early school-life because of **the great importance attaching to literature seems to me a perversion**...*[252]

> *The mere absorbing of facts and truths is so exclusively individual an affair that it tends very naturally to pass into **selfishness**. There is no obvious social motive for the acquirement of mere learning; there is no social gain in success thereat."*[253]

Thus Dewey and his colleagues decided the only way they could get students to become less independent and more collective was to **get rid of their literacy ability.**

• **More Emphasis on Group Work – Less Emphasis on Individual Work and Independent Thinking:** As Dewey said:

> *You can't make socialists out of individualists. Children who know how to think for themselves spoil the harmony of the collective society, which is coming, where everyone is interdependent.*[254]

• **"The goal was to produce inferior readers with inferior intelligence** dependent on a socialist educational elite for guidance, wisdom, and control." G. Stanley Hall tried to even extol the virtues of being illiterate:

> *The knowledge that illiterates acquire is probably on the whole more personal, direct, environmental and probably a much larger proportion of it practical. Moreover, they escape much ' eyestrain and mental excitement, and other things being equal, are probably more active and less sedentary...*[255]

• **"Look-Say" Method of Reading – First Taught with *Dick and Jane Books* and later with the "Whole Language Method."** It was a reading method no longer using phonics to sound out the words. Children were to memorize a small number of sight words serving as the stimuli, and repetition of the same words as the conditioning response. Of course, not a great deal of reading took place, with just a small number of sight words, The first place this method was used was in the public schools in Iowa. Immediately, their schools began to be plagued with reading problems never before seen. But that did not prevent the "experts" from promoting it, for those were the results they wanted.

• **The National Education Association helped to spread the Look-Say Method** and Dewey helped to make the NEA became more powerful. The NEA was started back in 1857 in Philadelphia. Its goal was to someday establish a national system of education. The Prussian system was their ideal. The NEA is coming closer and closer to that goal, and is now the most powerful and largest labor union the Democratic Party has.

• **The illiteracy rate in USA is now 14% of adults** - 32 million; 19% of high school graduates; 63% of prison inmates (DOE, 4/28/13) According to the Employment Policies Institute of Washington D.C., it is even much higher - **38% of adults.**

• **Teach "global citizenship:"** Global Government under the United Nations is the ultimate goal of the NEA, as was written back in 1946, one year after the United Nations was founded.

In the struggle to establish an adequate world government, the teacher has many parts to play. He must begin with his own attitude and knowledge and purpose. He can do much to prepare the hearts and minds of children for global understanding and cooperation..."

Joy Elmer Morgan, "The Teacher and World Government," 1946 *NEA Journal*. Morgan was editor of the *NEA Journal* for 31 years, 1921-1954. He, along with a very tight, small group held the reigns over the NEA and shaped its liberal, globalist world view.

• **Socialists Had Not Yet Succeeded in Their Goals**: In spite of all the attack on literacy and the spreading of socialism through our schools, somehow good teachers managed to still educate students in somewhat the basics of a decent education. Test scores were still fairly high; students were still basically moral and decent. Then something happened that changed all that drastically:

• **1962 - The Pivotal Year - God was officially taken off the ship with the Supreme Court Ruling of "Separation of Church and State."** Schools were no longer allowed to have Bible reading or prayer in the public schools. This has had an enormous effect not only on our schools but on the whole nation. Charts that the organization called Wall Builders created show the enormous changes in our nation that have taken place since 1962, divorce rates, crime rates, teen age pregnancy rates, rate of STDs (sexually transmitted diseases), suicide rates – all have skyrocketed since that important date of 1962. While test scores on the SAT have steadily gone down. Obviously, it was not good for our nation to remove God and the Bible from the public schools.

• **Secular Humanism:** The void that was left when prayer, the Bible and Judeo/Christian religion was removed is now filled with secular humanism, social engineering, diversity instruction (mainly promoting acceptance of homosexuality, redefining marriage and family), multiculturalism, new-age religions, native-American religions, eastern religions, pro-Islam teachings, anti-Christian teachings, and teachings worshiping mother earth through environmentalism.

• **Age of Psychology:** More and more psychologists have gotten on board with their "touchy-feely, sensitivity training" and more experimental programs introduced into the schools without any prior proven success. Some of those psychologists were Carl Rogers, B.F. Skinner, and William Spady.

• **Outcome-based Education,** based on attitudes and feelings not academics. It turns education upside down. Instead of knowledge and facts as the foundation of learning, feelings and attitudes become the most important.

• **1979 U.S. Department of Education** came on board in fulfillment of the promise Jimmy Carter gave to the NEA for their endorsement and campaigning for him. This was done in total violation of the 10th Amendment of the Constitution, which states that "powers not delegated to the United States [federal government] by the Constitution, nor prohibited by it to the States, are reserved to the States respectively, or to the people." Education was never meant to be under federal control. Our founding fathers believed education should be left under the control of parents through local government.

• Note: Not only had the NEA been pushing for a national office of education for many years, so had the United Nations. Now the United States could join the international community by being represented with an official minister of education. The U.S. "Office of Educational Research and Improvement" (OERI) was created, which could be closely linked to those that other nations had such as the Paris "Center for Educational Research and Improvement" (CERI) and which would better match a similar office in the U.N. "Office of Economic Cooperation and Development (OECD). The U.S. assistant secretary for OERI would now attend all the UN

OECD meetings and receive his marching orders relating to international restructuring efforts and programs, all of which would be implemented in the future in the United States, such as: site-based management, school-to-work, community education, Concerns-Based Adoption Model (CBAM) for staff development (a program for psychological manipulation of teachers who resist change.)[256]

• **1984 – A Nation at Risk** was published, which greatly alarmed Americans about the state of our education and caused drastic reform methods to begin taking place – exactly what the globalists wanted. The report stated:

> *Each generation of Americans has outstripped its parents in education, in literacy, and in economic attainment. For the first time in the history of our country, the educational skills of one generation will not surpass, will not equal, will not even approach, those of their parents.*

• **1985-1988 Soviet/U.S. education agreements began** during Ronald Reagan's presidency and Soviet leader Micheal Gorbachev. These agreements have brought us "Direct Instruction dog training via Skinner/ Pavlov" and much more psychological training and testing. Traditional academic education and the absorption of knowledge has been replaced with the Soviet philosophy that children are to be trained as lab rats, teaching them only low level basic skills for the globalist workforce.[257]

• **School-based health clinics** are becoming more a part of each school where Planned Parenthood representatives can help any girl get an abortion without parental notification. Most of these services are being paid for with Medicaid, which is just about breaking the system.

• **Political correctness gone amuck:** Text books, tests, even story books are being rewritten to make sure all words are now politically correct. Author Dianne Ravitch discovered an elaborate protocol of beneficent censorship endorsed and implemented by test and textbook publishers and the federal government to screen every sentence for potential bias. Here are some examples: a biography of Gutzen Borglum was eliminated because he designed the Mount

Rushmore Monument. Why? The Lakota Indians consider the Black Hills a sacred place to pray and consider the sculptures of Washington, Jefferson, Lincoln, and Teddy Roosevelt an abomination. A passage about owls was eliminated because the owls are taboo for the Navajos. California has asked for any reference to French fries, coffee, bacon, butter, ketchup, mayonnaise to not be included because they are unhealthy. (*"Forbidden Topics, Forbidden Words"* by Dianne Ravitch.) In New York State's high school English exam, excerpts from great literature have been altered to make them more P.C.; "cowboy or cowgirl" is changed to "cowperson,"

• **Political Correctness Gets Even Worse in College**: More than two-thirds of colleges and universities have speech codes even though, at least at public universities, they are unconstitutional. The codes are aimed at forbidding the free speech of conservatives, Christians, and humor magazines (since liberals have no sense of humor). Many of the speech codes are as silly and intolerant as the British speech code at Stockport College which made international news by banning 40 "offensive" words. Lady and gentleman are banned because of "class implications," "history and chairman are sexist, "normal couple" is simply unacceptable, and "slaving oyer a hot stove" is offensive to the plight of real slaves. (*London Telegraph* 6/11/00).

• **Multiculturalism, Racism and Diversity Instruction**: Colleges and universities have hired highly-paid itinerant facilitators to train incoming freshmen to feel guilty if they are white and to think politically correct thoughts about race and diversity. Two of the films widely used at these Soviet-style re-education sessions are "Skin Deep," which presents intolerance and racism as the norm in America, and "Blue-Eyed," a 90-minute tirade designed to humiliate people with blue eyes and to empower people with brown eyes. *(Reason magazine,* Mar. 2000) Students have little or no academic freedom to escape from intolerant professors intent on indoctrinating their students.

• **Women's Studies**: At the women's studies program at the University of South Carolina, students must acknowledge the existence of racism, classism, sexism, heterosexism, and other institutional forms of oppression of women before being permitted to participate in class discussions. This is typical of the 900 women's studies courses taught nationwide.[258]

• **God is Being taken out of Everything on Campus:** At Sonoma State University in Rohnert Park, CA. where my husband works, the song "America The Beautiful" has been sung at graduation ceremonies. But the verse "God shed his light on thee" has been changed to "Love shed her light on thee."

• **Transformation of Society:** This is a speech given in 1989 by a former Federal Department of Ed Representative – Dr. Shirley McCune - to the National Governors Association in Wichita, Kansas - that reveals what the ultimate plans are for transforming society to a central-planned society:

> *What is happening in America today and what is happening to Kansas in the Great Plains is not simply a chance situation in the usual winds of change. What it amounts to is a total transformation of our society...so we have to anticipate what the future is and then move back and figure out what it is we need to do today. That's called anticipatory socialization or the social change function of schools."* The Governors all applauded.

> *You have to understand the breadth of the task that's before us. You cannot think about restructuring of education without understanding that our total society is in a crisis of restructuring and you can't get away from it ... what we are facing is a **total restructuring of the society...** these changes would be profound, economic, demographic, and a **complete transformation of our society - and would impact virtually every aspect of our individual and collective lives** - the manifestation of a new era of civilization, **the movement from a national to a global society.** Virtually every institution is forced to restructure to meet a changed environment and changed needs.*

REFORM – what does it really mean? According to one blogger, "it's all about the cheddar, isn't it? All of this "reform" stuff never has really been about the children. It's about business. **R-E-F-O-R-M = Ruining Education For Our Resources & Money.** This, ladies and gentlemen, is what school "reform" has always been about. © JRAT, April 4, 2013.[259]

V. Modern Federal Legislation and Policies Giving More Federal Control over Education Schools and more Global Influences. Here are the series of education bills passed by the four U.S. presidents following 1989 helping to bring about the education transformation of society that Shirley McCune was predicting and bringing us to Common Core. [If anyone thinks CC was a simple "State standard initiative," they need to read this information.]

- **1988:** Marc Tucker became the president of the National Center for Education and the Economy (NCEE) where he joined with Hillary Clinton, Mario Cuomo, and Ira Magaziner to get States to **move away from local control of their schools and migrate to national standards**.
- **1990:** George H. W. Bush signed an international agreement entitled, "World Education for All (EFA), the result of a **United Nations "World Conference on Education for All"** summit.
- **1991:** Tucker and Lauren Resnick created New Standards that pushed **standards-based reform.**
- **1991 - America 2000:** by George Herbert Bush. It was a series of goals that gave more power to the federal government over State and local schools.
- **1992:** Tucker writes the infamous "Dear Hillary Letter." This letter, written to Hillary Clinton, addressed Tucker's ideas for radical education reform after Bill Clinton's presidential win. The goal is "to **remold the entire American system**" into "a seamless web that literally extends from cradle to grave and is the same systems for everyone," coordinated by "**a system of labor market boards at the local, state and federal levels**" where **curriculum and "job matching"** will be handled by counselors "accessing the integrated computer-based program."

• **1994:** Tucker's ambitious plan was implemented in **three laws passed** by Congress and signed by President Clinton: academics and teacher licensures, the School-to-Work Act Opportunities Act, and the reauthorized Elementary and Secondary Education Act (ESEA) called "Improving America's Schools Act of 1994."

1) The Goals 2000 Act under Clinton (1994)– expanded Bush's goals with more mandated dumbed-down national education goals, national standards, curriculum, assessments (primarily based on attitudes not factual knowledge).

2) School-to-Work - (1994) created education/business partner-ships, changing the purpose of education from acquiring broad-based knowledge to supplying workers for business. Schools are now job-training centers with narrowly defined career choices, approved by government economic forecasters, which match students and adults with government-preferred industries. [Note: **The final plank of the Communist Manifesto calls for the "Combination of education with industrial production."]** Schools will soon become "one-stop" centers, where students and the community can get all services.

3) Workforce Investment Act - (1998) created a nationwide network of workforce boards of "government-appointed representatives" from business, education, and government, who all work to implement and manage the system through local "one-stop" centers (public schools).

The Three R's are replaced with the Five L's "Limited Learning for Life-Long Labor" Children are trained for just one career (often chosen for them) This was started under Clinton and was known as "school-to-work" or school-to-career."

Under Common Core it is now known as "college or career readiness." As we have already read, Common Core is not preparing students for a true university level education, but only for a junior college level or for one certain career.

• **1996:** An organization called **ACHIEVE, Inc.** was formed by some of the nation's governors and corporate leaders. (Many of them **tied to Marc Tucker and the NCEE**). The goals from an Education Summit in Palisades, NY were to ACHIEVE the goals of the 1994 school reform bills.

• **1998:** Tucker and Judy Codding created America's Choice, a comprehensive school reform program, that made sure the **national standards** were further implemented into schools.

• **2001:** George W. Bush renames ESEA "The No Child Left Behind Act" and signed it into law. **NCLB** was supposed to get rid of all of the above, but it didn't happen. They are now all firmly cemented in place with more federal controls. NCLB adds more federal controls by including a forced federal test, at the NAEP.

• **NAEP** - (National Assessment of Education Progress) otherwise known as the Nation's Report Card that would test one State against another. It used to be the one and only test administered by the federal government. That will be different with Common Core.

• **2004: Microsoft (Bill Gates) contracts with UNESCO** (the United Nations Educational, Scientific and Cultural Organization) to fulfill part of UNESCO'S **Millennium Campaign Goals— universal education** and educating for a global economy. A "master curriculum" for teacher training in information technologies based standards, guidelines, benchmarks, and assessment techniques is to be developed. UNESCO / Gates Foundation Agreement

• **2005: Bill Gates funds the New Commission on the Skills of the American Workforce—created by Tucker;** States begin adopting its education reform initiative, "Tough Choices or Tough Times." In 2008, Utah's Governor Huntsman touts it and joins with 5 others states (Massachusetts, Delaware, Arizona, New Mexico, and New Hampshire) who adopt it in order to "reinvent their educational systems."

• **2008: Gates Foundation**, along with two other foundations, created **Strong American Schools** (a successor to the STAND UP campaign launched in 2006, which was an outgrowth of **UNESCO's Millennium Campaign Goals for Universal Education**). It calls for American education standards.

• **2008: Gates Foundation** funds the International Benchmarking Advisory Group report for Common Core Standards on behalf of the **National Governors Association, Council of Chief State School Officers**, and **ACHIEVE, Inc.** titled, "Benchmarking for Success: Ensuring U.S. Students Receive a World-Class

Education." This report shows the **United Nations is a member of the International Benchmarking Advisory Group for Common Core Standards**. The member of mention is the Organization for Economic Cooperation and Development (OECD) which developed UNESCO's Millennium Declaration—partnering with the World Bank and the International Monetary Fund.

The report states: While states must take the lead, the federal government can help. And the federal government can do that best by playing an enabling role grounded in **a new vision for the historic state-federal partnership in education**.

• **2009:** Marc Tucker writes a chapter in the book "Change Wars: The Inspiring Future for Educational Change." One chapter is called **International Benchmarking as a Lever for Policy Reform**. The book says the **UN's OECD** launched a Program for International Student Assessment in 2000 to **monitor the outcomes of education**. Linda Darling-Hammond also contributes a chapter. Darling-Hammond heads the SBAC (see 2009, December below)

• **April, 2009: Gates Foundation** members, along with a few dozen others, participate in a Washington conference and produce "Smart Options: Investing the Recovery Funds for Student Success." These ideas were funded by the 2008 Stimulus (ARRA-American Recovery and Reinvestment Act) and supported Race to the Top. **Priority 1: Develop Common American Standards— also called Career-Ready Standards— by Jan. 2012**.

• **2009, July, Race to the Top** under Obama provided the funding of $4.5 billion stimulus money for governors wishing to sign on to Common Core - 2008-10 under President Obama, which brings us even more top-down, total government, socialistic control of our schools, curriculum, standards, and assessments with teachers having to teach to the test each and every day and constant data of students, teachers, and administrators.

> *Government is implementing policies that will lead to poverty, not prosperity, by adopting failed ideas of a state-planned and managed economy similar to that of the Soviet Union. Individual choice is narrowed. It is based on a utilitarian worldview that measures human value*

only in terms of productive capability for the "best interests of the State." Individual freedom is subservient to a collective society. Senator Michelle Backmann

• **2009 (summer):** Council of Chief State School Officers, National Governors Association, and ACHIEVE, Inc. agree to **partner on a common core standards project**.

• **2009 (fall):** The U.S. Dept. of Ed signals it will fund $360M for summative assessments aligned to Common Core Standards and begins planning meetings. Two consortia begin competing for this funding: Smarter Balanced Assessment Consortium and Partnership for the Assessment of Readiness for College and Careers. **States begin adopting Common Core Standards and join one of the consortia in order to receive No Child Left Behind waivers** from the U.S. Department of Education Secretary, Arne Duncan.

• **2009 (December):** Utah becomes a governing member state of Smarter Balanced Assessment Consortium (SBAC) and is obligated to use the assessments created by the SBAC which is **led by Bill Ayers' friend, Linda Darling-Hammond**. Judy Park, Associate Superintendent, Utah State Office of Ed, eventually co-chairs the Consortia.

• **2009 (December): Gates Foundation gives the National PTA a $1 million grant to mobilize parents for Common Core Standards**.

• **June, 2010:** National Governors Association and State Education Chiefs **launch Common State Academic Standards**.

• **April 2011:** The SBAC Overview Curriculum and Assessment Conference issues a report stating that **governing member states must adopt Common Core** by Dec. 31, 2011.

• **2011:** The American Legislative Exchange Council's (ALEC) education task force calls for the demise of the Common Core Standards, but puts it on hold after receiving a **$376,635 grant from the Gates Foundation**.

• **2011: Bill Gates speaks at the November G20 Summit** in Cannes and issues his report, "Innovation With Impact: Financing 21st Century Development" stating, "My report will address the **financing needed to achieve maximum progress on** the **Millennium Development Goals**, and to make faster progress on development over the next decade."

• **2011: Obama Education Secretary Arne Duncan announces** "Today, I promise you that the Department of Education will be a committed partner in the national effort to build a more environmentally literate and responsible society... **We must advance the sustainability movement through education**... Education and sustainability are the keys to our economic future- and our ecological future."

• **2012:** States begin to recognize the loss of local control and enormous cost of implementation of the Common Core Standards. **Many states begin pushing back**. The Heritage Foundation and the Cato Institute call the standards unconstitutional per federal education law.

• **2012:** States not signed on to Common Core and not meeting the Annual Yearly Progress requirements of NCLB petition congress for relief. Lawmakers working on options are undercut when the **Obama White House circumvents congress to grant waivers from NCLB if states adopt Common Core.**[260]

Our Ship of Education is now OVERLOADED WITH BUREAUCRACY – Federal Office of Secretary of Education, Secretary of Health and Human Welfare, Office of Labor, Federal Department of Education, Ten Regional Education Laboratories, State Secretary of Education, State School Board, State Department of Education, County Superintendent, County Department of Education, School District Superintendent, School Board, local school principal and all his assistants and staff, then finally come the teachers and the students.

Money has to go through about fourteen layers deep of bureaucracy before salaries trickles down to the poor teachers in the schools. **Picture a gigantic web and a mass of confusion – that is our modern ship of American Education.**

The Hidden Cs of Common Core

Chapter XI

Successes Made in the Battle Against Common Core, What Can We Still Do? Classical English Literature Recommended Reading List, Thoughts About Education and Teaching

Governor Mike Pence surrounded by happy children who were supposed to be no longer under the yoke of Common Core (or are they?).

Indiana's experiment with Common Core was supposed to be over. As the nation watched, Governor Mike Pence signed legislation March 24, 2014, requiring the State to come up with its own academic standards, making Indiana the first State to totally pull its support for Common Core. Governor Pence made the following statement:

"I believe our students are best served when decisions about education are made at the state and local level,

By signing this legislation, Indiana has taken an important step forward in developing academic standards that are written by Hoosiers, for Hoosiers, and are uncommonly high."

How Did this Supposed Success Happen? Two mothers led the battle to get rid of Common Core in Indiana, Erin Tuttle and Heather Crossin. They discovered it early in 2011 by the strange math that was in their children's Catholic school. They then discovered it was in the public schools as well. The more they investigated it, the more the red flags went up. They formed an organization called Hooziers Against Common Core and began to inform many other parents. They and other concerned parents spoke to State Senators Dennis Kruze and Scott Schneider, who began to do their own research and agreed with the parents. Senator Schneider drafted SB 91 and Senator Kruze shepherded it. It put Common Core on hold last year and this year, Governor Pence signed legislation to throw it out.

However, as we Soon Found out – this Success was just for Appearances Sake: The governor of Utah let the cat out of the bag –the new standards that the Indiana State Board of Education voted in – are a mirror image of Common Core.

In a press conference, March 28, when Governor Gary Herbert of Utah was asked what he thought of Indiana voting out Common Core, this was his reply:

I've talked to Governor Pence about what they're doing there. In essence, they're creating what's called the Indiana Core. It's not the Common Core. It's the Indiana Core, but their standards are almost mirroring exactly what's commonly referred to as the Common Core standards. So they're just doing it in a different way, which is what we've already been doing in Utah.[261]

Indiana's new Math Standards Worse than Before: According to Sandra Stotsky, the two men most responsible for the new bad math standards in Indiana need to be "written up for posterity to remember." According to one expert, a Mr. Wu, math professor at Berkeley, "the standards made no mathematical sense." Professor James Milgram said *"...the high school standards were bizarre."* Stotsky stated:

> *Pence has gone from having one of the best sets of math standards to the absolute worst. Fordham can be thanked for its role in this debacle. People who know no math will decide what the K-12 math curriculum is.*[262]

What About Other States? As you see below, many States have legislation to also put Common Core on hold:

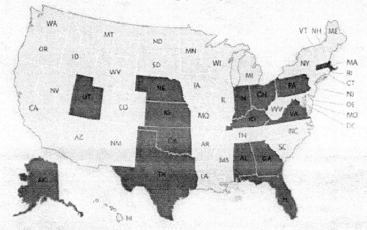

Not So Fast: States Increasingly Wary of Common Core

Indiana is not alone in the battle against Common Core. At least 15 other States, either are not using, or have grown increasingly wary of, Common Core. The map shows the current status of States that either never adopted the standards, or have put Common Core on hold, or have downgraded some aspect of it – like dropping out of the testing consortium.

Following are the States and the Names of the Consortium they have dropped out of:
1. Utah (Smarter Balanced)[263]
2. Oklahoma (PARCC) - [264]
3. Georgia (PARCC) - [265]/
4. Alabama (Smarter Balanced & PARCC - as an advisory state) [266]
5. Indiana (PARCC). Even before Governor Mike Pence had signed legislation March 24, 2014, to get out of Common Core all together, he had already dropped PARCC in August of 2013.[267]
6. Kansas (Smarter Balanced) [268]
7. Pennsylvania (Smarter Balanced & PARCC) - [269]
8. Alaska (Smarter Balanced) - [270] (Alaska joined SBAC in the spring of 2013 as a non-governing state. Joining in the capacity that they did, they did not commit to using the SBAC assessments and they did not have a governing vote. Alaska has in essence adopted the CCSS, they just did not say they did.)[271]

States That are Actively Considering Withdrawing from a Testing Consortium:
Michigan (Smarter Balanced)[272]
Kentucky (PARCC)[273]
North Carolina (Smarter Balanced)[274]
Iowa (Smarter Balanced) - The Iowa Legislature put it on hold and has to approve its use. [275]

States that never Joined any Consortium.
1. Virginia
2. Texas
3. Nebraska
4. Minnesota

What Indiana is Replacing Common Core with?   According to Eric Weddle, a reporter for the *IndyStar.com* "Whatever the answer, there is sure to be much debate as parents, teachers and others read and comment on the proposed frameworks, something that was missing when Common Core standards were pushed upon the State with no input or knowledge that they even existed."

What will it be called? "College and career ready" academic standards for grades K-12. That is a little worrisome, because "college and career ready" has usually been the term used when talking about Common Core.

States that have Some Pushback Against Common Core

State pushing back against Common Core	Never adopted	Paused implementation	Downgraded participation in or withdrew from national tests
Alabama			X
Alaska	X		X
Florida			X
Georgia			X
Indiana		X	X
Kansas			X
Kentucky			X
Massachusetts		X	
Nebraska	X		
Ohio			
Oklahoma			X
Pennsylvania		X	X
Texas	X		
Utah			X
Virginia	X		

Notes: Pennsylvania has resumed implementation.

Thanks to the Heritage Foundation for the above information, March 2014.

Weddle writes that the new set of standards for Indiana are a 98-page draft that includes more than 1,000 benchmarks on what skills students are expected to learn in math and English at each grade level so they can graduate prepared to attend a university or start working. Some standards are very simple and others contain multiple goals.

Similarities to Common Core? Critics of Common Core and some lawmakers have warned they don't want to see significant similarities between the national standards and the new draft. Others state that "any rigorous plan to meet federal requirements must have similarities with Common Core."

Governor Mike Pence praised the educators and state workers who played a role in creating the draft and said the following:

> *I am confident that at the end of this process, Indiana will have a set of uncommonly high standards, written by Hoosiers for Hoosiers, which ensure every child finishes school ready for success in college or in the workplace," he said in a statement. To read the full draft of Indiana's k-12 standards go to this website.*[276]

Obama Administration Warns Indiana with a Threat that they could Lose their NCLB Waiver: On May 7, 2014, the federal DOE sent a letter to the Indiana Department of Education telling them that since they are no longer using CC standards that they could lose their waiver to get out of NCLB. It stated:

> *Because the [Indiana Department of Education] will no longer implement those [CC] standards, IDOE must amend its [Elementary and Secondary Education Act] flexibility request and provide evidence that its new standards are certified by a state network of [Institutions of Higher Education] that students who meet the standards will not need remedial coursework at the postsecondary level.*

So much for State-led: *The letter from the U.S. Education Department demonstrates "just how weak the phrases 'state-led' and 'voluntary' became when used to describe Common Core," wrote Brittany Corona, a domestic policy researcher at the Heritage Foundation.*[277]

Even Liberal California is Having some Impact Fighting Common Core: On April 30, at a rally on the East side of the State Capital building in Sacramento, about 150 people gathered to support Assemblyman Tim Donnelly, who presented a bill to empower the local school districts to say no to Common Core and the Assessment testing. A good third of the people gathered at the rally were children. Later these children spoke at the Education Committee hearing in support of the bill along with about 30 adults.

This was one of two bills presented that went down in dust with Californian's liberal Education Committee. The first bill was one presented by Assemblyman Curt Hagman of the Los Angeles area that was asking for a very logical request that we postpone the Assessment test for another year, until we have enough computers and the technology in place for it. It also was voted down unanimously without a single vote in favor of it. But at least the committee is hearing from people who do not like Common Core.

Children at the Rally Against Common Core, April 30, 2014 with Assemblyman Tim Donnelly who presented an anti-Common Core bill

Sandra Stostky, Professor Emerita, from the University of Arkansas, was one of the featured speakers at the rally. Behind her can be seen Sandra Smith with her sign "Democrats Against Common Core." She also spoke and introduced her four sons, the reason she is so adamantly fighting Common Core.

Other featured speakers were: Assemblyman Tim Donnelly, Assemblyman Shannon Grove, Attorney Brad Dacus from the Pacific Justice Institute, who created the opt out form for parents to opt their children out of the Assessment test; Lydia Guttierez, a 2nd grade teacher who is running for Superintendent of California; Orlean Koehle, State President of Eagle Forum and Director of Californians United Against Common Core; Angela Weinzinger, a School board trustee for the Travis Unified School District, who started the face book page, Parents and Educators Against Common Core Standards, that now has over 18,000 members.

Katherine Duran, the "suspended Mom" also spoke with her son Christopher standing by her side, Professor Dave Scanlan, who teaches computer science at Sacramento State University, spoke about the dangers of using Wi-Fi with its pulsed radiation in the classroom. He told how he has convinced all of his students to take Wi-Fi out of their homes and connect to the internet with a wired connection.

Various other people, some teachers, some concerned parents, and some young people spoke at the rally and expressed their concerns and dislike for Common Core.

The rally was organized and presented by three groups: Californians United Against Common Core, Eagle Forum of California under the direction of Orlean Koehle and Democrats Against Common Core, founded and led by Sandra Smith.

Brad Dacus, on the left, Sandra Smith, Orlean Koehle speaking, with Assemblyman Tim Donnelly and Lydia Gutierrez on the right

We are hoping this will be one of many rallies and that the momentum will continue to grow in California against Common Core as it has in other States.

Another Success – Chicago Teachers Union Passed a Resolution Against Common Core: May 7, 2014, the teachers' Union of the third largest school district in the nation, just passed a resolution against Common Core, joining the teachers' union of New York.

Here are some of the reasons they give for rejecting Common Core:

> *Among other things, the CTU resolution, passed by delegates to its governing body, contends that standards contain "numerous developmentally inappropriate expectations," "reflect the interests and priorities of corporate education reformers," and "emphasize pedagogical techniques, such as close reading, out of proportion to the actual value of these methods." It adds that the upcoming aligned tests will consume "tremendous amounts of time and resources for test preparation and administration."* [278]

Whatever Will We Do If We Dump Common Core? A component of pushing CCSS involves panicking the public into believing that in the absence of CCSS, States will have no standards. This message was promoted by Melinda Deslatte, *Associated Press,* March 30, 2014, *"If Not CCSS, Then What?"* in her coverage of the Louisiana capitol:

> *Lawmakers can only take one approach to make critics... happy: Get Louisiana out of Common Core and its related testing. **But if legislators do that, what education standards do they put in place? How quickly could they develop them? How much would state-specific standards cost? And how disruptive would a change be in schools already transitioning to Common Core?*** [Emphasis added.]

This is a summation of an article written by Mercedes Schneider that starts out by the words: **"Allow me to expose this nonsense for what it is."**

1. No one advocating for CCSS was educated via CCSS. They were all educated under some "education umbrella" other than the Core.
2. These "corporate reformers" are saying that anything that is not CCSS is "substandard," yet they were all themselves so substandardly educated – "in which case, why should anyone bother heeding any advice they should push onto the public? In

short, they declare themselves as not educated well enough to listen to."

3. Every corporate reformer's child, who currently attends an elite private school, is exempt from CCSS. Note that none of the **top 50 best private day schools in America** (as rated by thebestschools.org) advertise adherence to CCSS.

4. These private schools have much more available for the privileged, elite students. They advertise and offer "a huge array of special programs to "educate **the whole person**, inside and outside of the classroom": a wide variety of musical groups, study abroad and exchange programs, and co-curricular activities. Students are required to pass a swim test, learn CPR, and complete community service hours as part of their graduation requirements.

5. Thus CCSS is just **"potted meat"** – **"education for the masses."**

6. **Whatever will States do without CCSS?** Before there was CCSS, every state had standards in place. Go back to them. According to Fordham Institute that had rated all of the State's standards before Common Core, three States had superior math standards: Indiana, California and D.C. Let the other States adopt theirs. Massachusetts had superior English Language Arts (that Sandra Stotsky had helped develop). Let the other States adopt theirs.

Mercedes adds a little side bar about what has happened in Indiana:

> *And yet, in another irony of late, CCSS-superior Indiana has **pretended to dump** CCSS in order to have "its own" state standards– which has amounted to little more than an attempt to covertly retain CCSS. **Allow me to reiterate:** The Fordham Institute–an organization that wants CCSS– graded Indiana's standards as superior–and yet Indiana chose not to simply return to its former "CCSS-superior" standards–though it could have done so.*

And concerning what has happened in Louisiana, Mercedes writes:

...Fordham gave Louisiana's ELA standards the same grade as it gave CCSS ELA– a B-plus– so it seems that pro-CCSS organizations like Fordham have no justification for promoting CCSS ELA as "superior" to Louisiana's ELA standards.

*Nevertheless, CCSS is sold to the American public as both necessary and "superior"– further proof that **CCSS** is not a set of standards but a political ploy.*

Mercedes Answers More of the Questions from the AP Reporter:
"If legislators do that (dump CCSS), what education standards do they put in place?"

- Legislators need not "put standards into place."
- Each state can return to the standards in place prior to the CCSS "bait-and-switch."

How quickly could they develop them?

- "No need to re-invent. Each state already had a set of standards in place. Once freed of CCSS, the education stakeholders in each state are then able to revisit and modify its standards as each state sovereignly sees fit."
- But do this in the open – "not via secretive committee meetings and clandestine arrangements" as with CCSS.

How much would state-specific standards cost?

- No one was too concerned about this question prior to and regarding CCSS implementation.
- Each state already has its former standards. It couldn't be that costly to bring them back.

And how disruptive would a change be in schools already transitioning to Common Core?

- "It is CCSS that is 'disruptive' as evidenced by the nationwide pushback.
- Much of this pushback is coming as parents and teachers are finding out that their children and students are being forced to use CCSS "by those above CCSS consequences – and yet benefiting from CCSS profits."
- "It is foolish to argue that states should keep the rigid, CCSS **non-standards** only to avoid change."

Mercedes stresses that those who should be involved in this process of "revisiting education" should be the "stakeholders," the parents themselves, and not by some "controlling top" forced upon us, the "helpless bottom" as CCSS is doing:

> *Revisiting education systems and assumptions is necessary—but it must emerge from the stakeholders. In order to improve the educational standards of any state, those with a vested interest in the quality of education for their children must be the ones to initiate, navigate, institute, and evaluate the standards (and curriculum and materials, and assessments) based upon outcomes they determine to be meaningful.*
>
> *Such cannot be accomplished from some controlling "top" and forced upon some helpless "bottom"– which is exactly what CCSS enforcement demands.*

Thus, I agree with another of Deslatte's statements previously highlighted in this post: *Lawmakers can only take one approach to make critics... happy: Get Louisiana out of Common Core and its related testing.* Proverbial nail hit squarely on its proverbial head.[279]

"Like locally-grown Washington apples, the core should be local and exceptional, not common."[280]

Exiting the Common Core Memorandum of Understanding: In a separate article written April 12, 2014, Mercedes Schneider writes that the State governors and the State superintendents were the only two that signed on to the MOUs. If those two are no longer in office, which is the case in most of the States, since most of the dates were in 2009 or 2010, then those MOUs are no longer binding. Even if both signators are still currently in office, as in Idaho, both the public and elected officials can pressure the two signators to write USDOE and declare a reversed, "State-led" decision. She urges us to challenge the MOUs! **Here are the main points of her important article:**

The (CCSS) memorandum of understanding (MOU) was the

agreement that State governors and State superintendents signed with the US Department of Education (USDOE) when they signed on to compete for RTTT funding.

States agreed to be "state led" according to the criteria set forth in the legal document composed as an appendix to accompany a State's Race to the Top (RTTT) application in each State's bid for RTTT money. As Mercedes adds, "So much for 'state led.'"

[How can this truly be a State-led program, when the federal government created the language and forced the States to sign a statement going along with that language to be able to get their RTTT money? It is like training a parrot to say "State-led, State-led," before they can get their special, tasty, expensive cracker.]

The CCSS MOU includes no provision for exiting CCSS. But it also includes no wording in which States are bound to CCSS if the original signators no longer hold the positions of governor and State education superintendent.

Only two signators were required - to bypass the "messiness" of the legislative process and bind States to CCSS via only two signatures in "top-down" fashion.

This allows more "ease to enter but also ease to exit": The "ease" in which the USDOE bound States to CCSS via two signatures - **inadvertently offers States** more **"ease" in exiting.** As Mercedes writes, "This is a very important!"

> *Since the MOU fails to include language binding States to CCSS if such States receive RTTT money (no doubt excluded so that USDOE might maintain it is not "forcing" States to accept CCSS in order to receive RTTT money), then even States that received RTTT money are able to exit CCSS and challenge any USDOE pressure to return RTTT money. If CCSS is truly not federally forced, then it will not pursue States choosing to be "State led" right out of CCSS.*

A "breach of RTTT contract" would underscore the violation of the ESEA law of 1965, that there should never have been a contract (MOU) between the USDOE and State governments over education standards. If the USDOE were to pursue States exiting CCSS for some labeled RTTT "breach of contract" that would only underscore USDOE's violation of the Elementary and Secondary Education Act (ESEA) of 1965, Subpart Two, <u>Section 9527(c)(1)</u>:

> *(c) PROHIBITION ON REQUIRING FEDERAL APPROVAL OR CERTIFICATION OF STANDARDS-*
> *(1) IN GENERAL- Notwithstanding any other provision of Federal law, no State shall be required to have academic content or student academic achievement standards approved or certified by the Federal Government, in order to receive assistance under this Act.* [Emphasis added.]

No need for legislative action: If both signators no longer hold the positions of governor and State superintendent, then the MOU cannot bind each state.

> *There is no need for legislative action to dispose of CCSS. In such cases, the current governor or state superintendent can formally declare a state's exit from CCSS. USDOE has no legal recourse, and neither does a non-signator governor nor non-signator superintendent who might push to keep CCSS.*

Agencies can Challenge a Contract that is Essentially Dead: If the current governor or State superintendent fail to admit no binding agreement for CCSS, then agencies can challenge them in court for supporting a contract created by those no longer in office.

Mercedes sites the example of New York, where neither former Governor David Paterson nor former Education Commissioner Richard Mills who signed the state on for CCSS are in office. "so, the CCSS MOU is dead."

> *US Secretary of Education Arne Duncan can praise current New York Education Commissioner John King all that he likes for sticking by the Core. King's name is not on the CCSS MOU; so, the situation is ripe for a lawsuit against King for attempting to uphold a dead contract.*

In states in which one signator is currently in office, such as Louisiana's case with Governor Bobby Jindal, both the public and elected officials can pressure Jindal and call his "anti-CCSS 'green card' bluff."

Mercedes suggests reminding Arne Duncan of his words on April 8, 2014, before the House Appropriations Subcommittee, *"I'm just a big proponent of high standards. Whether they're common or not is secondary."* [So, in other words, since Common Core is starting to get such a bad name, could Arne Duncan also be trying to wiggle out of using the label Common Core. If that is the case, would all the MOUs no longer be valid since the States were specifically signing on to CCSS?] And if Duncan refuses to comply, Mercedes suggests suing the USDOE for all the laws they have violated pushing Common Core on the States.

> *Yes, it is time-, money-, and energy-consuming, but we need to continue to fight with fervor against this twisting of the democratic process into a federally-enabled, mega-corporate feeding trough for education profiteers.*

If the CCSS MOU is Dead, the Assessments are as well: Mercedes ends her article with the following:

> *If the CCSS MOU is dead, then its testing-consortium appendages, the SBAC and the PARCC, lose their justification for existing. Thus, states that shed the CCSS MOU have no reason to follow through on SBAC or PARCC.* ***Challenge the CCSS MOU!***[281]

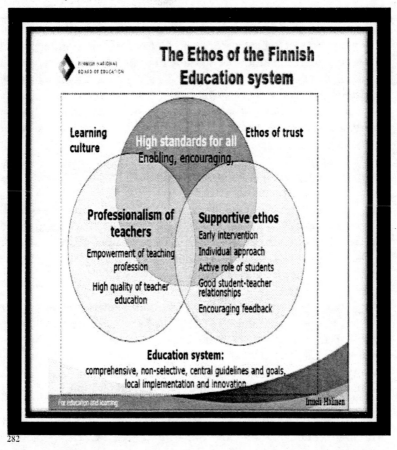

The Ethos of the Finnish Education system

FINNISH NATIONAL BOARD OF EDUCATION

Learning culture

High standards for all
Enabling, encouraging,

Ethos of trust

Professionalism of teachers

Empowerment of teaching profession

High quality of teacher education

Supportive ethos

Early intervention

Individual approach

Active role of students

Good student-teacher relationships

Encouraging feedback

Education system:
comprehensive, non-selective, central guidelines and goals, local implementation and innovation

For education and learning

Irmeli Halinen

282

Learn from Finland: The Finns have led the nations in international test scores and look what they say about testing. *"Who cares!" We prepare children to learn how to learn – not to take a test"*

The Art of Learning: Everybody's talking about Finland, the country that nearly tops the charts in reading, science, and math [scores]. But guess what? They don't really care. Here's what a representative from their Ministry of Education says: "We are not much interested in PISA [Program for International Student Assessment]. It's not what we are about." Instead he says, "We prepare children to learn how to learn, not how to take a test."[283]

Let's say No to Common Core and Get out of the Standards and the Assessment Testing. Let's follow Finland's example. We don't need the standards or the testing, and let's go back to the form of education that we had before Common Core. Teach children to enjoy education for the sake of education. Teach our children the joy of learning and prepare them for life as we did in the early days of our country.

Support Congressional Resolutions Against Common Core: This year 2014, a resolution was proposed by Sen. Lindsey Graham (R-SC) that supports the restoration and protection of State authority -- in all aspects of a child's education process. S. Res. 345 was co-sponsored by Sens. Chuck Grassley (R-IA), Thad Cochran (R-MS), Roger Wicker (R-MS), James Inhofe (R-OK), Tim Scott (R-SC), Ted Cruz (R-TX), Mike Lee (R-UT) and Mike Enzi (R-WY).

Work to Get Common Core out of Catholic Schools or any other Private Christian School. The following ten good suggestions can apply to any school. They come from an excellent article by Dan Guernsey that was published in the "Catholics is our Core. Org bulletin put out by the Cardinal Newman Society, Feb. 2013, "Examining Critical Issues in Faithful Catholic Education.

Ten Minimal Adaptations Catholic Schools Should Consider Making to the Common Core State Standards." Guernsey prefixes his list of suggestions with the following:

> *Since standards drive curriculum, a Catholic curriculum must include standards that are integrated with the magisterial teachings of the Catholic Church. For example, consider that Catholics have much to say about literature, history, science, and, above all, about Truth, goodness, and beauty. And, since the object of every academic discipline is truth, the Catholic curriculum should be based on the conviction that all truths ultimately*

converge in their source—God. This standard, among others, is sorely lacking in the Common Core.

2) **Renounce the English Language Arts (ELA) percentages for literary and informational texts** (which are not research-based). [He is referring to the 50% classical literature in elementary and only 30% in high school; the rest is all "informational texts."

• **Do not alter your literature selections based on the CC standards.**
   Stick with the best literature from recognized masters. Use great works with compelling themes that speak to the heart of the human condition across the ages. Do not remove poetry, drama or literature; conversely, do not artificially add more informational texts into your ELA program.

   • Throw out the Common Core Appendices and stick to your tried and true curriculum.

3) **Reduce textbook use when possible and move to actual documents and unadapted books.**
   • Set your teachers and students free with authentic, un-sanitized texts and original questions and assignments...

3) Respond to the texts, not the Standards.
   • Literary study should not be stuffed into a pre-determined standard or examined with canned questions.

   "Treating literature simply as grist for the mill of college and career readiness saps its transformative power of inquiry and translation of experience.

   • Development of reading skills/tools should not become the goal of reading great works.
   • Stay away from canned materials and exemplar units. Keep your teachers and instruction creative. Beware that computer-based instruction can also be overly scripted and become a crutch and distraction.

4) Do not take the Common Core's rightful emphasis on text-based arguments too far.

• Do not follow the Common Core's philosophy that the only way that a student can demonstrate knowledge gleaned from a text is using evidence from the text to support their claim.

...in Catholic schools, knowledge is attained and demonstrated when the human intellect, informed by the senses, judges things rightly. Our criteria include not only the text itself but also a rich and wonderful world outside the text (which the text might brilliantly unveil—sometimes with life-changing effect). Evidence and knowledge are certainly based on the text; however, they are ultimately grounded in truth, beauty and goodness. If we miss this, we miss everything about Catholic education.

• Allow discussion outside texts or ideas.
• Conduct a little test preparation. Teach older students how to sanitize their normal "human" responses for the purposes of the standardized test evaluation.

5) Avoid premature use of technology, peer-editing, research and rhetorical pedagogy in place of good old-fashioned writing instruction.

• Use pencil and paper when you teach writing to young children.

Technology is only a teaching tool, not a magic smart pill. Using technology to write can wait. Do not panic that your elementary students will be "left behind" if you are still teaching them to handwrite. None of us over 40 had computers in school, but we have managed somehow to be smart, productive, technologically proficient 21st century learners.

Technology is the easy part; thinking clearly and deeply is the hard part, and this can happen without extensive technology. We don't know what type of technology our students will have at their disposal in 15 years, but we do know what type of brains they will have; we need to prepare those.

• Avoid the early emphasis on peer-editing (a teaching technique and not a standard) and the too early emphasis on research. Young students deserve adult guidance at this stage and not the faux guidance of their peers who cannot teach what they do not yet know.

• Remember that the goal of writing is to communicate the truth. Writing should not be viewed simply through the Common Core lens of effective rhetoric, where students learn how to manipulate words and use standard grammar to produce a cogent, if not somewhat detached, argument.

6) **Create your own explicit standards for your junior high and high school literature classes.**

• List the critical texts, time periods, authors and genres that you expect your students to cover. The Common Core Standards only chunk and repeat the same empty skills year after year...it does not account for adequate content coverage or skills development necessary for effective high school literature.

7) **Do not alter your math progression.**

• Keep mastery of the standard algorithms using multi-digits at the levels they are currently found. Do not delay these for a year as suggested by the CCSS. Keep addition/ subtraction in 2nd-3rd grade, multiplication in 4th, division in 5th.

• Keep algebra in 8th grade as the norm for your school. A non-algebra track for struggling students can also be offered for those who fall short of the norm.

• Keep your geometry program unchanged. Do not follow the unorthodox and failed version presented in the Common Core.

• Develop explicit standards for classes necessary for future science, technology, engineering or math (STEM) majors. There currently are no explicit standards for classes such as pre-calculus, trigonometry, statistics, number theory, calculus, etc.

8) **Avoid the temptation to push "higher-ordered thinking skills" too quickly.**

• Give novices (that is, grade school students) the direct instruction that they need.

• Continue to emphasize memorization in the younger grades.

9) **Avoid teaching to the tests.** Focus on good instruction, not this or that test.

• Do still give norm-referenced tests with post-Common Core validity such as the Iowa's to assist with student formation.

Do plan for SAT/ACT testing courses to be formally placed in your high school curriculum. Teach students in a discreet course "how" to take a standardized test and respond to prompts in a Common Core expected manner.

10) Keep the greatest distance possible between your curriculum and the Common Core Standards.

• Do not cheerlead for the Common Core. Do not praise the Common Core: Let it sink or stand on its own without your prior validation. The Common Core Standards are untested.

• If you use the Standards, set them as sub-floor but not as a foundation for your Catholic education…Our foundation must always be Jesus Christ.

• Interpret the Standards as loosely and broadly as possible. Do not attempt to tie daily instruction and lesson plans directly to the Common Core Standards

"We do after all owe it to the world to witness to the Truth about authentic education and about the human person."

> *We also owe a duty to the majority of Catholic children who attended public schools to voice our opposition to the flawed program to which they are being subjected. Some public school supporters of the Common Core point to our schools and say, "See, if the Catholic schools are using it, it must be good!"*
>
> *With so many concerns, one wonders why Catholic schools would base their efforts on the Common Core at all. Catholic schools have had unparalleled and enviable success for decades using their own standards.*

Dr. Dan Guernsey is an advisor to The Cardinal Newman Society's Catholic High School Honor Roll,serves on the board of the National Association of Private Catholic and Independent Schools (NAPCIS), which provides consulting and accreditation services for more than 150 independent Catholic schools across the nation. He is headmaster of the Rhodora J. Donahue Academy of Ave Maria University,

Florida, and is establishing an education major program at Ave Maria University. [284]

List of What Parents and Educators Can Do:

• Do your own research, attend conferences, learn from others who are speaking out on these issues, get inspired, be persistent and never give up.

• Join with like-minded people. There is strength in numbers.

• We have to recommit at the local level, electing school boards willing to stand up to big money and the state and federal governments when they see policies that damage our children.

• We must elect congressmen willing to curtail destructive programs like No Child Left Behind and Race to the Top. Have them sign onto the resolution to defund Common Core.

• We can't vote every couple of years then sit back and do nothing. We have to make noise — lots of noise — to be sure those in power know what we want.

• We have to call and write. We have to testify and attend school board meetings. We have to remind these people who they work for.

• Write letters to the editor, call in on talk radio programs.

• Support legislation against Common Core.

• Sign Petitions on CUACC.org.

• **Opt Out of the Testing**: Opt Out groups were reporting record numbers of students in New York not taking the test, with sources estimating more than 33,000 opt outers. A recent report by the New York State School Boards Association estimates Opt Out at 5 percent, which would represent about 60,000 students in grades 3-8. It is believed Opt Out will grow when the math tests.[285]

• **Home School** - For the safety of your family, if a ship is sinking, it is best to jump ship. Either home school or put your children in private schools that have rejected Common Core. There are excellent ways that you can network with other home school parents so your children are not missing out socially.

Classical English Books and Plays– My Personal Recommended Reading List: As a former English teacher and avid reader, I highly recommend the following great books that have withstood the test of time. They are exciting, with thought provoking plots and deep meaning that take place in different periods of history. From these books, young people can learn to love reading and gain valuable lessons of wisdom, discernment, history, how to tell good from evil, truth from error, morals, ethics, virtues, true love, charity, and principles to live by, and why liberty, truth, and moral convictions are worth fighting for:

1776 by David Mc Cullough
A Christmas Carol by Charles Dickens
A Tale of Two Cities by Charles Dickens
Adventures of Tom Sawyer and Huckleberry Finn by Mark Twain
Alice in Wonderland / Through the Looking Glass by Lewis Carol
Animal Farm by George Orwell
Ann of Green Gables by L.M. Montgomery
Atlas Shrugged by Ayn Rand
Black Beauty by Anna Sewell
Brave New World by Aldous Huxley
Charlotte's Web by E. B. White
David Copperfield by Charles Dickens
Don Quixote by Miguel de Cervantes
Dr. Jekyll and Mr. Hyde by Robert Louis Stevenson
Emma by Jane Austin
Enders Game by Oscar Scott Card
Farenheit 451 by Ray Bradbury
Farewell to Arms by Ernest Hemingway
Fellowship of the Ring by JRR Tolkien
Gone with the Wind by Margaret Mitchell
Great Expectations by Charles Dickens
Gulliver's Travels by Jonathan Swift
John Adams by David Mc Cullough
Little Women by Louisa May Alcott
Les Miserables by Victor Hugo
Lord Jim by Joseph Conrad
Lord of the Flies by William Goldbert
Lord of the Ring by JRR Tolkien
Miracle at Philadelphia by Catherine Drinker Bowen
My Antonia by Willa Cather
Moby Dick by Herman Melville
Nineteen Eighty Four by George Orwell
Of Human Bondage by Somerset Maughan
Oliver Twist by Charles Dickens
Pilgrim's Progress by John Bunyan

Pride and Prejudice by Jane Austin
Robinson Crusoe by Danial Defoe
Rebecca by Daphne De Murier
Swiss Family Robinson by Johann David Wyss
The Adventures of Sherlock Holmes by Sir Arthur Conan Doyle
The Bible
The Call of the Wild by Jack London
The Chronicles of Narnia by C.S. Lewis
The Complete Works of Shakespeare
The Constitution of the United States of America by James Madison
The Count of Monte Cristo by Alexander Dumas
The Federalist Papers by Alexander Hamilton
The Five Thousand Year Leap by Cleone Skousen
The Fountainhead by Ayn Rand
The Great Gatsby by F. Scott Fitzgerald
The Hunt for Red October by Tom Clancy
The Hobbit by JRR Tolkien
The Iliad by Homer
The Law by Frederick Bastiat (explains socialism in France)
The Pearl by John Steinbeck
The Three Musketeers by Alexander Dumas
The Odyssey by Homer
The Old Man and the Sea by Ernest Hemingway
The Sound and the Fury by William Faulkner
The Wind in the Willows by Kenneth Grahame
Twenty Thousand Leagues Under the Sea by Jules Verne
Uncle Tom's Cabin by Harriet Beecher Stowe
Where the Red Fern Grows by Wilson Rawls
Wuthering Heights by Emily Bronte

There are many other great classics that you, as the reader, could add to the list. I recommend that the parent read the book first to make sure it has the redeeming qualities that you would want to pass on to your child. Reading a good book is like spending many hours in the presence personally of the author. If the words of the author are not what you want instilled in the hearts and minds of your child, don't allow it in your home and don't allow your child to read it at school. Insist on an alternative assigned book.

Thoughts About Schools, Education and Teaching:

Remember the old song that used to be sung back in the early 1900s to 1960s called "School Days"?

School Days, School Days, good old Golden Rule days,
Reading and writing and 'rithmetic, hark to the tune of the
hickory stick.
I was your girl in calico, you were my bashful barefoot bow.
You wrote on my slate, I love you so,
When we were a couple of kids.

Here is a modern interpretation of the words of the song and what they mean today

- **School days** - *8 a.m.-6 p.m., year round school, with early preschool; the school has become the center of the community.*
- **Golden Rule** – *has a new meaning - "He who has the gold rules," in this case the federal government has the gold and dictates to the States what they must do to get the gold.*
- **Reading, Writing, and 'Rithmetic** – *They were known as "the Three Rs." They have now been replaced with "the five Ls, "Limited Learning for Life-Long Labor," the new meaning of education through "School to Work" and Common Core.*
- **Hickory Stick** - *not used on children any more. It is the big stick hanging over the heads of teachers and administrators – the threat of firing or no more funding if a school district, principal or teacher does not go along with the program.*
- **The girls don't wear calico anymore.** *The vast majority of them wear short shorts or short skirts, low-cut spaghetti-strapped tops that show their belly buttons where there is a ring hanging out. Often they have rings in their tongues, their lips, their nose, their eyebrows, several in their ears.*
- **The boys are not bashful.** *Many of them are rather brazen and use the foulest language that would make your hair curl. Their pants are usually the baggy kind that are worn low around their hips. If anyone tugs hard they fall off. They are not barefoot unless they are an environmentalist. In that case, they don't shower or take baths or wash their clothes.*
- **The kids don't write notes on slates.** *But, they do write notes on things that resemble slates –computers, iPads, smart phones. They don't really write - they text, and it is best not to repeat some of the dirty, suggestive language that some are sending out as text*

messages or the naked pictures that are sent. It is called "sexting." Modern day "slates" have the ability to keep track of everything that is written on them and to keep enormous personal data on every person using them.

"Oh, for the good old days of school when the true "Golden Rule" was taught and lived, morals were taught and lived, and education really meant that our youth were well prepared to be happy, productive citizens of this great nation." Orlean Koehle

"Education is not the filling of a pail, but the lighting of a fire."
William Butler Yeats

"The more a society drifts from truth, the more it will hate those who speak it." George Orwell

" If Congress... may establish teachers in every State, county, and parish, and pay them out of the public Treasury; they may take into their own hands the education of children establishing in like manner schools throughout the Union... I would venture to declare it as my opinion... it would subvert the very foundation and transmute the very nature of the limited Government established by the people of America..." James Madison, 1792

"If you think education is expensive, try ignorance."
Harvard President Derek Bok

"Children who know how to think for themselves spoil the harmony of the collective society which is coming where everyone is interdependent." John Dewey - 1899

"The battle for mankind's future must be waged and won in the public school classroom. The classroom must and will become the arena of conflict between the old and the new, the rotting corpse of Christianity and the new faith of humanism."
John Dunphy, Humanist Magazine, January-February 1983

The Hidden Cs of Common Core

"Freedom is never more than one generation away from extinction. We didn't pass it to our children in the bloodstream. It must be fought for, protected, and handed on for them to do the same."

Ronald Reagan

"I am a teacher.... The life I lead is the most agreeable I can imagine. [In the] classroom ... there await me a group of intelligent and curious young ... [people] who read the books assigned them with a sense of adventure and discovery, discuss them with zest, and listen appreciatively to explications I may offer. What makes the process most satisfying is the conviction that ... education is mankind's most important enterprise."

an American college teacher, 1962

"We lead students to the fountain of knowledge. Some will drink deeply, some will take a few swallows, and some will just sip. An increasing number will, as at the dentist, merely rinse before spitting out." an American college teacher, 1995

"The philosophy of the classroom of one generation will become the philosophy of the government of the next." Abraham Lincoln

"Those who can – teach, those who can't -- create common core standards" Lydia Gutierrez, candidate for State Superintendent of Public Instruction in California and a classroom teacher

"Common Core is another example of Washington trying to control all aspects of Americans' lives." Senator Ted Cruz, Texas

How Will They Know?
(Lyrics to a song by Natalie Sleeth)
How will they know, the ones for whom we care, that God is love and with us everywhere. That life is good with blessings all can share? How will they know unless we teach them so?
How will they learn that though they go astray, God will forgive and

help them find the way? How will they feel the spirit day by day? How will they know unless we teach them so?

How will they grow in wisdom and delight? How will they choose to follow what is right? How can they trust the future will be bright? How will they know unless we show them so?

How will they live when they at last are grown? What will they give to children of their own? Will they reflect the values we have shown? How will they know as on through life they go? How will they know unless we strive to teach them so?[268]

A Little Girl Putting the Map together of the USA

A little girl went to her father and asked him if he could show her what the United States looked like. Her Father remembered a map he had seen of the USA in a magazine. He cut it out and then cut it into small pieces. He gave them to her with some tape and said, *"Go into the other room and see if you can put this together. This will show you our whole country today."*

After just a few minutes, she returned and handed him the map, correctly fitted and taped together. The father was surprised and asked how she had finished so quickly.

"Oh," she said, *"On the other side of the paper is a picture of Jesus. When I got all of Jesus back where He belonged, then our country just came together."*

Behold the ships, which though they be so great, and are driven by fierce winds, yet are they turned about with a very small helm." James 1:3

Let us do our utmost to get Jesus back where he belongs in our nation, and also to right the sails and turn the helm of our sinking ship of education. What a difference that would make!

The Hidden Cs of Common Core

End Notes

[1] http://thecommoncore.com/mission.

[2] http://southdakotansagainstcommoncore.com/2013/10/14/cc-math-standards-not-designed-for-four-year-university/.

[3] Common Core State Standards Training Manual, French Valley Elementary School, Winchester, CA., "The 4Cs," 4/14/2013, page 11.

[4] https://search.yahoo.com/yhs/search;_ylt=AuBRM_chGD1R2FXpo BOAmwp.lVM6?p=I+Choose+C++You+Tube+&type=2button&fr=ush-mailn&hspart=att&hsimp=yhs-att_001&type=yahoo_pc_mail.

[5] http://www.thenewatlantis.com/publications/the-truth-about-ddt-and-silent-spring.

[6] Cindy Long, "Move Over Melville, Common Core Doesn't Cut Literature, it Compliments it," *NEA Today*, Winter 2014, Washington D.C., pp. 68-69.

[7] http://www.mariettatimes.com/page/content.detail/id/551888/Know-the-facts-of-Common-Core.html?nav=5007

[8] Emmett McGrourty, nspoken at a public forum, Salt Lake City, Utah, July 10, 2012, sponsored by the Utah Education Coalition.

[9] Ibid

[10] http://whatiscommoncore.wordpress.com/2013/06/06/whats-wrong-with-social-justice-rabbi-lapin-explains/.

[11] http://www.crossroad.to/Books/BraveNewSchools/5-Earth.htm.

[12] http://prichblog.blogspot.com/2012/03/common-core-good-teaching-and-cold.html.

[13] http://atthechalkface.com/2014/03/09/how-do-we-take-back-our-curriculum-from-common-core/.

[14] www.achieve.org/stayinformed.

[15] http://www.teachthought.com/featured/what-close-reading-actually-means/.

[16] http://pioneerinstitute.org/blog/blog-education/do-cold-readings-of-our-historical-documents-level-the-playing-field/.

[17] *http://stateimpact.npr.org/florida/2014/03/21/new-florida-writing-test-will-use-computers-to-grade-student-essays/.*

[18] http://prichblog.blogspot.com/2012/03/common-core-good-teaching-and-cold.html.

[19] www.sfppr.org; *www.marygrabar.com*; *www.dissidentprof.com*

[20] http://www.uaedreform.org/wp-content/uploads/2000/01/ZimbaMilgramStotskyFinal.pdf.

[21] http://www.commoncoremovie.com/.

[22] http://www.foxnews.com/us/2013/08/30/new-age-education-fuzzy-math-and-less-fiction/#ixzz2dxfKr6rY.

[23] http://parentsacrossamerica.org/2011/04/james-milgram-on-the-new-core-curriculum-standards-in-math/.

[24] Sandra Stosky on a CWFA Conference call, July 10, 2013.

[25] http://www.hslda.org/commoncore/Analysis.aspx#FAQ.

[26] http://www.dese.mo.gov/divimprove/curriculum/documents/cur-ela-comcore-35commonalities-11.pdf

[27] http://www.ed.gov/blog/2011/08/education-is-social -justice/.

[28] http://www.americanthinker.com/2014/03/changing_the_sat_for_social_Justice.html.

[29] http://teainpolicics.wordpress.com/2013/05/12/common-core-or-rotten-to-the-core-you-decide/.

[30] Orlean Koehle, *Common Core, a Trojan Horse for Education Reform*, 2012, p. 21.

[31] Ibid.

[32] http://whatiscommoncore.wordpress.com/2013/06/06/whats-wrong-with-social-justice-rabbi-lapin-explains/.

[33] Op.Cit. *American Thinker*.

[34] http://www.edutopia.org/blog/common-core-been-here-before-allen-mendler.

[35] Betsy Kraus, *Catholic Children in Grave Danger, A Report on Common Core in Catholic Schools*, May, 2013, p.15.

[36] http://www.pressharold.com/controversy-deepen-over-virtual-schools_2012-09-12.html.

[37] http://accomplishedcaliforniateachers.wordpress.com/2011/07/22/my-teacher-the-computer/.

[38] http://www.riverjournalonline.com/categoryblog/3175-irvington-schools-flipped.html.

[39] http://www.knewton.com/flipped-classroom/.

[40] http://wifiinschools.org.uk/20.html.

[41] http://www.funderstanding.com/theory/constructivism.

[42] http://www.vlrc.org/articles/110.html.

[43] http://www.gatesfoundation.org/media-center/speeches/2009/07/bill-gates-national-conference-of-state-legislatures-ncsl.

[44] http://cdn.lexile.com/m/uploads/downloadablepdfs/WhatDoestheLexileMeasureMean.pdf.

[45] http://www.theolympian.com/2013/09/09/2712706/no-longer-swearing-by-cursive.html

[46] *Ibid.*

[47] http://deutsch29.wordpress.com/2014/01/18/lets-help-neas-dennis-van-roekel-forsake-his-common-core-guessing/.

[48] Orlean Koehle, *By Stealth and Deception, USA Transformation and its Parallel to the European Union*, Xlibris, 2010, pp. 123-124.

[49] *Ibid, p.* 125.

[50] http://www.foxnews.com/us/2014/02/22/name-game-amid-opposition-states-change-title-common-core/

[51] http://www.foxnews.com/us/2014/02/22/name-game-amid-opposition-states-change-title-common-core/

[52] http://www.glennbeck.com/2014/02/04/mike-huckabee-advocates-for-rebranding-common-core/

[53] Betsy Kraus, *Catholic Children in Grave Danger, A Report on Common Core in Catholic Schools*, May, 2013, p.7.

[54] DVD "Exposing the Global Road to Ruin through Education"

[55] http://ourvoicewashingtonea.org/wp-content/uploads/2013/12/Order-on-Motion-for-Summary-Judgment.pdf.

[56] "Changing Grades," *Education Reporter*, December, 2013.

[57] Orlean Koehle, *Common Core, a Trojan Horse for Education Reform*, 2012, pp. 72-74.

[58] E-mail Nov. 11, 2013.

[59] http://www.cardinalnewmansociety.org/CatholicEducationDaily/DetailsPage/tabid/102/ArticleID/3061/Common-Core-Partnership-Reveals-Growing-Impact-on-Curricula.aspx#sthash.73rC8vTC.dpuf.

[60] http://www.cardinalnewmansociety.org/Portals/0/Common%20Core/Primer/Andrew%20Seeley%20The%20Common%20Core%20vs%20the%20Classical%20Roots%20of%20Catholic%20Education.pdf.

[61] http://www.news.va/en/news/pope-francis-on-clerical-sexual-abuse-not-one-step.

[62] http://freedomoutpost.com/2012/12/is-texas-cscope-curriculum-pro-islam-anti-christian/

[63] http://www.joannejacobs.com/tag/sandra-stotsky/#sthash.VgHhtuCK.dpuf.

[64] Koehle, *Common Core, A Trojan Horse for Education Reform*, p. 3.

[65] http://www.pbs.org/newshour/bb/arnie-duncan-education-agenda/.

[66] *http://pjmedia.com/blog/the-show-of-support-for-common-core-in-georgia/?singlepage=true.*

[67] http://abcnews.go.com/m/story, "6 States Receive $280M in Early Learning Grants," 12/19/13.

[68] http://www.healthofchildren.com/C/Cognitive-Development.html#b.

[69] Kraus, *Op.Cit.*, p.2.

[70] Kevin Eggers speaking for the Eagle Forum of California State Conference, Sacramento, July 17, 2012, http://www.youtube.com/watch?v=qvREXBUxdIc

[71] http://ppjg.me/2010/03/17/what-is-communitarian-law/

[72] *World Book Dictionary, Vol. 1 A-K,* World Book Inc. Chicago, 1984.

[73] *Noah Webster's First Edition of an American Dictionary of the English Language, 1828 Edition,* Foundation for American Christian Education, San Francisco, CA.

[74] file:///C:/Users/wort/Downloads/Womb_To_Tomb-Anita_Hoge-1995-299pgs-EDU.sml.pdf.

[75] http://thedailynewsonline.com/opinion/article_87cb30e8-2ac0-11e3-bcee-0019bb2963f4.html.

[76] "ADHD: Classroom Crutch," *Education Reporter*, December 2013, p. 4.

[77] http://www.scribd.com/doc/61537521/Common-Core-State-Standards-and-Race-To-The-Top-Flowchart.

[78] http://www.corestandards.org/public-license.

[79] Kraus, *Op.Cit.* pp. 6-7.

[80] http://www2.ed.gov/programs/racetothetop/phase1-applications/colorado.pdf.

[81] http://toped.svefoundation.org/2012/06/05/estimating-common-core-costs/.

[82] Betsy Kraus, www.scribd.com/doc/179787173/Catholic-Education-in-America-To-Deceive-the-Elect.

[83] E-mail from Sandra Stotsky as part of TAE Network, April 1, 2014.

[84] *Ibid*, pp. 14-15.

[85] Koehle, Op. Cit. pp. 152-157.

[86] http://www.txcscopereview.com/2014/cscope-is-alive-and-damaging/.

[87] http://www.newburyportnews.com/opinion/x1387865702/Column-The-mystery-behind-Common-Core.

[88] Alex Newman, "Common Core, A Scheme to Rewrite Education, *New American,* August 19, 2013, p. 7.

[89] http://blogs.wsj.com/ceo-council/2008/11/18/gerstners-education-fix-fewer-districts-national-standards/.

[90] http://online.wsj.com/news/articles/SB122809533452168067.

[91] Koehle, Op.Cit., pp. 73-75.

[92] http://online.wsj.com/news/articles/SB122809533452168067

[93] http://www.redstate.com/2013/07/08/lamar-alexander-the-consummate-statist/.

[94] http://truthstreammedia.com/all-day-school-chris-christie-weighs-in-on-schools-serving-kids-dinner/.

[95] http://online.wsj.com/news/articles/SB122809533452168067.

[96] http://www.achieve.org/michael-cohen.

[97] http://www.parcconline.org/project-management-partner.

[98] http://achieve.org/print/contributors

[99] *http://whatiscommoncore.wordpress.com/2012/04/06/what-is-achieve-inc-and-why-should-you-care/*

[100] http://achieve.org/college-and-career-ready-agenda.

[101] Koehle, Op.Cit. p. 7.

[102] http://www.nga.org/cms/home/news-room/news-releases/page_2009/col2-content/main-content-list/title_common-core-state-standards-development-work-group-and-feedback-group-announced.html.

[103] http://www.kjonline.com/news/citing-costs-lepagequits-governors-group_2012-09-30.html

[104] http://www.corestandards.org/

[105] http://whatiscommoncore.wordpress.com/2012/04/06/what-is-achieve-inc-and-why-should-you-care/.

[106] http://www.deliveryinstitute.org/funders.

[107] http://www.pearson.com/about-us/where-we-are.html.

[108] http://www.pearson.com/about-us/education.html.

[109] http://isteve.blogspot.com/2013/10/david-coleman-architect-of-common-core.html.

[110] http://blogs.kqed.org/mindshift/2013/04/some-ask-whats-the-value-of-common-core-state-standards/.

[111] http://dianeravitch.net/2012/05/19/who-is-david-coleman/

[112] https://press.collegeboard.org/releases/2012/remarks-president-david-coleman-college-board-national-forum.

[113] http://www.achieve.org/adp-benchmarks.

[114] E-mail from Sandra Stotsky sstosksy@aol.com, March 4, 2014.

[115] http://www.philanthropyroundtable.org/events/speaker_bios/david coleman.

[116] https://www.youtube.com/watch?v=eJZY4mh2rt8.

[117] http://stopcommoncorewa.wordpress.com/2014/02/25/fact-sheet-on-common-core-s-developers-writers-validation-committee-and-standards/.

[118] Dianne Ravitch, Op.Cit., Who is David Coleman?

[119] http://www.nytimes.com/2012/05/16/education/david-coleman-to-lead-college-board.html?_r=0

[120] Ibid.

[121] http://www.philanthropyroundtable.org, op.cit.

[122] http://www.catalyst-chicago.org/news/2005/08/18/grow-network-tells-teachers-parents-what-test-scores-mean.

[123] http://forward.com/articles/182587/david-coleman-the-most-influential-education-figur/?p=all.

[124] Sol Stern, "The Bomber as a School Reformer," *City Journal*, Oct. 6, 2008.

[125] http://www.ohio.com/news/bill-ayers-defends-weather-underground-bombings-1.395109.

[126] http://www.humanevents.com/2008/10/21/bill-ayers-scary-plans-for-public-schools, by Phyllis Schlafly.

[127] http://www.theobamafile.com/_associates/BillAyers.htm.

[128] Jerome R. Corsi, PhD., *The Obama Nation, Leftist Politics and the Cult of Personality,* Threshold Editions, 2008, p. 71, 87.

[129] Ibid.

[130] http://www.commoncoreie.org/uploads/8/7/14/8714202/common_core_hsandbook.pdf.

[131] http://northdenvernews.com/stunning-revelation-bill-gates-has-spent-2-3-billion-on-common-core/.

[132] http://www.huffingtonpost.com/mercedes-schneider/a-brief-audit-of-bill-gat_b_3837421.html.

[133] http://www.*washingtonpost*.com/blogs/answer-sheet/wp/2013/05/12/gates-gives-150-million-in-grants-for-common-core-standards/

[134] http://www.breitbart.com/Big-Government/2014/04/16/Common-Core-the-Fordham-Institute-and-the-D-C-Edu-Blob.

[135] Ibid.

[136] http://www.amazon.com/Must-Take-Charge-Chester-Finn/dp/0029102766/ref=tmm_pap_title_0.

[137] http://northdenvernews.com/stunning-revelation-bill-gates-has-spent-2-3-billion-on-common-core/.

[138] Ibid.

[139] "Push Against Common Core Gains Momentum," *Education Reporter*, May 2013, p. 4.

[140] http://www.pta.org/about/newsdetail.cfm?ItemNumber=3558 and PTA.org/CommonCore.

[141] http://www.huffingtonpost.com/alan-singer/cuomo-common-core-and-pearson_b_1293465.html.

[142] Education Reporter, op.cit.

[143] http://businessroundtable.org/media/multimedia/john-engler-supports-common-core-mike-huckabee-show.

[144] http://www.philanthropyroundtable.org/file_uploads/K-12_NYC_Meeting_Notes_2009.pdf

[145] http://blogs.edweek.org/edweek/marketplacek12/2014/01/chamber_calls_for_support_of_common_core_in_2014.html

[146] http://www.businessforcore.org/.

[147] https://www.uschamber.com/press-release/us-chambers-institute-competitive-workforce-receives-26-million-grant-gates-foundation.

[148] http://www.gatesfoundation.org/How-We-Work/Quick-Links/Grants-Database/Grants/2013/11/OPP1081590

[149] https://www.youtube.com/watch?v=AF3fCvQPwco&feature=youtu.be.

[150] http://theassailedteacher.com/tag/corporate-takeover-of-schools/.

[151] http://dianeravitch.net/2013/12/12/breaking-news-pearson-foundation-fined-millions-for-violating-laws/

[152] http://onlineathens.com/opinion/2014-03-08/blackmon-common-core-just-symptom-real-problem-education.

[153] DVD of Kitty Werthmann speaking and https://pl-pl.facebook.com/notes/jos%C3%A9-sixpack/dont-let-freedom-slip-away-kitty-werthmann-born-1926-endured-in-austria-under-th/429131782114.

[154] http://www.nydailynews.com/opinion/common-core-great-literature-article-1.1394249#ixzz30rmgbFBa.

[155] Orlean Koehle, *Common Core, A Trojan Horse for Education Reform,* p. 33.

[156] http://www.tpnn.com/2014/04/08/common-core-lesson-teaches-that-america-is-a-racist-nation/.

[157] http://politichicks.tv/column/warning-graphic-common-core-approved-child-pornography/

[158] http://dailycaller.com/2013/09/12/fifty-shades-of-the-common-core-how-much-porn-is-too-much-for-high-schoolers/#ixzz2yCxnphGf.

[159] http://www.theblaze.com/stories/2014/05/06/watch-what-happens-when-one-parent-speaks-out-at-a-school-board-meeting-about-a-controversial-book-assigned-to-his-daughter/.

[160] Ze'ev Wurman, e-mail, May 7, 2014.

[161] http://www.foxnews.com/opinion/2014/01/17/parents-upset-by-x-rated-sex-ed-poster-in-middle-school/

[162] *Ibid.*

[163] http://www.truetolerance.org/2011/what-parents-should-know-about-glsen/.

[164] "http://www.timesunion.com/local/article/School-apology-Th.ink-like-a-Nazi-task-vs-Jews-4428669.php#ixzz2QFwDZ1AE."

[165] http://abclocal.go.com/kabc/story?id=9527060.

[166] Op.Cit. www.timesunion.com.

[167] Terrence O. Moore, *The Story Killers, A common Sense Case Against the Common Core*, 2013.

[168] http://www.nextgenscience.org/toward-integration-ngss-and-common-core-classroom.

[169] http://www.frontpagemag.com/2014/mary-grabar/common-cores-little-green-soldiers/.

[170] *Ibid.*

[171] http://www.edhelper.com/caring_for_earth.htm.

[172] http://www.foxnews.com/us/2014/05/02/proposed-science-standards-spark-climate-change-debate-in-coal-heavy-wyoming/?intcmp=latestnews.

[173] http://federalexpression.wordpress.com/2012/09/05/rescue-mission-planet-earth-a-childrens-edition-of-agenda-21/.

[174] www.cuacc.org/audio/video.

[175] http://townhall.com/columnists/erickerickson/2014/04/18/the-common-core-conundrum-n1825826/page/full.

[176] http://truthinamericaneducation.com/common-core-state-standards/common-core-math-problems/.

[177] http://rare.us/story/common-core-math-homework-baffles-north-carolina-dad-with-ph-d/#sthash.h1a7K3c5.dpuf.

[178] http://rare.us/story/common-core-math-continues-to-stump-nations-smartest/#sthash.RZtbfmTk.dpuf.

[179] http://www.theblaze.com/stories/2014/03/25/frustrated-father-who-obliterated-common-core-in-viral-post-shares-how-his-sons-teacher-reacted/.

[180] http://dailycaller.com/2014/03/18/how-moronically-hard-can-common-core-math-make-subtraction-video/.

[181] http://thecolbertreport.cc.com/videos/nemi1a/common-core-confusion.

[182] http://www.utahnsagainstcommoncore.com/drafter-says-math-standards-were-for-social-justice/.

[183] http://deutsch29.wordpress.com/2013/10/13/the-common-core-public-license-guess-who-wins/.

[184] Al Duncan, *The Master Plan,* Duncan Publications, Nice, CA, 1999, pp. 52-53.

[185] http://www.npr.org/2013/06/10/190160772/amid-data-controversy-nsa-builds-its-biggest-data-farm.

[186] http://archive.frontpagemag.com/readArticle.aspx?ARTID=5841

[187] http://www.susanohanian.org/core.php?id=443.

[188] http://andreagabor.com/2013/10/08/inbloom-education-technology-and-the-murdoch-klein-connection-a-son-of-frankenstein-b-movie-sequel/

[189] E-mail from Allyson Williams in Utah, Jan. 23, 2014, alyowil@gmail.com.

[190] https://www.edsurge.com/n/2014-04-21-inbloom-closes-its-doors.

[191] E-mail from Christina Marie in Nevada, Jan. 23, 2014,

[192] http://www.foxnews.com/us/2014/05/13/price-for-nevada-dad-to-see-state-school-files-on-children-10g/.

[193] http://www.principlesoffreedomforum.com/2014/02/27/data-collection-your-school-and-you/.

[194] http://missourieducationwatchdog.com/home-school-public-school-student-parents-is-your-school-district-contracting-with-third-party-vendors-and-providing-student-data/.

[195] http://america2e.com/forum/topics/parents-outraged-school-survey?xg_source=msg_mes_network.

[196] http://www.examiner.com/article/8-california-school-districts-granted-nclb-waiver.

[197] http://www.usnews.com/news/articles/2013/11/14/education-department-loosens-nclb-waiver-requirements.

[198] http://ir.lawnet.fordham.edu/cgi/viewcontent.cgi?article=1001&context=clip

[199] http://deutsch29.wordpress.com/.

[200] http://www.sandiegoreader.com/news/2013/dec/03/stringers-sweetwater-district-spent-arne-duncan-/?page=1&

[201] http://missourieducationwatchdog.com/when-data-privacy-bills-dont-protect-privacy-a-mom-takes-on-ngos-governmental-agencies-and-politicians/

[202] http://www.pacificjustice.org/california-common-core-data-opt-out-form.html

[203] http://www.safeinschool.org/2011/02/latest-in-scientific-world-on-health.html

[204] http://www.safeinschool.org/2011/02/latest-in-scientific-world-on-health.html

[205] http://www.disabilityscoop.com/2013/03/20/autism-rate-1-in-50/17540/.

[206]http://www.earthcalm.com/emf-radiation-cause-of-autism/#sthash.T81OBXGu.dpuf

[207] http://www.edweek.org/ew/articles/2014/03/21/26fieldtests ep.h33.html?intc=mvs

[208] Orlean Koehle, *Common Core, a Trojan Horse for Education Reform*, 2012, p. 57.

[209] http://whatiscommoncore.wordpress.com/tag/sir-michael-barber/.

[210] Ibid.

[211] www.parcconline.org/sites/parcc/...SirMichaelBarber.ppt.

[212] *Recommendations for Transitioning California to a Future Assessment System*, Department of Education, California, January 2013, p.3.

[213]http://comsewogue.k12.ny.us/files/news/letter%20to%sen.%20lavelle%20and%20attachment.pdf.

[214] http://www.reviewjournal.com/news/parent-questions-whether-schools-can-require-students-field-test-new-exams.

[215] http://www.latimes.com/opinion/opinion-la/la-ol-common-core-test-optout-20140408,0,4198942.story#ixzz302MksjSv.

[216] ttps://search.yahoo.com/yhs/search;_ylt=AgOvyy09lB9NWqVw JBP8Wpt.lVM6?p=Katherine+Duran+and+Tim+Donnelly+on+the+Glen+Beck+show&type=2button&fr=ush-mailn&hspart=att&hsimp=yhs-att_001&type=yahoo_pc_mail.

[217] http://pix11.com/2014/04/01/opting-out-of-controversial-common-core-testing-is-common-sense-brooklyn-parents/#axzz2zwHfiSb1.

[218]

https://docs.google.com/spreadsheet/lv?key=0AuLBonoXvLu9dFF1Nmty eWxGTmpRazYtcXovVGFMeVE&usp=drive_web&pli=1.

[219] "Spotlight on Sonoma County Schools, 2013-2014," Sonoma County Office of Education, www.scoe.org.

[220] http://accomplishedcaliforniateachers.wordpress.com/2011/03/11/common-core-confusion/

[221] http://en.wikipedia.org/wiki/Core_Education_%26_Technologies_Ltd

[222] http://core-edutech.com/home.php.

[223] https://learnweb.harvard.edu/wide/en/commoncore/

[224] http://marniepehrson.com/unplugged/2013/11/29/breaking-the-spirits-of-the-best-and-brightest/. marnie@marniepehrson.com.

[225]http://www.washingtonpost.com/blogs/answer-sheet/wp/2013/01/29/a-tough-critique-of-common-core-on-early-childhood-education/.

[226] http://americanprinciplesproject.org/app-education/early-childhood-standards-of-common-core-are-developmentally-inappropriate/.

[227] Perry Chiaramonte, *Fox News,* December 8, 2013.

[228] http://blogs.kqed.org/mindshift/2013/04/some-ask-whats-the-value-of-common-core-state-standards/

[229] http://www.washingtonpost.com/blogs/answer-sheet/wp/2014/02/23/why-test-based-school-reform-isnt-working-by-the-numbers/.

[230] http://dianeravitch.net/2013/11/14/teacher-meg-norriss-to-her-students-i-love-you-and-believe-in-you/.

[231] http://www2.turnto10.com/news/2012/dec/14/providence-teacher-resigns-youtube-video-ar-1276535/.

[232] http://truthinamericaneducation.com/common-core-state-standards/a-wyoming-schools-common-core-gag-order/

[233] *http://wyomingagainstcommoncore.wordpress.com/about/.*

[234] http://www.kake.com/home/headlines/Parents-homeschooling-children-in-response-to-Common-Core-standards-241101171.html?ref=171

[235] http://www.catholictradition.org/common-core.htm.

[236] http://deutsch29.wordpress.com/2014/01/18/lets-help-neas-dennis-van-roekel-forsake-his-common-core-guessing/.

[237] The Problems with the Common Core, Stan Karp, Rethinking Schools, Volume 28 No.2 - Winter 2013/14 FROM Sandra Stotsky.

[238] http://www.washingtonpost.com/blogs/answer-sheet/wp/2013/11/02/catholic-scholars-blast-common-core-in-letter-to-u-s-bishops/.

[239] (http://www.pe.com/local-news/riverside-county/corona/corona-headlines-index/20110210-more-college-students-require-remedial-courses.ece)

[240] http://www.bus.lsu.edu/accounting/faculty/lcrumbley/study.htm.

[241] http://www.invisiblechildren.org/2010/11/18/75-of-inmates-are-illiterate-19-are-completely-illiterate-ruben-rosario/.

[242] http://www.cde.ca.gov/nr/ne/yr11/yr11rel54.asp.

[243] George B. de Huszar, *Basic American Documents,* Littlefield, Adams & Co., Ames, Iowa, 1953, p.66.

[244] John Taylor Gatto, *The Underground History of American Education,* 2001, Oxford Village Press, N.Y.,pp. 132,133, 135.

[245] Berit Kjos, *Brave New Schools,* Harvest House Publishers, Eugene, Oregon, 1995, p. 149.

[246] http://www.scribd.com/doc/4068145/Personal-Account-of-Horace-Manns-Visit-to-the-Schools-of-Prussia.

[247] Samuel Blumenfeld, NEA, *The Trojan Horse in American Education*, Paradigm Company, Boise, ID. p. 17.

[248] http://en.wikipedia.org/wiki/G._Stanley_Hall.

[249] Blumenfeld, *Op. Cit.*, p. 51.

[250] Ibid, p. 83.

[251] Barbara M. Morris Report, "Are Public Schools Religious Seminaries?," Ellicott City, MD., June, 1974,Vol 5, No. 3.

[252] http://www.thenewamerican.com/reviews/opinion/item/12048-john-dewey-and-the-decline-of-american-literacy.

[253] Blumenfeld, *Op .Cit..* p. 105.

[254] http://blottingoutgod.com/2013/02/21/the-nea-agenda-how-john-deweysocialism-influenced-public-education/

[255] Blumenfeld, *Op Cit.* p. 106.

[256] *The Deliberate Dumbing Down of America,* by Charlotte Iserbyt, pp. 151 and 191.

[257] http://www.deliberatedumbingdown.com/OtherPDFs/Iserbyt_Soviets_in_class.pdf

[258] *Washington Times,* 5/16/02) "Thought Control Replaces Academic Freedom" on Phyllis Schlafly web site, *Eagleforum.org*, April 2003.

[259] http://georgiateachersspeakout.com/2013/04/03/bill-gates-and-his-common-core-curriculum-and-his-profitable-common-apps-need-merit-pay-to-shut-the-mouths-of-outspoken-teachers/

[260] Oak Norton, webmaster for Utahns Against Common Core March 1, 2012 "Think Common Core State Standards are State led? Get the facts."

[245] Stotsky's response in an e-mail message, April 21, 2014.

[246] http://www.sltrib.com/sltrib/mobile/54627081-68/utah-state-standards-consortium.html.csp.

[247] http://truthinamericaneducation.com/common-core-assessments/oklahoma-pulls-out-of-parcc/ (the Tulsa World article is no longer on the website).

[248] http://www.ajc.com/news/news/breaking-news/georgia-decides-against-offering-common-core-stand/nYzDr.

[249] http://blogs.edweek.org/edweek/curriculum/2013/02/alabama_withdraws_from_both_te.html.

[250] http://truthinamericaneducation.com/common-core-assessments/pence-pulls-indiana-out-of-parcc/. and

http://indianapublicmedia.org/stateimpact/2013/07/29/gov-pence-signals-intent-to-withdraw-from-common-core-consortium-parcc/.

[251] http://m.cjonline.com/news/2013-12-10/kansas-opts-create-its-own-common-core-tests.

[252] http://blogs.edweek.org/edweek/curriculum/2013/06/pennsylvania_Signals_departure_from_test_consortia.html.

[253] http://www.newsminer.com/news/education/alaska-changes-school-testing-consortium/article_05509298-7d77-11e3-9606-001a4bcf6878.html.

[254] http://blogs.edweek.org/edweek/curriculum/3023/12/consortium_watch_kansas_drops_html.

[255] http://blogs.edweek.org/edweek/curriculum/2013/12/consortium_watch_kansas_drops_.html.

[256] http://www.newsobserver.com/2014/01/02/3502892/common-core-backlash-casts-shadow.html.

[257] http://caffeinatedthoughts.com/2013/05/iowa-puts-common-core-assessments-on-hold/.

[258] www.doe.in.gov/standards/standardsreview.

[259] http://truthinamericaneducation.com/common-core-state-standards/ut-gov-herbert-reveals-in-gov-pences-knowledge-of-common-core-rebranding/.

[260] http://www.nola.com/opinions/baton-rouge/index.ssf/2014/03/bills_to_undo_common_core_up_f.html#comments.

[261] http://www.theblaze.com/stories/2014/05/07/federal-govt-issues-warning-to-state-that-wants-to-opt-out-of-common-core/.

[262] http://stopcommoncorewa.wordpress.com/2014/03/28/the-task-is-set-and-needs-to-be-carried-out/.

[263] http://www.washingtonpost.com/blogs/answer-sheet/wp/2014/04/18/arne-duncan-dismisses-critics-lots-of-drama-lots-of-noise/.

[264] http://blogs.edweek.org/edweek/teacherbeat/2014/05/chicago_union_passes_resolutio.html.

[265] http://deutsch29.wordpress.com/2014/04/12/exiting-the-common-core-memorandum-of-understanding/.

[266] http://www.huffingtonpost.com/2012/11/16/standardized-testing-a-fo_n_2145623.html.

[267] http://www.businessinsider.com/finlands-education-system-best-in-world-2012-11?op=1

[268] http://www.cardinalnewmansociety.org/Portals/0/Common%20Core

/Primer/Dan%20Guernsey%2010%20Minimal%20Changes%20to%20the%20Common%20Core.pdf.

[269] http://www.nystoptesting.com/.

[270]Natalie Sleeth, "How Will They Know," words and music, Hinshaw Music, Inc., Chapel Hills, NC, 1985.

Bio for Orlean Koehle

Orlean Koehle has been serving as the State President of Eagle Forum of California since 2002. In 2012, she started Californians United Against Common Core (CUACC.org) and serves as its Director. She is a former speech/drama and journalism teacher, who came back to teaching after raising her six children. She was disturbed by all the changes she saw and began researching and writing to find out where these changes were coming from. Her two latest books *Common Core, the Trojan Horse for Education Reform* and now *the Hidden C's of Common Core* have answered many of her questions.

Orlean is the author of four other books: *Looking at Lincoln*, the history of Lincoln, Nebraska; *The Golden Rule School*, which seeks to bring morals, ethics, and character education back into the public schools; *By Stealth and Deception, USA Transformation and its Parallel to the European Union*, which exposes the hidden history of the United States over the past 100 years; and *Just Say No to Big Brother's Smart Meter*, which tells of the dangers Smart Meters and the two year battle in California to be able to get an opt out ruling from the California Public Utility Company, a battle Orlean and Eagle Forum were a big part of.

Orlean and her husband, Dr. W. Kurt Koehle, PhD, live on acreage outside of Santa Rosa, CA. Kurt is formerly from Southern Germany, where he and Orlean lived for several years when they were first married. Kurt is an administrator at Sonoma State University. They have six children and six grandchildren.

Orlean can be contacted at 707-539-8393 or caleagle@sbcglobal.net.

Her books can be ordered at Turn the Helm Publishing, www.TurntheHelm.org.

An e-book version will soon be available.